Regional Planning: Concept, Theory and Practice

By the same author:
Basics of Economic Geography

About The Author

Prof. Dr. Kanan Chatterjee obtained her P.G. and Ph.D. degree in Geography from University of Calcutta. She started her teaching carrier in North Bengal University, 1976 and University of Calcutta, 1979. The areas of her interest are Social and Economic Geography. Prof. Chatterjee was awarded U.G.C. Emeritus Fellowship in 2013. She visited countries of Europe (1996) and U.S.A. (2013) for academic exercise. Prof. Chatterjee conducted U.G.C. Emeritus Fellowship Project, U.G.C. Major Research Projects, D.R.S. Projects etc. A number of research scholars were awarded Ph.D. degree under her supervision and guidance. She has contributed a large number of research papers in peer-reviewed journals of national and international repute. Prof. Chatterjee edited and authored a number of books in various fields of Geography. She is a life member of various learned national and international bodies like Asiatic Society. Prof. Kanan Chatterjee has distinguished herself as a devoted teacher and a promising geographer.

REGIONAL PLANNING
Concept, Theory and Practice

Professor Kanan Chatterjee

CONCEPT PUBLISHING COMPANY PVT. LTD.
NEW DELHI-110059

ISBN-13: 978-93-5125-239-9 (HB)

First Published 2017

Published and Printed by

Since 1974

Concept Publishing Company Pvt. Ltd.

Regd. Office:

A/15-16, Commercial Block, Mohan Garden,
New Delhi-110059 (INDIA)

Phones : 25351460, 25351794, *Fax* : 091-11-25357109

E-mail : publishing@conceptpub.com

Website: www.conceptpub.com

Editorial Office: H-13, Bali Nagar, New Delhi-110 015, India.

Cataloging in Publication Data—DK Courtesy: D.K. Agencies (P) Ltd. <docinfo@dkagencies.com>

Chatterjee, Kanan, author.

Regional planning : concept, theory and practice / Professor Kanan Chatterjee.
pages cm
Includes bibliographical references and index.
ISBN 9789351252399 (HB)
ISBN 9789351252405 (PB)

1. Regional planning. 2. Regional planning—India—West Bengal—Case studies. I. Title.

HT391.C43 2017 DDC 307.12 23

Dedicated to

my students

University of Calcutta

Preface

Regional planning has an economic bias and is primarily concern with the centrally directed allocation of resources between regions to active certain regional and national objectives. Regional planning involves the physical, economic and social planning of development with regions and sub-regions and has more of land-use content.

Indeed, planning is not really planning unless it is related to implementation programmes and administration. There is a growing awareness of the need for regional planning in many countries of the world. In sum, this awareness has proved positive action. This has certainly been the case in the United Kingdom. The need for regional planning is now widely accepted even in government circles. There are many fundamental problems yet to be resolved.

The problem is to find areas suitable for inter-regional resource allocation and intra-regional planning providing a framework for more local plans. The next problem relates to the hazy nature of regional goals and objectives. There is a lack of general guidelines on the most desirable future inter- and intra-regional distribution of population and employment. The third problem concerns the relation between the principles of regional analysis and the practice of regional planning. Finally, there is the problem of administration. This constitutes a major constraint on effective regional planning in many countries and certainly in India.

However, despite the problems, significant process has been made in regional planning in many countries and India in particular. But the problems should not be ignored. They can provide a valuable guideline to future research priorities. Research is needed into technical areas—such as the role of growth centres, industrial location factors in practice and regional information systems and into industrial areas—such as the relationship between regional planning and adjacent planning levels and the most satisfactory form of regional machinery. All of these require more regional planners and improved educational programmes.

This book contains seven chapters dealing with Concept, Scope, Content and Objectives of Regional Planning (Chapter-1), Aspects of Regional Planning (Chapter-2), Theories and Regional Growth (Chapter-3), Planning and Development (Chapter-4), Regional Planning and Development (Chapter-5), Case Studies in Indian Context (Chapter-6), and Regional Planning—Development Strategies and Possibilities (Chapter-7).

This book is intended as a general and introductory text in regional planning. It has been designed and written with the requirements of undergraduate and postgraduate courses. It may also prove useful to researchers in this field of study. It is hoped that it will be of particular use to students in urban and regional planning, geography, economics and other related subjects.

Prof. Kanan Chatterjee
Emeritus Fellow
Former Professor
Department of Geography
University of Calcutta
Kolkata, West Bengal

Acknowledgements

The author is grateful to the University of Calcutta, Kolkata, West Bengal for providing her with infrastructural facilities for processing of this book. Appreciation is also extended to her research scholars for their co-operation, effort and assistance in pursuing the publication work.

Contents

List of Figures

List of Tables

List of Plates

Chapter 1
Regional Planning—Concept, Scope, Content and Objectives

Concept of Region

It is very difficult to define a region because the concept has been used by different people to mean different things. The concept is generally linked with 'space' and has special dimensions, though it is also used as something 'subjective' (a mental construct) or 'spaceless'. The followers of the subjective approach treat region only as an 'idea' by accepting the nation as one-point economy, and arbitrarily dividing it into as many regions as the need be, independent of considerations of space. The concept is favoured by many economist, engaged in the formulation of regional growth theory. However, for most geographers and public in general, region is an objective reality linked with space and defined in terms of (and through) space. The major problem that has to face in such an analysis is the ambiguity that surrounds the term 'region'. Thus, sometimes a district is taken to be a region, sometimes a state and sometimes a group of states (or part of them) is regarded as region. However, if one states clearly the object of one's enquiry, the confusion can be considerably reduced for depending on the purpose of one's enquiry definition (or more accurately, the delimitation) of region will vary. As far as the methods of delimiting a region are concerned, they can be grouped under three categories: homogeneity, nodality and programming. "The first stresses homogeneity with reference to someone or combination of physical, economic, social or other characteristic; the second emphasizes the so-called nodality or polarization, usually around some centre urban place; and the third is programming or policy-oriented concerned mainly with administrative coherence or identity between the area being studied available political institutions for effectuating policy decisions."

The idea of homogeneity emphasizes uniformity while the idea of nodality underlines interdependence. The one gives a formal region and the other a functional region. A formal region is a geographical area which is homogeneous in terms of selected geographic criteria (as similar topography or climate), or selected economic criteria (such as similar per capita income level, similar production structure, similar consumption pattern, uniform unemployment situation etc.) or social and/or political criteria (e.g. party allegiance). When physical homogeneity is stressed, i.e. when uniformity in topography or climate is taken into account in actual delineation of regions, we get the natural regions or physical geographic (or physiographic) regions. When we stress economic homogeneity, i.e. when we emphasize uniformity or similar in per capita income levels, production structure, consumption pattern etc., we get economic regions. When homogeneity in some social factor(s) is stressed, we get what are generally called socio-cultural regions. Against all such classifications, the functional region emphasizes interdependence (or linkage). It is composed of heterogeneous units such as cities, towns and villages, which are nevertheless functionally interrelated. Obviously, the functional region is a nodal region, since it emphasizes intra-regional spatial differentiation. Population and economic activities are seen as concentrated in or around some specific foci of activities (e.g. large urban structures). The functional interrelationships are usually revealed in flows of people, factors, services, commodities or communications.

Definition of Region

A.J. Herbertson felt that a region is "a complex of land, water, air, plant, animal and man regarded in this spatial relationship as together constituting a definite portion of the earth's surface."

V.B. Stanberry makes a distinction between a geographic region and a functional region by saying that "geo-physical regions may be described as areas bounded by definite physical conformations or areas having similar physical characteristics."

According to B.A. Botkin, "A region is the geographer's term for an environmental type in which the geographic elements are arranged in certain definite and constant relations. From the concept of natural regions—physiographic, geological, climatic, biotic etc.—the human geographer, correlating social with organic factors, has developed the concept of cultural landscape, and the human use of region. From human geography, in turn, the sociologists and the ethnologists have derived the concept of sociological region and the culture area. In the natural, social and engineering sciences regionalism as a discipline has not only opened up new research leads but also supplied the techniques of regional planning."

E. Reclus (1885) more specifically in the Géographie Universelle that the regional concept was framed: a popular term relating to regional spaces and which serves as the basis for administrative divisions of nation-states.

Darwin, that the regional concept split with the "pays" concept, and the natural region was considered a spatial unit defined by physical criteria: soil, relief, vegetation, climate… Whether they were large or small, these regions provided the framework for determinist research on the man-environment relationship.

Vidal de la Blache (1889, 1910) cast a different shade of meaning on this approach with the concept of homogeneous regions and based regional geography on a possibilities' vision: the bond between nature and societies creates a history and common geography for men who have been able to take advantage of the milieu in which they live. Vidal de la Blache stated that in the twentieth century the role of societies is marked by the establishment of the means of communication and concentrations of economic activity that account for the distortions of spatial homogeneity.

Scope of Regional Planning

The regional planner while visualizing the spatial processes attempts to identify the flows that reflect interdependences among the spatial units in terms of economic activities that bind them. Thus, it is possible to identify in the interrelated spatial sub-systems, one which acts as the dominant over the others; the development of this type of spatial system could be explained in economic terms by factors such as transport cost economics of scale and of agglomeration, while the core one emerges as the dominant, highest order 'pole' in a hierarchical structure of spatial system. Such is the case of the dominant areas of the Western countries. The real spatial process is undeniable and the development planner is confronted with the problem of delineating a system of meaningful regions for descriptive and analytical purposes with the given variables that characterize the space. This spatial characterization is based upon the principles that the composing units of a territory are different in terms of chosen criteria, that these differences are significant; and that these differences can be approved empirically (Hilhorst, 1971) and helps in identifying meaningful sets of homogeneous areas of varying character—the most complex are being the set of socio-economic region of various levels of development. The identified homogeneous area serves better understanding of the region and is also useful for development planning purpose. According to the Soviet Geographers, the regionalization process emerges not as a cutting up of the country into territorial parts for the convenience of research, but as a systematic uncovering of actually existing integrated territorial economic units (Rodoman, 1967). The choice of regionalization techniques thus rests upon the positivistic approach towards the realization of goal objectives under a given situation and in creating a best suited operational index of measuring the spatial pattern of regional elements of a given territory or identification of such regions characterization by given elements. The growing regional imbalances of today in India are a major concern of Indian Planners (Pathak, C.R., 1997). In the problem of extending the benefits of economic progress to the less developed regions and a widespread diffusion of the benefits of industry and other development programmes as step to even out regional inequalities, the first step would be a systematic identification of problematic or backward areas and emphasized an area approach for their development and evolve some objective criteria for demarcating areas in which the planning body would participate more actively in promoting accelerated development (*Regionalization and Regional Planning*, C.R. Pathak, 1997). The basic objective of human development is to enlarge the range of the people's choices to make development literally with a paradigm shift and it unfolds itself at the global level.

Content of Regional Planning

Throughout the first half of the twentieth century, the influence of planning broadened within Europe as various national and local statutes increasingly guided new development. European governments became directly involved with housing provision for the working class, and decisions concerning the citing of housing construction shaped urban growth. In the United States, local planning in the form of zoning began with the 1916 New York City zoning law, but it was not until the Great Depression of the 1930s that the federal government intervened in matters of housing and land-use. During Second World War, military mobilization and the need to coordinate defence production caused the development of the most extensive planning frameworks ever seen in the United States and Britain. Although, the wartime agencies were demobilized after hostilities ended, they set a precedent for national economic and demographic planning, which, however, was much more extensive in Britain than in the United States.

During the post-war period European governments mounted massive housing and rebuilding programmes within their devastated cities. These programmes were guided by the principles of modernist planning promulgated through the Congrès International d'Architecture Moderne (CIAM), based on the ideas of art and architectural historian Siegfried Giedion, Swiss architect Le Corbusier and the International school rooted in Germany's Bauhaus. High-rise structures separated by green spaces prevailed in the developments built during this period. Their form reflected both the need to produce large-scale, relatively inexpensive projects and the architects' preference for models that exploited new materials and technologies and could be replicated universally. Government involvement in housing development gave the public sector a more direct means of controlling the pattern of urban growth through its investments, rather than relying on regulatory devices as a means of restricting private developers.

The Regional Comprehensive Plan (RCP) serves as the long-term planning framework for the region. It provides a broad context in which local and regional decisions can be made that move the region towards a sustainable future—a future with more choices and opportunities for all residents of the region.

It better integrates our local land-use and transportation decisions, and focuses attention on where and how we want to grow. The Regional Planning contains an incentive-based approach to encourage and channel growth into existing and future urban areas and smart growth communities.

The planning process should be responsive to the planning issues arising from growing cultural diversity and should seek where possible to actively affirm and support the needs of the new local communities which are emerging. The areas where immigrants settle have the potential to develop a new local diversity which can re-vitalize them and support urban regeneration. New approaches to work practices, new types of entrepreneurship, links with home countries and other innovative approaches which immigrants may bring can become a basis for stimulating new local economic activity. Development plans may need to specifically recognize these changes and seek to create conditions which enable the potential for local initiatives to be realized. Views on the acceptability of different types and mixes of retail, commercial and other business activities at neighbourhood or community level should be teased out and reviewed, taking account of input from immigrant communities.

There are several steps that are involved in the process of regional planning, these are:

- Identifying the regionalism present;
- Demarcating the region;
- Determining the needs of the region;
- Making a plan for the region;
- Implementing the plan within the framework of the state and federal sovereignties; and
- Review of the plan as it goes into effect.

All these steps involved survey, planning and programming, design and techniques of development, management, utilization, information and education, programme application and feedback. The next stage is the plan formulation. It involves proper assessment of the regional as well as external resources—natural, financial and human—the assessment of the felt needs and the fixation of priorities. The stage of implementation is by far the most crucial stage in planning. This is more so in a country like India. Implementation requires efficient administrative, managerial and technical services.

Objectives of Regional Planning

The objectives should be explicit, detailed and quantitative, and should focus on 'ends' and not 'means'. A list of specific goals is preferable to general statements. The background material should be explanatory rather than historical and narrative. The objective of regional planning guidelines should provide a long-term strategic planning framework for the development of the region for which the guidelines may be prepared. The planning framework referred to, should consider the future development of the region. It would address the whole of the region to which the guidelines relate, in accordance with the principles of proper planning and sustainable development, the following matters—

(a) Projected population trends and settlement and housing strategies;
(b) Economic and employment trends;
(c) The location of industrial and commercial development;
(d) Transportation, including public transportation;
(e) Water supply and waste water disposal facilities;
(f) Waste disposal;
(g) Energy and communication networks;
(h) The provision of educational, healthcare, retail and other community facilities;
(i) The preservation and protection of the environment and its amenities, including the archaeological, architectural and natural heritage; and
(j) Such other specific and localized matters as may be prescribed.

While making regional planning guidelines, the regional authority shall take account of the proper planning and sustainable development of the whole of the region to which the guidelines relate, the statutory obligations of any local authority in the region and any relevant policies or objectives for the time being of the Government including any national plans, policies or strategies to be of relevance to the determination of strategic planning policies.

The main objectives of regional planning refer to:

- Reflect the vision, principles and outcomes of the Land-use Framework;
- Define regional outcomes (economic, environmental and social) and a broad plan for land and natural resource use for public and private lands;
- Align provincial strategies and policies at the regional level;
- Consider the input from the communities, stakeholders and the public;

- Determine specific trade-offs and appropriate land and natural resource management for specific landscapes within a region;
- Define the cumulative effects management approach for the region and identify targets and thresholds; and
- Provide direction and context for local plans within the region.

Concept of Planning Region

When one comes to define regions for planning purposes, administrative convenience assumes paramount importance. This is so because in actual implementation of development plans, the existing administrative boundaries cannot be easily ignored. In fact, it is generally these boundaries that have to be accepted as demarcating the different regions. Political realities and availability of data for specific administrative units only make this practically essential. However, in enthusiasm of practical (administrative) considerations, one must not forget the importance of the factors of homogeneity and nodality, for the neglect of these factors can introduce distortions in the whole planning process.

Keeping these arguments in view, Keeble defined planning to be an area that is large enough to enable substantial changes in the distribution of population and employment to take place within its boundaries, yet which is small enough for its planning problems to be viewed as a whole. Klaassen believes that a planning region "must be large enough to take investment decision of an economic size, must be able to supply its own industry with the necessary labour, should have homogeneous economic structure, contain at least one growth point and have a homogeneous economic structure, and contain at least one growth point and have a common approach to an awareness of its problems." According to another definition, a planning should have the following characteristics : (a) it should be large enough to contain a range of resources to serve a desired degree of economic viability and at the same time not too large to make the comprehensive approach too general; (b) its resource position is such that a satisfactory level of product combination for consumption and for exchange would be feasible; (c) the internal homogeneity of resource structure should logically link up the anticipated future so as to make future relevant to the present; (d) the region should be internally cohesive area; and (e) that planning region is essentially operational in character, therefore, a high degree of flexibility and elasticity should be maintained in the process of regional delineation.

What is Planning?

Planning has been going on throughout history and it is tempting to explain it a way merely starting that has a natural urge to plan, it is part of his organizational make-up. This could be the psychologist's approach, setting 'planning' up as one of the basic 'social drives' of society—a drive which is not biologically inborn, but which is learned in society and upon the satisfaction of which rests the survival of society.

Individual definition of planning are abundant, but a general theory of planning has not yet been written. Indeed, with a subject which is so obviously evolutionary and responsive to its own history of development and to the wider developments taking place in society as a whole, it is perhaps too much to expect a final statement on what constitutes 'planning' and this will certainly not be attempted here. In addition, certain alternative types of planning of some relevance to the regional form can be indentified within this general framework.

Stages of Planning

- The identification of the problem;
- The formulation of general goals and more specific and measurable objectives relating to the problem;
- The identification of possible constraints;
- The projection of the future situations;
- The generation and evaluation of alternative courses of action; and
- The production of a preferred plan, which in its generic form may include any policy statement or strategy as well as a definitive plan.

According to Friedman's concept, "Planning is primarily a way of thinking about social and economic problems, planning is oriented predominantly towards the future, is deeply concerned with the relation of goals to collective decisions and strives for comprehensive in policy and programme. Wherever, these modes of thought are applied, there is a presumption that planning is being done."

Types of Planning

(i) *Physical planning*: Physical planning is the planning of an area's physical structure—land, use, communications, utilities and so on, and has its origins in the regulation and control of town development, which outstrip the ability of the market mechanism to cope.
(ii) *Economic planning*: Economic planning is concerned more with the economic structure of an area and its overall level of prosperity. It works more through the market mechanism than physical planning which relies heavily on direct controls.
(iii) *Allocative planning*: Allocative planning is concerned with co-ordination, the resolution of conflicts ensuring that the existing system in ticking over efficiently through time in accordance with evolving policies. Hence, it is sometimes known as regulatory planning.
(iv) *Innovative planning*: Innovative planning is concerned with improving/developing the system as a whole, introducing new aims and attempting to mould change on a large scale. It is known as development planning.
(v) *Multi or single objective planning*: Planning has certain aims in the planner's region—goals and objectives. It may have single and multi-goals and objectives. These goals and objectives are usually of social and/or economic nature.
(vi) *Indicative planning*: Indicative planning merely lays down general guidelines and is advisory in nature.
(vii) *Imperative planning*: Imperative or command planning involves specific directives.
(viii) Resource planning.
(ix) Agricultural planning.
(x) Industrial planning.
(xi) Infrastructural planning.
(xii) Rural planning.
(xiii) Urban planning.
(xiv) Demographic planning.
(xv) Socio-cultural planning.

Planning may be classified on the basis of following aspects:

Imperative and Indicative Planning

From the organizational angle, planning can be regarded as imperative or indicative. When the public sector takes up the task of marshalling the productive resources of the country to achieve the desired goal, as it was in the former USSR, then it may be called imperative planning.

When the mainspring of economic growth is left to the private sector, it may be called indicative planning. In indicative planning, the major sectors may be fully or partly owned by the government, but the government rarely intervenes directly in the affairs of the individual firms so long as they function within the framework of the economic policy enunciated by the government. Planning thus becomes indirect and involves the collaboration and co-operation between the public and private sectors. Indicative planning can be passive or active depending upon the degree of control of the public sector on the economy.

Whether a country or nation follows imperative or indicative planning mechanism depends upon the political system in operation. Communist ideology tends to opt for imperative planning whereas democratic and socialist republics like India tend to opt for indicative planning.

Normative and Systematic Planning

The planning process can be divided into two types, like normative planning and systematic planning. Normative planning seeks the best possible results in relation to established goals. It involves: (a) defining the goals and objectives; (b) the phasing of the plan and defining the sequences and linkages; (c) linking and integrating the sectoral and functional elements of the plan; (d) linking and integrating the territorial plans; and (e) determining the contribution that specialists can make and coordinating their activities. Here, the planner's function is confined to the preparation of the plan, while its implementation is left to the politicians and the politico-administrative institutions. There is little emphasis on the social and institutional dimensions of planning. It does not take into account the consequences of implementation of the plan in a hostile social environment and hence, does not possess the flexibilities for it to become operational under different sets of conditions. Physical planning is normative in approach.

Systematic planning treats planning as a social process operating in varying socio-technical contexts. The planning system consists of different objects or elements with varying attributes or characteristics which interact with each other to give rise to a set of relationships which may or may not be in a state of equilibrium. For planning purposes the national territory may be considered as a system, the boundaries of which are relatively closed in terms of political, administrative and economic exchanges. Smaller territorial units may be called subsystems which in turn may consist of even smaller inter-linked units.

Temporal Planning

From the temporal point of view, planning can be of short-term or long-term. Short-term planning is designed to solve pressing problems which do not require large-scale changes in the social and economic order. For example, the short-term plans may be used to increase production and employment opportunities, to adjust production to market demand and supply or to meet targets set by the long-term plans.

The long-term plans aim at the institutional and structural changes necessary for achieving the long-term social and economic goals of the society. National economic planning can, therefore, be subdivided into:

(1) The short-run allocative form concerned with the stabilization of the short-run fluctuations of the economy; and
(2) The long-run innovative form concerned with the achievement of more fundamental changes such as attaining certain rates of economic growth.

The dictionary meaning of '*ad hoc*' is to adopt or do something for a particular purpose. *Ad hoc* plans may be made or implemented for a particular purpose, possibly to overcome some pressing and unforeseen problem. Hence, they are expected to be of short-term in nature (e.g. plans to combat spread of diseases like malaria in selected areas, construction of local embankments, wells or tube-wells according to necessity etc.). In India '*ad hoc*' planning has featured substantially in the planning process to meet emergency requirements.

Levels of Planning

The terms—macro-level, meso-level and micro-level—are often used to indicate the three major areas or territorial levels of operation. Thus, planning regions of various ranks may be derived by grouping areas according to purpose and scale of plan.

At the macro-level, planning is likely to be concerned with problems requiring interrelated solutions and calling for comprehensive resource development decisions (e.g. development of hydrographic resources, irrigation system, food self-sufficiency, power supply, location of industries of national importance etc.). Since, the scale of these problems may transcend state or local governmental jurisdiction, the planning units envisaged at this level may include areas involving more than one state or parts of two or more states. The macro-planning regions are expected to have following characteristics:

(1) Within their confines a complete matrix of essential resources for integrated development; and
(2) A higher degree of mutual interdependency within it or internal cohesion to enable it to form an economic system of its own with its own specialization; thereby having the potentiality to develop complementary exchange relationships with other regions.

The macro-regions are sub-divided into meso-regions which form the primary economic units for the purpose of planning. The main purpose of delineating meso-regions is to identify viable areal units for effective exploitation, conservation and utilization of resources. Economic viability at the minimum level is the primary consideration for grouping areas to form meso-regions. The resource pattern of the meso-region may be such as to promote specialization in some major means of production. This may be achieved by grouping areas characterized by a certain association of resources and complementary characteristics or tied by extensive intra-areal activities or flows.

At the micro-level, the region should have some unifying core (related to a problem or interest). It should include all territory, tributary to the core. The areas within micro-region should be devoid of serious conflicting interests. The micro-regions are intended to be suitable units for formulation of area development plans, as they are sufficiently close to the grassroots, affording opportunities for people's participation in the planning process. There may be three types of micro-regions:

(1) Nodal regions consisting of urban centres and their zones of influence;
(2) Rural areas with a large number of minor nodes without any organizational hierarchy, which may have potential to develop into growth points in future; and
(3) Problem or backward areas such as hill area, famine or flood prone or a reclamation area.

Regional planning is thus similar to other types of planning in that it possesses the same basic features and may be a combination of the variety of alternative forms already outlined. But it is also distinct from other types of planning in that it is planning for a region. In general terms, a region is a flexible concept, referring to a continuous and localized area intermediate between national and urban levels.

- **National level planning:** Planning at the national level of government tends to be strongly economic in content. National economic planning can be sub-divided into the short-run allocative form concerned with the stabilization of the 'ups and downs' of the economy, and the long-run innovative forms concerned primarily with the achievement of certain rates of economic growth.
- **State level planning:** Planning at state level deals with the economy, demography, education, health, employment and the quality of life of the state-population.
- **Local authority level:** Planning at the local authority level concerns with grassroots level rural as well as urban planning. Local plans are formulated in details the ways in which the policy and general proposal are to be worked through.
- **Intermediate level:** Intermediate level has gained momentum in many countries. It straddles the national-local gap. It is concerned with the planning for an area with distinctive economic and social characteristics, opportunities and problems—setting it apart from other regions. Economic

factors are again of major importance when dealing with areas at this level.

- **Sub-regional levels:** The sub-regional level is perhaps the most difficult to define. It is something of a 'hybrid', relating to a part of a larger region and although it may not be too clearly definable, it has certain logic in practical terms. It is more localized area with its own particular structure, problems and potential. There is more emphasis on physical elements at this level, and the sub-regional level can be regarded as the highest one at which physical elements are major components of the plan.

'Intra' and 'Inter' Regional Planning

The primary role of regional planning is to deal directly with the functional problems of the regional level. This has given rise to two approaches, i.e. intra- and inter-regional planning.

- **Intra-regional planning:** Intra-regional planning is planning within region, but at a level higher than the local authority. The prime aim of intra-regional planning is to achieve a satisfactory relationship between people, jobs and the environment within the region. More specifically, social objectives are concerned with factors such as the provisions of housing, social, cultural and recreational facilities; economic objectives relating to the control of the diseconomies of the congested cities and the distribution of new investments; and aesthetic objectives relating to issues such as the quality of urban form and the prevention of urban sprawl can be identified. It is also multi-objectives drawing in particular on the national economic objectives of economic growth, full employment, social equity and giving them a spatial dimension.
- **Inter-regional planning:** Inter-regional planning is planning between regions. The prime aim is obviously more economic in nature relating to the achievement of a satisfactory relationship between people and jobs. The problems of economic malaise in certain areas have given rise to more economic planning approach concerned with the inter-regional allocation of resources.

Principles of Regional Planning

Planning has been identified as a future oriented problem solving process, which may be classified in a variety of ways. Regional planning fits into this general classification, but differs from other forms of planning in that it is specifically concerned with the regional levels. This level lie somewhere between the national and local levels and the region is a continuous and localized area at this level. To some, the region is a real entity that can be positively identified as a 'Natural Region'; to others, it is merely a product of the imagination, a method of classification. It should be, however, noted that a good planning requires a good authority, where the land should be better utilized, which can be identified for development of transport linkages, power and wholesale marketing for the traders and making them available of the same to the consumers.

The regional planning involves basic parameters for identification of an aerial unit on the basis of regularity in the chosen or selected criteria. For instance, the Calcutta (now Kolkata) Industrial region demands its analysis based on the predominant industrial or non-agricultural functions of the area which includes sub-units. This may include east bank of river Hooghly and west bank of river Hooghly is further divided into micro-regions based on service, commercial and industrial activities or combination of them. The regional planning discipline can be further classified into various regions for which it is done. It should be noted here that a regional planning may be classified into short-term and long-term; spatial and sectoral; allocative and indicative; normative and systematic; imperative and indicative etc. Chandrasekhara in 1971 advocated the delineation of planning regions according to the minimum resource potentials for different regions so that the benefits of the activity in the former may flow into the latter. Such planning regions are required to have within them three primary requirements for generating economic activities like land, raw materials and power. According to him, these would enable each planning region to achieve a degree of self-sufficiency in food and employment potential in the agricultural and non-agricultural sectors to meet the needs of the region's population and power base to serve both industry and agriculture. These factors are considered to be necessary to achieve a certain degree of economic viability. The scheme of the Town and Country Planning Organization divided the country into thirteen macro-regions and thirty five meso-regions.

According to him, this scheme of planning regions need not come into conflict with the existing state boundaries which will serve as administrative units responsible for the implementation of the policies drawn up within the regional framework. Political boundaries and administrative regions are mostly independent of the regional boundaries conceived on the bias of various criteria chosen for planning purposes. The entire problem of development lies with the maintenance of balance which may not be easily viable. Indigenous technical knowledge no doubt exists, especially in countries with histories of old civilizations, like India, but when set in the context of current global context of technological innovations, it is important to give them the form of acquired technical knowledge (Chowdhury, 2001).

Many planners have opined that the lack of infrastructure is the stumbling block to the development of backward areas, but if infrastructure is developed without the planning for the structure of economic development which would require such infrastructure; it will strengthen its backwardness rather than energize the regional economy. The development must be ingrained in the resource base. The demand of land for rural and urban settlement development has been increasing and gradually agricultural lands, wetlands and fringe areas around the settlements are being converted for residential uses. The planning mechanism gives us the opportunity to analyse the given parameters on earth or which is applicable to both physical and cultural aspects; that may apply to the direct and indirect attempt to modify social problems and find solutions for the same.

Although the term "regional planning" is nearly universal in English-speaking countries, the areas covered and specific administrative set-ups vary widely. In North America, regional planning may encompass more than one state, such as the Regional Plan Association, or a larger conurbation or network of settlements. North American regional planning is likely to cover a much larger area than the Regional Assemblies of the UK; both, however, are equally "regional" in nature. Regions require various land-uses; protection of farmland, cities, industrial space, transportation hubs and infrastructure, military bases, and wilderness. Regional planning is the science of efficient placement of infrastructure and zoning for the sustainable growth of a region. Advocates for regional planning such as new urbanist Peter Calthorpe, promote the approach because it can address region-wide environmental, social, and economic issues, which may necessarily require a regional focus. A 'region' in planning terms can be administrative or at least partially functional, and is likely to include a network of settlements and character areas. In most European countries, regional and national plans are 'spatial' directing certain levels of development to specific cities and towns in order to support and manage the region depending on specific needs.

Specific interventions and solutions will depend entirely on the needs of each region in each country, but generally speaking, regional planning at the macro level will seek to:

- Resist development in flood plains or along earthquake faults. These areas may be utilized as parks, or unimproved farmland.
- Designate transportation corridors using hubs and spokes and considering major new infrastructure.
- Some thought into the various role's settlements in the region may play, for example some may be administrative, with others based upon manufacturing or transport.
- Consider designating essential nuisance land-uses locations, including waste disposal.
- Designate Green belt land or similar to resist settlement amalgamation and protect the environment.
- Set regional level 'policy' and zoning which encourages a mix of housing values and communities.
- Consider building codes, zoning laws and policies that encourage the best use of the land.

According to the most conventional definitions a Planning Region should have the following characteristics:

- It should be large enough to contain a range of resources conditions and attributes so as to serve as desired economic viability and at the same time not too large to make the comprehensive approach to generate.
- Its resources position should be such that a satisfaction level of product combination for consumption and for exchange would be feasible.
- The internal homogeneity of resources should be logically linked up to the anticipated future so as to make the future relevant to the present.

- The region should be internally cohesive.
- The planning region is essentially operational and therefore, a high degree of flexibility and elasticity should be maintained in the process of regional delineation.

The ambiguity in identifying or defining terms and specifying their coverage can be a problem when these are used for generating data for spatio-temporal comparisons or for taking administrative and legal decisions. As a result, often, efforts are made to define the relevant terms rigorously so that there is no ambiguity in the official information system or administrative decisions/orders. This helps provide an unambiguous terminology for communication among policy-makers, researchers and administrators associated with urban governance. This is not to suggest that all the terms, currently being used in planning, administrative or legal documents have clear-cut definitions, or that the data generated by using these terms are strictly comparable over time and across official agencies.

Basic Principles of Regional Planning

Planning is deciding in advance what to do, how to do it, when to do it and who to do it. It involves anticipating the future and consciously choosing the future course of action. According to Haimann, "Planning is the function that determines in advance what should be done." While planning, two aspects are considered like Region specific functions which are determined in respect to raw materials and markets. Region with non-specified functions that may be useful for backward areas though it is necessary to study the problem of relative economic efficiency in total, which is both the allocative and technical efficiency. Proper spread of industries has been accepted as one of the important means of promoting balanced regional development.

Regional planning was practised as a tool to plan the most economical development of resources in a region in ancient time. Techniques, policy and the task of regional planning change with time, technology, philosophy, politics and economy of a country, but the basic principles seem to operate throughout. La Play introduced a formula of interaction among place, work, folk and organism, function, environment. They act, react and interact in a cyclic order. La Play's formula was extended by Patrick Geddes. Patrick Geddes explained the relationship between physical and socio-economic aspects with the help of valley section.

The Valley Section of Geddes mainly employed by the Geographer-planner epitomizes the 'synoptic approach', i.e. the method of taking a bird's eyeview of problems. The Valley Section should be regarded as a microcosm of nature: stretching from the coastal plains of India to the backbone of the Western or the Eastern Ghats. The Valley Section not only suggests that each landscape (natural and cultural) tends to have a distinctive mode of life, but also offers clues to spatial relations and to the life-cycle of towns and villages with changing geographic values. The Valley Section should be taken as an illustration of innovation of regional planning, the principles, the methods, the approach, and in fact the whole story of development, in areal and time dimensions, are the bases for the projected regional development.

The first principle of a regional planner is to take a bird's eye-view of the area—particularly, its problems and existing resources. Basic principles vary from place to place, from region to region, from country to country. In UK, the planning policies insist on restructuring, renovation and vertical extension of the region. In France, diversion and dispersion of settlement and activities from the congested and saturated Paris basin to the outskirts. In a developing country like India the regional planning policies are related to the basic needs of human being—food, clothing and shelter. Priority should be given on issues. The first principle emphasizes to mitigate the regional imbalance between rich and poor, advanced and backward.

Spatial relations govern the second principle, that each region should be planned in coordination with the adjoining or farther regions, which are interlinked, physically, economically and socially. The development in one region produced chain effect on the regions which are interlinked. It is the geographic situation of the region (for example, North Brabant or the Randsatd in Netherlands or the Malnad in the Mysore State in India, and the prevailing national, political and economic policy that sometimes determine the region's development policy.

The third principle is that regional planning should be coordinated with the national planning policies and problems. In India, following the nation's development policy, the basic task of planning at regional level should mainly are three-fold:

- To contribute to the production of essentials like food, clothing and shelter.
- To develop on a priority basis, such resource as are of national importance and for which the region has the optimum conditions.
- To reduce inter-regional economic disparities chiefly by decentralized industrial development.

There is, in fact, no logical reason to expect that one detailed inventory should be adequate for planning for the future, since land-use and land-cover patterns of any region change in keeping with demands for natural resources. Each classification is made to suit the needs of the user, and few users will be satisfied with an inventory that does not meet most of their needs. Even now, in spite of considerable progress the operational techniques are relatively crude. Among the developing countries the Indian approach to planning is one of the most sophisticated. The techniques and functions of planning in India, the focus will turn to method of analyzing the implications for development of alternative targets and the significance of such alternatives.

Chapter 2
Aspects of Regional Planning

Prerequisites of Planning

It is presumed that there exists in every country a central planning organization which manages the national economic model. It will commonly be a Development and Planning Ministry. Its fundamental purpose is to define social and economic objectives, to identify national needs, to determine how resources are deployed to best effect in fulfilling them, and to promote the environment in which progress can be made. This body will prepare and maintain a National Economic Development Plan. This is, logically, the synthesis of a series of sector studies. The Central Planning Organization could initiate a sector study by appointing and briefing a service institution, or company, or working party, and then allow the study to proceed unsupervised. This is not recommended without an external control mechanism, it is more probable than possible that the focus of the study will drift from the course set and produce a sector study which does not fulfil the intended purpose. Equally important, work may show that the original course should be modified. A mechanism which recognizes this in good time and makes the change as a positive decision will avoid delay and save effort. The mechanism proposed is that the central planning body appoints a Steering Committee with a wholly management function. As it befits the purpose of a national study, its members would be nationals. However, developing countries or those with little background in aquaculture might include representatives of development agencies or international experts. Both public and private sector representation are essential on such a committee. In all likelihood, a member of the central planning body would act as chairman. It is the Steering Committee which will set-up a Working Party to undertake the study, lay down the parameters within which it will be carried out, and exercise control. The Steering

Committee will be responsible for drafting the Terms of Reference for the study, appointing and briefing members of the Working Party, procuring funds and facilities, receiving and responding to interim reports at specified intervals, approving the final report(s) and sponsoring inclusion of the recommended programme in the National Economic Development Plan.

Working Group in the Regional Planning

The terms of reference are the rules which govern the study. They have a major bearing on how well it is done and should be drafted with the utmost care. The points to be covered are, therefore, discussed in some detail. The choice of title is important. It must describe accurately what any reader will wish to know if he or she refers to the document. The Working Party will comprise up to 6-10 members. Each will have a specific contribution to make and will take the lead in his own expert field. It is important to minimize overlap of interest and to establish clearly which member is responsible for a particular action. There will be a Coordinator who is appointed by the Steering Committee at the start to take part in drafting the Terms of Reference and nominating other Working Party members. The Coordinator will be chosen primarily for leadership qualities and ability to maintain momentum and direction. A background in aquaculture is desirable, but not essential as expert subject knowledge will be provided by other members. Organization and management skills are more relevant. They may be employed consultants or staff seconded from parent organizations for the duration of the study. They should, if possible, be nationals of the country and, as with members of the Steering Committee, both the public and private sectors should be represented. In practice, many of these people are willing to give their professional services free and this can be allowed for when preparing the budget. Not all these skills need to be provided by Working Party members. The budget will allow for investigations by co-opted consultants, and the Coordinator's authority to employ such people will be defined. The study will have been originated by the Central Planning Organization, which, for practical purposes, vests authority on the Steering Committee as managing agent. The Steering Committee will, in turn, delegate powers to the Working Party sufficient for it to carry out the assigned task. These delegated powers must be unambiguous and in a form which will be acknowledged by organizations and individuals whose cooperation is sought. This will accompany an obligation to respect information given in confidence. The Steering Committee must be available throughout the study to deal with problems raised by the Working Party and to resolve issues not covered by these powers. "Our dialogue sessions generate a wealth of information that will help us all — politicians, business community, advocates and citizens alike as we work towards a sustainable future for Metro Vancouver", said Metro Vancouver Board Chair Greg Moore. "Expert panelists and highly engaged participants have provided fresh and stimulating perspectives on regional issues and while Metro Vancouver may not be able to tackle all the challenges on its own, it can certainly serve as a catalyst in identifying actions and working, with partners, towards their implementation."

Dialogues in Regional Planning

Dialogue is the key challenge for the planners in the new administrative regions—and for the planners in the state and the municipalities. The Planning Act has really taken up dialogue—now as a defined tool. Danish planning has all the prerequisites to revitalize the spatial planning process and thus, the dialogue about where what will take place. It is well known that every municipality cannot do everything everywhere. Given the global competition, it is far more important that the municipalities and the administrative regions view themselves in a broader context and thereby cooperate about who should take on which task and where. Strategies—especially business development strategies must be coordinated and unified with territorial location to make each administrative region or municipality as robust and competitive as possible. Nevertheless, despite many years of discussion about coordinating spatial plans and spatial development, the municipalities desire to designate more land for such purposes as business and dwellings have led several of the final regional plans (2005) to reserve enough land for locating business and dwellings to last for many years and, especially for business purposes, based on projected future trends that are deeply retrospective. But, the regional spatial development plan cannot solve this conflict by vetoing the municipal plans as the regional councils can do today. This is because the regional spatial development plan does not make precise designations. This is the task of the municipalities, and if spatial development continues in an undesired direction, the state will have to intervene (which could result from a request from the regional councils). The regional councils must use dialogue. The regional councils have an opportunity to promote binding dialogue about the future of each administrative region through broad cooperation with business, knowledge institutions, the municipalities and the citizens. This dialogue can be prescribed in the regional spatial development plan, which can outline the desired development both in words and visually.

Regional economic growth forums are one of the most important regional agencies influencing the spatial development of the administrative regions. The regional business development strategy must, therefore, be part of the basis for the regional spatial development plan. So, the regional council must base its regional spatial development plan on the business development strategy of the regional economic growth forum, which is an annex to the regional spatial development plan. Conversely, the business development strategy of the regional economic growth forum must comply with the framework of the legislation that constitutes the overall basis for the regional spatial development plan, which means that the business development strategy must not contradict the desired future spatial development described in the regional spatial development plan.

These provisions make these two documents inextricably intertwined. This requires dialogue between the regional economic growth forums and the regional councils. One way that this dialogue can be promoted is by ensuring that the regional council is represented in the regional economic growth forum and because the regional council serves as a secretariat for the regional economic growth forum and can thereby ensure close coherence between the business development strategy and the regional spatial development plan. Any Business Promotion Act describes the tasks of the regional economic growth forums. The regional economic growth forums develop initiatives to improve the local conditions for economic growth, including the development of small-town (peripheral) regions, and they make recommendations to the regional council about using the regional council's money for business development and to the state about using money from the European Union Structural Funds.

The regional economic growth forums comprise representatives of the regional council, the municipal councils, local business, knowledge institutions and the confederations of employees and employers. Thus, this is quite a complex process with many conflicting interests that must unfold to create a consensus on the spatial development of the administrative region—and to create five strong administrative regions in Denmark in the face of global competition. This requires a broad overview, comprehensive thinking, clear strategies and professional regional management.

Planning for the Resources and Development

Planning for the resources is a rational inventory for its efficient utilization for the well-being of the human societies. Management relates to minimization of wastes in production and consumption, conservation of valuable resources, and preservation for future use by discovering substitution replacing the non-renewable by the renewable resources. Productive powers of natural, human and manmade resources are to be maintained and developed through positive control and directions. Exploitation of natural resources leads to economic development whereas its over-exploitation leads to exhaustion, ecological imbalances and environmental degeneration.

Acquiring resources is a dynamic concept and the resource potentialities may be enhanced by its development or discovery of new ones. Up till now more importance is given to the conservation and management of resources because of its scarcity in supply and its non-replaceability but the renewable resources also demand a serious attention as overuse of them would also make them scarce. So, the path of resource development should be sustainable and designed through continuous regeneration of renewable resources in order to remove inequality.

Regional Management of Resources

The idea of regional management will not be reserved solely for the regional council. Regional management is required as the comprehensive common projection of where dynamic spatial development can be created regionally. It might be the regional economic growth forum discussing regional spatial development with the municipalities, business and knowledge institutions. It might be municipalities in part of an administrative region that cooperate across municipal boundaries to undertake the regional management for their sub-region and thereby influence spatial development in the administrative region as a whole. Finally, the regional council has the opportunity to take the lead in the dialogue, or regional management that links globalization and the administrative region's strengths and weaknesses. The Ministry of Environment and Oxford Research published a report on regional management and planning.

What differentiates regional management from traditional management as far as resources are concerned is that this overall strategic plan cannot be implemented through a traditional decision hierarchy of resource utilization. Regional management is basically about getting a lot of different actors and individuals to move in the same direction. All the individual actors will tend to start to work based on their own visions and aims, and the challenge is to get these different driving forces to collaborate. Thus, regional management will largely mean understanding the complex network synapses that drive a region forward. Regional management, therefore, requires that visions and strategies be solidly anchored with the local actors. A common basic understanding of the vision and strategy must be established and disseminated, so that the individual actors can work for and not against the vision and strategy. This anchoring can be achieved, if the strategy is developed in dialogue in which the numerous actors participate actively—and it is here that the experiences from the dialogue projects established as a result of the government's regional economic growth strategy and the 2003 National Planning Report can contribute.

The management of resources and planning for their uses gives two impacts—firstly one that relates to the growth impulses generated from inside and the other those exogenously set from outside. As a matter of fact, both the forces are complementary to each other and could be distinguished only in terms of their role in regional development. Regional level management of resources is an integral part of national economic development and has an objective of long-term improvements in the welfare of the people to achieve equity in the share of national wealth.

Thus, more than ever before, the key is the process and the administrative region's ability to design the spatial development process. The regional council's dialogue with the regional economic growth forums and the future committees comprising the chair of the regional council and the mayors of the municipalities in the administrative region will be crucial. If the process is carried out successfully, the results are expected to be anchored locally, and the correlation between the regional spatial development plan, the regional economic growth strategy and the larger and more powerful municipalities will lead to the municipalities using the regional strategy and the regional spatial development plan as overall guidelines for their municipal planning.

Thus, the challenge for regional management will be to lead the development processes in a non-hierarchical political space while the regional spatial development plan functions in a hierarchical administrative system. If this succeeds, this is likely to give the regional spatial development plan inherent clout. The consensus created through the dialogue will lead to the municipalities being able to recognize their own interest in supporting the common vision, the common projection of the future spatial development of the region. Pursuant to legislation, the regional councils will have several ways to implement the regional spatial development plan. One is using money in accordance with sector acts to support the strategies and visions of the regional spatial development plan. Further, the regional councils may propose new spatial planning initiatives to the state and the municipalities within the administrative region. The proposals made to the municipalities may focus on municipal planning and local planning. The Planning Act prohibits municipal plans from contradicting the desired future spatial development described in the regional spatial development plan. The regional council may, therefore, veto proposals for municipal plans that contradict the plan. The regional council's veto must be based on overall considerations for the comprehensive spatial development of the administrative region, including considerations for sustainable spatial development in the region. This thereby emphasizes that this veto is not a veto of the details of the municipal plan as in the present regional planning. For example, locating a hotel outside the tourism centres broadly indicated by the regional spatial development plan cannot justify a veto. But a municipality's intention to locate districts for polluting industrial activities precisely where consensus has been obtained to promote the administrative region's tourism sector would probably justify a veto.

After the regional spatial development plan has been prepared in dialogue and coordination with the regional economic growth forums and the municipalities, it must be published as a proposal with opportunities for submitting comments and objections. Further, the regional spatial development plan is intended to be part of the basis of municipal planning. This is why the Planning Act stipulates that the regional councils must publish a regional spatial development plan before the end of the first half of the regional and municipal election period. This is coordinated with the stipulations of the Planning Act on the municipal planning strategies that then become part of municipal planning. Further, the regional council may publish a proposal for a regional spatial development plan whenever it finds this appropriate.

Finally, the regional council has a role in mediating between the municipalities within the administrative region when a municipality objects to a neighbouring municipality's plan proposal because it is of considerable importance for the development of the objecting municipality. One municipality might also plan in accordance with the consensus obtained about the regional spatial development plan; whereas another municipality's planning contradicts this. The regional spatial development plans will play a crucial role in the interaction between economic factors and spatial development.

One might claim, slightly polemically, that one must move away from the view that towns and regions inherently promote innovation and development and therefore, can be planned by regulating land-use. Instead of towns and regions as individual actors, the focus seems to be on the economic actors in a town or region creating regional spatial development. This signals a new spatial planning system based on:

- The actions of companies and citizens—and the regional or spatial implications of these actions;
- The interaction between the economic actors—in the spatial development of this interaction; and
- The territorial space, which is both a result of and a prerequisite for the behaviour of the economic actors.

Thus, we need to plan based on the comprehensive spatial context. The main challenge for future regional spatial development is linking what the report calls "business development in a globalized economy" and what the report calls "urban and regional development"—the planning based on regulating land-use. This link also affects the national planning carried out by the State. National planning reports present the vision of the Government of Denmark on the spatial development of Denmark as a whole and an overall position on the desired spatial development in the various parts of Denmark. The analysis and descriptions of comprehensive spatial ways of presenting the problems in the reports offer the potential to view the development of an individual administrative region in relation to what the state considers important.

Chapter 3
Theories and Regional Growth

Economic Base Theory

E.M. Hoover and Joseph Fisher have observed that a regional growth takes place in sequences. To start with a region may be having a self-sufficient subsistence type of economy with a population growth at par the available natural resources. With the development of economy and transport, a region may produce surplus in some products, that may be put into interregional trade to improve income and employment levels. Similarly, to explain the mechanism of regional growth, the theory of Economic Base was introduced. The economic base concept emerged in the 1920s. Economic Base Analysis was developed by Robert Murray Haig in his work on the *Regional Plan of New York* in 1928.

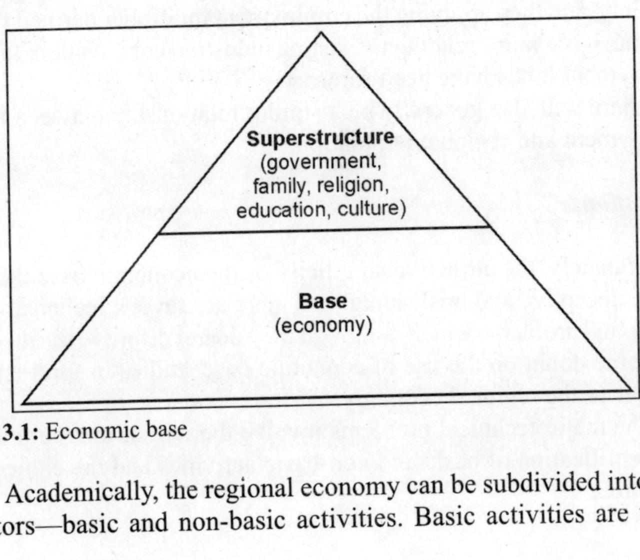

Fig. 3.1: Economic base

Academically, the regional economy can be subdivided into two sectors—basic and non-basic activities. Basic activities are those which export goods and services to points outside the economic confines of the community, or which market their goods and services to persons who come from outside the community's economic boundaries. Non-basic activities are those which provide for the needs of persons resident within the community's economic limits. They do not export any finished goods or services, but are primarily local in their productive scope and market areas. Implicit in this division of activities is the cause and effect relationship which constitutes economic base theory. An increase in the amount of basic activity within a region will increase the flow of income into the region, increasing the demand for goods and services within it and affecting a corresponding increase in the volume of basic activity. Alternatively, a decrease in basic activity would lead to a fall in income coming into the region and a decline in demand for the products of the non-basic sector. Hence, basic activity as its name suggests has prime mover role with any changes having a multiplier effect on the regional economy.

The economic base multiplier is usually calculated in terms of employment and can be expressed as:

$$\frac{\text{Total employment in basic and non-basic activities}}{\text{Total employment in basic activities}}$$

By evaluating the future prospects of the basic activities in the regional economy, and then applying the employment multiplier derived from the total: basic ratios relating to existing industrial composition, future employment totals have been forecast.

There will also generally be a similar relationship between total employment and regional population.

Limitations

Unfortunately, the attractive simplicity of the economic base theory can be deceptive and misleading, and there are several technical and conceptual problems which, although they do not disprove the theory, cast some doubt on the use of economic base studies in forecasting changes in the regional economy.

The major technical problems involve the unit of measurement, the identification of basic and non-basic activities and the choice of study area.

- Employment as a unit of measurement does not consider the fact that equal changes in employment in two basic industries playing widely differing wage levels, such as farming and computer technology, may have significantly different multiplier effects, nor does it consider changes in productivity whereby a firm may increase output dramatically leading to higher wages and more spending without increasing its labour force.
- The identification of basic and non-basic activities is a particularly thorny problem. In most economic base studies, the general practice with respect to industrial and commercial firms has been first to divide them into those that are wholly basic, then those that are wholly non-basic, and finally, those that are 'mixed'.

The basic/non-basic allocation of the 'mixed' firms can be done by either direct survey of the individual firms or by some indirect approach making use of information already available such as the levels and kinds of employment in individual industries.

The indirect approach to the basic/non-basic split may use one or a combination of three methods, none of which is completely satisfactory.

- The assumptions or arbitrary method simply assumes that all primary and manufacturing industry is basic, and all service industry is non-basic.
- The second method that of Location Quotients (LQ) has greater academic respectability but very little if any more reliability than the first method. The location quotient for each industry in a region can be derived from following ratio:

$$\text{LQ} = \frac{\text{Percentage of regional employment in industry A}}{\text{Percentage of national employment in industry A}}$$

Ratios greater than unity are taken to indicate an export or basic activity, and the number of workers surplus to those necessary to give an LQ of I (that is surplus to regional self-sufficiency) are assumed to serve the export market. Ratios of less than unity indicate a local or non-basic activity.

- The third method, minimum requirements, is a modification of the LQ method, using the minimum distribution of employment necessary to support a regional industry rather than the average distribution.

The fact that all three methods can produce very different estimates of basic and non-basic activities for any one particular region underlines the difficulty of indentifying the split.

- The choice of study area constitutes the technical problem. The basic/non-basic split changes as the analyst proceeds from the one extreme of a small hamlet to the other of the entire nation.

Additional to these technical problems are a number of more conceptual problems. Although basic industry probably is a major factor behind many changes in the regional economy, there can be little doubt that in certain situations well developed non-basic activities will themselves attract basic industries to a region and may, therefore, be amongst the determinants of that area's level of economic activity. It also appears more than likely that the basic/non-basic ratio will actually change with the very growth or decline.

By concentrating on basic or export activity, the theory also unfortunately turns a blind eye to the importance of imports. An increase in basic employment and income may have a very limited multiplier effect on non-basic activity, if much of the extra income flows out of the region in the form of expenditure on imports. Although, it must be noted that the influence of the trade factor may not always be negative, for as the regional economy grows, there may come a point when it can produce a service or good for itself rather than importing it. The resultant increase in non-basic activity may attract new basic industry, which again generates yet more non-basic activity. The fundamental point here of course is that an economy may grow not only by increasing exports from basic industries but also by replacing imports.

Relevance of the Theory

Economic base theory has the undoubted advantages of simplicity and easy application and can shed useful light on a region's economic structure and the general impact of short-run changes. In certain situations, for example when dealing with small regions with a high level of dependence on specialized export activities, the limitations are least severe and it can provide a very useful basic for short-run forecasting. It can also serve as an important point of departure for more elaborate models.

Rostow's Theory of Stages of Growth

W.W. Rostow put forward a theory called stages of growth which has equal importance both in the spheres of economic and regional development. He put forward that a regional growth takes place in sequential stages that may explain a country or a nation's process of development. The Rostow's Stages of Growth Model is one of the major historical models of economic growth. It was published by American economist Walt Whitman Rostow in 1960.

W.W. Rostow (1916-2003)

Plate No. 3.1

The model postulates that economic growth occurs in five basic stages:

1. Traditional society,
2. Preconditions for take-off,
3. Take-off,
4. Drive to maturity, and
5. Age of high mass consumption.

Rostow's model is one of the more structuralist models of economic growth, particularly in comparison with the 'backwardness' model developed by Alexander Gerschenkron, although the two models are not mutually exclusive.

Rostow argued that economic take-off must initially be led by a few individual sector. This belief echoes David Ricardo's comparative advantage thesis and criticizes Marxist revolutionaries' push for economic self-reliance in that it pushes for the 'initial' development of only one or two sectors over the development of all sectors equally. This became one of the important concepts in the theory of modernization in social evolution.

Traditional Societies

An economy in this stage has a limited production function which barely attains the minimum level of potential output. This does not entirely mean that the economy's production level is static. The output level can still be increased, as there was often a surplus of uncultivated land which can be used for increasing agricultural production. States and individuals utilize irrigation systems in many instances, but most farming is still purely for subsistence. There have been technological innovations, but only on *ad hoc* basis. All this can result in increases in output, but never beyond an upper limit which cannot be crossed. Lacking modern science and technology, such innovation as occurs spreads slowly and inconsistently and is sometimes reversed or lost. Trade is predominantly regional and local, largely done through barter, and the monetary system is not well developed. Wars, famines and epidemics like plague cause initially expanding population to halt or shrink, limiting the single greatest factor of production: human manual labour large volume of fluctuations in trade due to political instability are frequent; historically, trading was subject to great risk and transport of goods and raw materials was expensive, difficult, slow and unreliable. The manufacturing sector and other industries have a tendency to grow but are limited by inadequate scientific knowledge and a "backward" or highly traditionalist frame of mind which contributes to low labour productivity. In this stage, some regions are entirely self-sufficient. In settled agricultural societies before the Industrial Revolution; a hierarchical social structure relied on near-absolute reverence for tradition, and an insistence on obedience and submission. This resulted in concentration of political power in the hands of landowners in most cases; everywhere, family and lineage, and marriage ties, constituted the primary social organization, along with religious customs, and the state only rarely interacted with local populations and in limited spheres of life. This social structure was generally feudalistic in nature. Under modern conditions, these characteristics have been modified by outside influences, but the least developed regions and societies fit this description quite accurately.

Pre-conditions to Take-off

In the second stage of economic growth, the economies undergoe a process of change for building up of conditions for growth and take off. Rostow said that these changes in society and the economy had to be of fundamental nature in the socio-political structure and production techniques. This pattern was followed in Europe, parts of Asia, the Middle East and Africa. There is also a second pattern in which he said that there was no need for change in socio-political structure because these economies were not deeply caught up in older, traditional social and political structures. The only changes required were in economic and technical dimensions. The nations which followed this pattern were in North America and Oceania (New Zealand and Australia). There are three important dimensions to this transition: firstly, the shift from an agrarian to an industrial or manufacturing society begins, albeit slowly. Secondly, trading and other commercial activities of the nation broaden the market's reach not only to neighbouring areas creating international markets. Lastly, the surplus attained should not be wasted on the conspicuous consumption of the landowners or the state, but should be spent on the development of industries, infrastructure and thereby prepare for self-sustained growth of the economy later on. Furthermore, agriculture becomes commercialized and mechanized *via* technological advancement; shifts increasingly towards cash or export-oriented crops; and there is a growth of agricultural entrepreneurship. The strategic factor is that investment level should be above 5 per cent of the national income. This rise in investment capacities depends on many sectors of the economy. According to Rostow, capital formation depends on the productivity of agriculture and the creation of social overhead capital. Agriculture plays a very important role in this transition process as the surplus quantity of the produce is to be utilized to support an increasing urban population of workers and also becomes a major exporting sector, earning foreign exchange for continued development and capital formation. Increases in agricultural productivity also lead to expansion of the domestic markets for manufactured goods and processed commodities, which adds to the growth of capital allocation in the industrial sector. Social overhead capital creation can only be undertaken by government, in Rostow's view. All these changes effectively prepare the way for "take-off" only if there is basic change in attitude of society towards risk taking, changes in working environment, and openness to change in social and political organizations and structures. The pre-conditions of take-off closely track the historic stages of the (initially) British Industrial Revolution.

Take-off

This stage is characterized by dynamic economic growth. As Rostow suggests, all is premised on a sharp stimulus (or multiple stimuli) that is/are any or all of economic, political and technological change. The main feature of this stage is rapid, self-sustained growth. Take-off occurs when sector led growth becomes common and society is driven more by economic processes than traditions. At this point, the norms of economic growth are well established and growth becomes a nation's "second nature" and a shared goal. In discussing the take-off, Rostow is noted to have adopted the term "transition", which describes the process of a traditional economy becoming a modern one. After take-off, a country will generally take as long as fifty to one hundred years to reach the mature stage according to the model, as occurred in countries that participated in the Industrial Revolution and were established as such when Rostow developed his ideas in the 1950s. According to Rostow, there are three main requirements for take-off:

(a) The rate of productive investment should rise from approximately 5 per cent to over 10 per cent of national income or net national product;
(b) The development of one or more substantial manufacturing sectors, with a high rate of growth; and
(c) The existence or quick emergence of a political, social and institutional framework which exploits the impulses to expansion in the modern sector and the potential external

economy effects of the take-off, i.e. the needed capital is mobilized from domestic resources and is steered into the economy and not into domestic or state consumption.

Industrialization becomes a crucial phenomenon as it helps to prepare the basic structure for structural changes on a massive scale. Rostow says that this transition does not follow a set trend as there are a variety of different motivations or stimulus which began this growth process.

Table 3.1: Take-off

Country	*Take-off Period*
Great Britain	1783-1802
Russia	1890-1914
United States	1843-1860
Germany	1850-1873
Canada	1896-1914
China	1952
India	1952

The take-off also needs a group of entrepreneurs in the society who pursue innovation and accelerate the rate of growth in the economy. For such an entrepreneurial class to develop, firstly, an ethos of "delayed gratification", a preference for capital accumulation over expenditure, and high tolerance of risk must be present. Secondly, entrepreneurial groups typically develop because they cannot secure prestige and power in their society *via* marriage, *via* participating in well-established industries, or through government or military service (among other routes to prominence), because of some disqualifying social or legal attribute; and lastly, their rapidly changing society must tolerate unorthodox paths to economic and political power. A country's making it through this stage depends on the following major factors:

- Existence of enlarged, sustained effective demand for the product of key sectors.
- Introduction of new productive technologies and techniques in these sectors.
- The society's increasing capacity to generate or earn enough capital to complete the take-off transition.

- Activities in the key sector should induce a chain of growth in other sectors of the economy that also develops rapidly.

An example of a country in the Take-off stage of development is Equatorial Guinea. It has the largest increase in GDP growth since 1980 and the rate of productive investment has risen from 5 per cent to over 10 per cent of income or product.

Drive to Maturity

After take-off there follows a long interval of sustained growth known as the stage of drive to maturity. Rostow defines it "as the period when a society has effectively applied the range of modern technology to the bulk of its resources." Now regularly growing economy drives to extend modern technology over the whole front of its economic activity. Some 10-20 per cent of the national income is steadily on rise, permitting output regularly to outstrip the increase in population. The make-up of the economy changes unceasingly as technique improves, new industries accelerate, and older industries level off. The economy finds its place in the international economy: goods formerly imported are produced at home; new import requirements develop, and new export commodities to match them. The leading sectors will in an economy be determined by the nature of resource endowments and not only by technology.

Table 3.2: Maturity Stage

Country	*Maturity Year*
Great Britain	1850
Russia	1950
United States	1900
Germany	1910
Canada	1950

The structural changes in the society during this stage are in three ways:

- Workforce composition in agriculture shifts from 75 per cent of the working population to 20 per cent. The workers acquire greater skill and their wages increase in real terms.

- The character of leadership changes significantly in the industries and a high degree of professionalism is introduced.
- Environmental and health cost of industrialization is recognized and policy changes are thus made.

During this stage a country has to decide whether the industrial power and technology it has generated is to be used for the welfare of its people or to gain supremacy over others, or the world into a prime example of a country in the Drive to Maturity stage is South Africa. It is developing a world-class infrastructure—including a modern transport network, widely available energy, and sophisticated telecommunications facilities. Additionally, the commercial farm sector shed 1,40,000 jobs, a decline of roughly 20 per cent, in the eleven year period from 1988 to 1998.

This diversity leads to reduction in poverty rate and increasing standards of living, as the society no longer needs to sacrifice its comfort in order to build-up certain sectors.

Age of High Mass Consumption

The age of high mass consumption refers to the period of contemporary comfort afforded many Western nations, wherein consumers concentrate on durable goods, and hardly remember the subsistence concerns of previous stages. Rostow uses the Buddenbrooks dynamics metaphor to describe this change in attitude. In Thomas Mann's 1901 novel, *Buddenbrooks*, a family is chronicled for three generations. The first generation is interested in economic development, the second in its position in society. The third, already having money and prestige, concerns itself with the arts and music, worrying little about those previous, earthly concerns. So too, in the age of high mass consumption, a society is able to choose between concentrating on military and security issues, on equality and welfare issues, or on developing great luxuries for its upper class. Each country in this position chooses its own balance between these three goals. There is a desire to develop an egalitarian society and measures are taken to reach this goal. According to Rostow, a country tries to determine its uniqueness and factors affecting it are its political, geographical and cultural structure and also values present in its society. Historically, the United States is said to have reached this stage first, followed by other Western European nations, and then

Japan in the 1950s. The theory of Rostow has been criticized in various aspects. His theory was termed to be historical in the sense that the end result is known at the outset and is derived from the historical geography of a developed bureaucratic society. It had also been termed mechanical in the sense that the underlying motor of change is not disclosed and therefore, the stages become little more than a classificatory system based on data from developed countries. His model was based on American and European history and defines the American norm of high mass consumption as integral to the economic development process of all industrialized societies. Rostow's model did not apply to the Asian and the African countries as events in these countries are not justified in any stage of his model. The stages are not identifiable properly as the conditions of the take-off and pre-take-off stage are very similar and also overlap. According to Rostow, growth becomes automatic by the time it reaches the maturity stage but Kuznets asserts that no growth can be automatic there is need for push always.

Central Place Theory

W. Christaller (1893-1969)

Plate No. 3.2

The idea of central place theory was first put forward by Walter Christaller in 1933 in his book *Die Zentralen Orte in Suddeutschland*. It was based on his study of Southern Germany. His basic assumption was that towns act as central places for the countryside and come into being to carry out the tasks which the life of the countryside creates. Christaller believed that all consumer oriented functions belonged to the central place and suggested that the processing of raw materials could be done at a central place. He indicated that industries like food processing, dairies, sugar refineries and fruit preservation plants could be located in central places of higher order. The central functions considered by him were trade, banking, administration, education, commerce and transportation.

Basic Concepts implied in Central Place Theory

Centrality has been defined as the degree to which a town serves its surrounding area and can be measured in terms of goods and services offered. This gives rise to two basic concepts implied in Christaller's theory:

- *Threshold Population*: The threshold is defined as the minimum population required for supporting the service activity, i.e. to make an offering viable.
- *Range of Goods and Services*: This is the maximum distance over which people will travel to purchase goods or services offered at a central place. At some range from the centre the inconvenience of travel measured in terms of time, cost and trouble will outweigh the value or need of the good or an alternative nearer centre becomes available.

Assumptions

The assumptions adopted by Christaller for formulating his model are:

(1) Development takes place on an isotropic surface, that is, a flat uniform plain of equal population density and even distribution of natural resources. Population was assumed to be farmers.
(2) Movement in every direction is unimpeded and involves equal unit cost.

Hexagonal Market Areas

According to Christaller, mathematically the most efficient system would consist of hexagonal market areas, each tangential to the other, around a system of central places. It is assumed that a farmer is selling his produce at point 'A' and other farmers are willing to travel distance 'a' to purchase from this farmer. Since, travel is assumed to be equally easy in all directions the market area for the farmer at 'A' is given by the circle with radius 'a'. Beyond 'a' the benefits of purchase are outweighed by the travel costs involved. If retailing is profitable, other enterprising farmers may develop their own circular market areas and spatial competition will develop between the providers of the particular service activity. If with improved transport and communication consumers are willing to travel further and with improved production producers can lower their prices, market area will expand with radius 'b' to cover most of the landscape. In the next stage market areas with radius 'c' will overlap. In this overlap zone, consumers may use more than one centre. If they are rational and are seeking to minimize transport cost they will choose the nearest centre. This results in the division of the overlap zone and development of hexagonal market areas. With the consideration of more than one service activity, the situation can develop in several ways. The original central places may attract additional services such as doctors and banks, with threshold populations and markets areas similar to the original service activity. Smaller central places may also develop at the points where the hexagonal service areas meet, perhaps providing more 'low order' service activities. As these service activities require smaller threshold populations and market areas, the resultant central places will be more numerous than the original centres.

In addition, certain of the original central places may attract more 'high order' service activities such as a cinema or a super market, requiring a large threshold population and market range. There will be a limited number of these higher order central places. Already three levels in a hierarchy of central places are apparent, with a 'nesting' pattern of lower order trade areas within the trade areas of higher order centres. Figure 3.2 illustrates this hierarchy. 'A' centres may possess service activities 1 to n, with 1 being the local store and n a large supermarket. 'B' centres would possess a more limited range of activities, perhaps from 1 to (n-10), while the smaller 'C' centres would only possess a small number of service activities, perhaps from 1 to (n-20).

In his study of Southern Germany, Christaller identified seven levels of central place ranging from the small hamlet to the metropolitan city (Table 3.3).

Three Principles of Organization

Each central place is able to offer all goods of the lower order centres and in addition a distinctive range of goods related to the increased size of its hinterland. On this basis a series of ranks may emerge which has been referred to as the urban hierarchy. Christaller believed

Table 3.3: Christaller's Central Places in Southern Germany

General Hierarchy	*Christaller's hierarchy*					*English equivalent*
	Central place	*Towns*		*Hinterland*		
		Distance (km.)	*Population ('000s)*	*Distance (km.)*	*Population ('000s)*	
1st (lowest)						Roadside hamlet
2nd	Marktort	7	0.8	45	2.7	Village
	Amtsort	12	1.5	135	8.1	
3rd	Kreisstadt	21	3.5	400	24.0	Sub-town
	Bezirkstadt	36	9.0	1200	75.0	
4th	Gaustadt	62	27.0	3600	225.0	Town
5th	Provinzhaupstadt	108	90.0	10800	675.0	Major town City
6th	Landstadt	186	300.0	32400	2025.0	Major city
7th	Reichstadt					World city

that the hierarchy of central places may be organized according to one or the other of the three following principles:

1. ***Marketing Principle:*** He introduced the concept of *k* value which may be defined as the total number of settlements (markets areas) of a certain order served by a central place of next higher order. In this hierarchy a central place of a particular order has the allegiance of one-third of each of the six sub-centres located at the corner of the hexagon plus its own population [i.e. (1/3×6) + 1 = 3]. This gives rise to a it value of 3. Thus, market areas at each level will follow the geometrical progression of 1, 3, 9, 27, 81.
2. ***Transportation Principle*****:** This assumes significance where the cost of transportation is significantly high. In this hierarchy a central place of a particular order has the allegiance of half of each of the six sub-centres located at the corner of the hexagon plus its own population. This gives rise to a *k* value of 4 [i.e. (1/2×6) + 1=4].
3. ***Administrative Principle*****:** This is based on the idea that administratively each centre should have complete control of the six surrounding areas with no divided allegiance giving rise to a *k* value of 7 (i.e. 6 plus its own population).

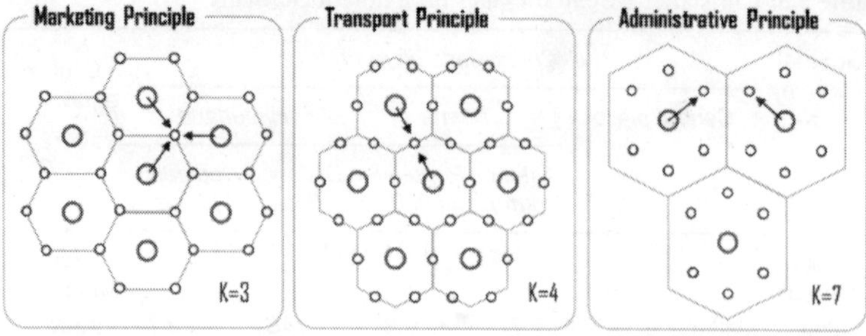

Fig. 3.2: Alternative hierarchies ($k = 3$, $k = 4$, $k = 7$)

Table 3.4 shows progression of complementary regions and number of centres under the three principles:

Table 3.4: Progression of Complementary Regions and Number of Settlements under the Three Principles of Settlement Hierarchy

Marketing principle (k = 3)		*Transportation principle (k = 4)*		*Administrative principle (k = 7)*	
Number of complementary regions	*Number of centres*	*Number of complementary regions*	*Number of centres*	*Number of complementary regions*	*Number of centres*
1	1	1	1	1	1
3	2	4	3	7	6
9	6	16	12	49	42
27	18	64	48	343	294
81	54	256	192	2401	2058
243	162	1024	768	16807	14406
729	486	4096	3072	117649	100842

Criticisms

Christaller's theory has been criticized for contradicting the basic hierarchical rules. Some of the criticisms are as follows:

- The theory relates only to service elements.
- The assumption of even plain and uniform distribution of natural resources results in deviation from reality as resource localization often distorts the regular hierarchy.
- The assumption of uniform population distribution and the rationality of the consumers causing them to patronize the

nearest centre do not conform with the reality; overlaps are bound to occur.

- The theory is apparently static as the increase in service activity of one centre is likely to have an impact on the service activity of competing centres.
- The hierarchy may also be distorted by the domination of large centres which may create shadow effect discouraging the growth of appropriately sized smaller settlements. An alternative distortion could be caused by the development of a dispersed city, which although physically separated, function together as one unit.
- The choice of criteria to rank the central places also presents a problem. Christaller realized that population alone was an insufficient measure of centrality and in addition he used an index based on the number of telephone installations. Subsequently, new methods have been devised by other researchers, like the Haydock method and Davies functional index based on location coefficients.
- The hexagonal lattice was mathematically drawn and non-existent in reality.
- While Christaller postulated a stepped and ranked distribution, Zipf (1941) envisaged a gradual gradation in his Rank Size Rule.
- An area where the model can be expected to fit is a poor and thinly settled agricultural region which is nearly self-contained. According to Berry (1971) with higher population density, increasing income, better accessibility and with centres protecting themselves through product specialization against the protection of distances, as in the developed countries, the propositions of central place theory have little validity.

Growth Pole Theory

Many of the criticisms levelled at the Central Place Theory as a model of regional spatial structure can be answered by the theory of growth poles. French economists, specially Perroux, who believed that basic fact of spatial, as well as industrial development is that growth does not appear everywhere and all at once; it appears in points or development poles, with variable intensities; it spreads along diverse channels and with varying terminal effects to whole of the economy. More specifically Boudeville defines a regional growth pole as a set of expanding industries located in an urban area and inducing further development of economic activity throughout its zone of influence.

Basic Concepts of Growth Pole Theory

The basic concepts and subsequent refinements and developments are to be found in the core literature of Perroux, Boudeville, Hansen, Hermansen, Hirschman and Myrdal. Perroux's original work focuses on the development of growth poles in economic space. This was a deliberate attempt to break away from the limiting geographical dimensions adopted by Christaller and Losch. But it was Boudeville who extended the original theory to include more comprehensively the geographical dimension. Following Darwent (1969), Moseley (1974) and Glasson (1975) used the term 'growth centre' for the geographical identity. According to Hermansen (1972), a nodal region qualifies to be called a development pole only when it contains propulsive firms and leading industries.

A **Propulsive Firm** is: (i) relative large, (ii) generate significant growth impulses into its environment, (iii) has a high ability to innovate, and (iv) belongs to a fast growing industry. A **leading industry** is: (i) a relatively new and dynamic industry with an advanced level of technology injecting an atmosphere of growth mindedness into a region, (ii) it has a high income elasticity of demand for its products which are usually sold to national markets, and (iii) it has strong inter-industry linkages with other sectors.

The growth of such poles can have two discernible impacts:

(1) **Spread effects** cause the dynamic and propulsive qualities of the growth pole to radiate outward into surrounding space.

(2) **Polarisation** of other economic units into the pole of growth can take place due to various agglomeration economies. This leads to geographical polarization with the flow of resources to and concentration of economic activity at a limited number of centres within a region. The three following types of agglomeration economies have been identified.

(i) *Economies internal to the firm*: These are the lower average costs of production resulting from an increased rate of output. Such large scale production allows technical economies, such as job specialization, various management, marketing and financial economies.

(ii) *Economies external to the firm, but internal to the industry*: These are the reductions in the cost per unit of production as the industry expands in a particular location. This results from the close locational proximity of linked firms. The advantages include development of a large and skilled labour pool, easy interchange of products, possibility of firms existing to process waste materials and development of specialized services (e.g. research facilities, repair services etc.) available to all firms.

(iii) *Economies external to the industry, but internal to the urban area*: These are the reduction of average costs of each firm as many industries grow in one place. Such urbanization economies include the development of urban labour markets, access to large market, and the provision of wide range of services by both public and private sectors for both people and industry. Such services may include the availability of improved transport, commercial and financial facilities and the development of a wide range social, cultural and leisure facilities.

Apart from the presence of a complex of leading industries, a highly developed infrastructure providing facilities for the centre of a wider region, may also facilitate polarization. According to Hirschman polarization effects can discourage growth in the following ways:

(i) The industries in the hinterland may find it difficult to compete with the industries in the growth pole,

(ii) With better investment opportunities in the growth pole, the investors may be tempted to invest in the growth poles rather than the backward hinterland,

(iii) It might be drained off the best part of its labour force, so instead of absorbing the disguised unemployment the progress of the growth pole may denude its hinterland.

(iv) The role of growth centres in regional development was linked by Berry to diffusion process. New innovations associated with

> growth are likely to filter down from large centres to the smaller ones and to spread from the centre to the surrounding region. Growth centres can be expected to serve as filtering enhancement devices when keyed to an accessibility policy that brings the peripheries within the orbit of the metropolis. The coordinated operation of filtering and diffusion can result in rapid integration of the nation's economic space.

Misra, Sundaram and Rao (1974) highlighted following inadequacies of the growth pole hypothesis, especially when applied to the developing countries:

1. Inapplicability to Varied Regional Problems: Frontier regions seem to be the most fertile areas for the application of the growth pole hypothesis, e.g. successful development of Brasilia project in Brazil. In well-populated, resourceful, but culturally backward areas the growth policy have failed to be a success, as in Visakhapatnam port with the shipyard as the core, Rourkela and Bhilai with modern steel plants as the cores in India. In these cases, the leading industries failed to generate developmental impulses in the hinterland. In the densely populated and economically backward regions of northern Bihar, eastern Uttar Pradesh and Telengana, (now new State) in Andhra Pradesh, where agriculture have been predominating traditionally, lack of industrial resources and urbanization seemed to be the major deficiencies. In the industrially advanced mineral rich area growth pole hypothesis formed the basis of the development programmes undertaken here. However, the impact of these development projects (like Chittaranjan, Durgapur, Asansol, Dhanbad etc.) on the surrounding region was very limited. The metropolitan regions of India with their leading industries and other characteristics of growth poles have had a parasitic effect on the hinterland, as their regions have grown at the cost of the adjoining rural villages which have remained backward.

2. Functional Rigidities: Growth pole hypothesis had its roots and relevance to the western countries whose economy already reached the social transformation threshold needed for accelerated industrialization. On the other hand, growth poles in countries like India have to perform three basic functions, like provision of services, promoting economic growth and social change, instead of centring around industries alone.

3. Lack of Spill-Over Mechanism: The location of leading industries and innovative functions at a particular place can bring about economic development and social transformation, only if the institutional infrastructure exists for the diffusion of innovations. Development of a hierarchy of towns is as important element in this regard. The growth pole hypothesis has not dealt with the processes by which people's participation in the development project can be ensured.

4. Urban and Industrial Bias: Another important weakness inherent in the growth pole concept is its disregard for environmental quality and future design of human society. The idea that manufacturing can alone be propulsive and that large industrial units only can generate growth does not seem to have empirical validity. Because Japan's development was rooted in the strength of small enterprises, while in Punjab, economically the fastest growing State of India, growth has come from innovations in agriculture.

Growth Pole Theory and Regional Planning

In spite of its shortcomings in regional context, value of growth pole theory has been recognized in regional planning in different parts of the world. In Britain it was first adopted in 1963 in plans for North-East England and Central Scotland, later also for the North-West, South Wales, The Scottish Highlands and Eire. 'Growth point' policies have been favoured in developed and developing countries like Italy, France, Brazil, Venezuela, the USA, Soviet Union and India. The theory is particularly attractive as a policy tool for several reasons:

(a) Owing to the various agglomeration economies it tends to be a very efficient way of generating development;
(b) The concentration of investment in specific growth points costs less in terms of public expenditure than wholesale grants to large areas; and
(c) The spread effects out of the growth points will help to solve the problems of depressed regions.

Weberian Concept on Location of Industries

The first person to work up a comprehensive theory accounting for the location of manufacturing industry, was Alfred Weber. Weber was

A. Weber (1868-1958)

Plate No. 3.3

a German Economist who taught at the University of Prague from 1904-1907 and the University of Heidelberg from 1907-1933. In 1909, he published his famous *Theory of the Location of Industries* incorporating several ideas that has been partially formulated by Wilhelm Launhardt in the 1880s. Weber's basic principle was that a businessman would choose a location where his costs were least. Hence, the theory may also be treated popular as least cost approach.

For the purposes of his model he made the following simplifying assumptions:

- The unit of analysis is a simple isolated country, homogeneous in terms of climate, topography, race of people, technical skills of the population and is under one political authority.
- Some natural resources like water, sand, clays etc. are ubiquitous, where others like coal and iron ore occur only in fixed sites.
- Labour is not ubiquitous, with several fixed labour locations and fixed labour mobility.
- Transportation costs are a function of weight and distance increasing in direct proportion to length of shipment and weight of cargos.

Within these assumptions, Weber postulated that manufacturing place would be located in response to three forces, namely transport costs, labour costs and something he called agglomeration which will be defined in a moment.

Weber illustrated the concept of least transport cost using his famous locational triangle, where the optimum location (T) is a balance between the forces exerted by the material sources and the consumption point. The least cost approach can be clearly illustrated using Smith's diagrams. Average Cost (AC) varies according to location, but Average Revenue (AR) is assumed to be constant. The optimum location is O where the average costs are at a minimum and unit profits are at a maximum. To indicate whether the optimum

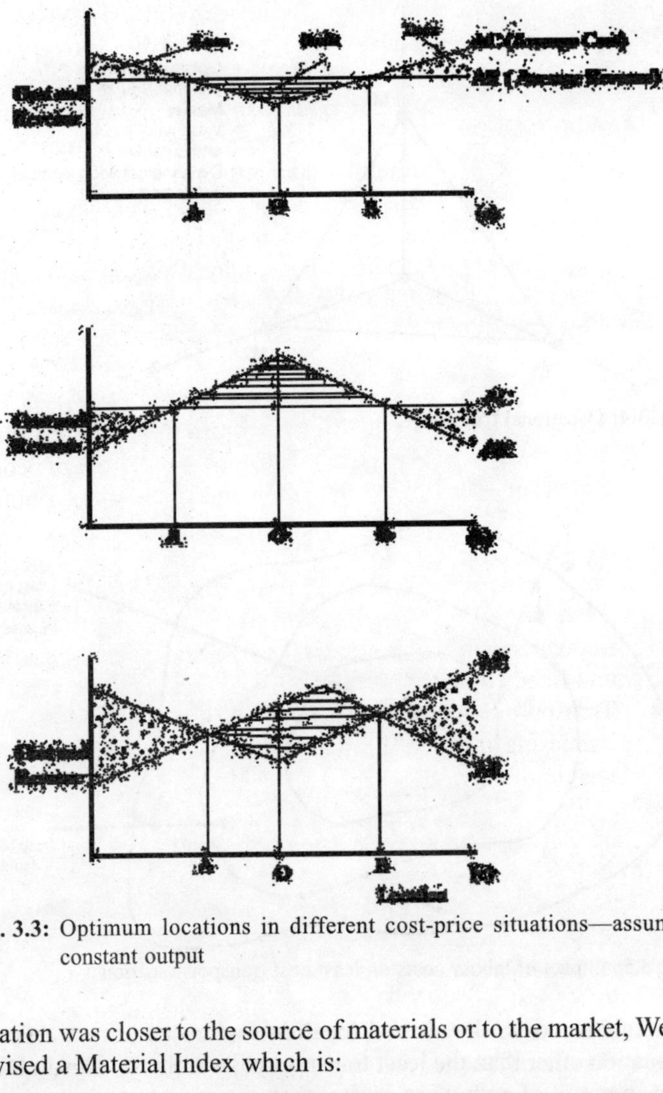

Fig. 3.3: Optimum locations in different cost-price situations—assuming constant output

location was closer to the source of materials or to the market, Weber devised a Material Index which is:

$$\frac{\text{(Weight of local material inputs)}}{\text{(Weight of the final products)}}$$

If the index was greater than one then the firm is material oriented; if the index was less than one it was market oriented.

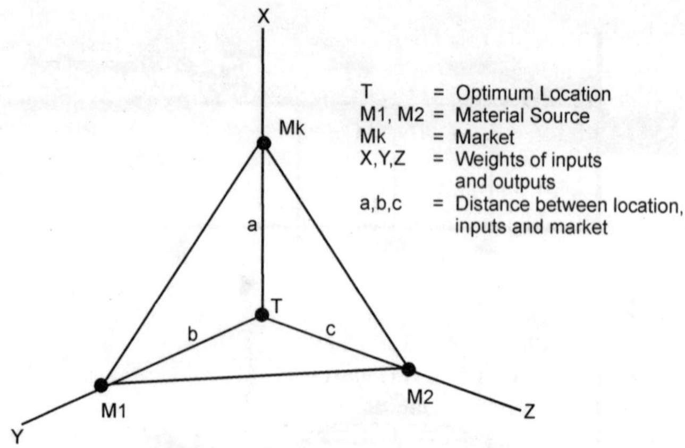

Fig. 3.4: Locational triangle

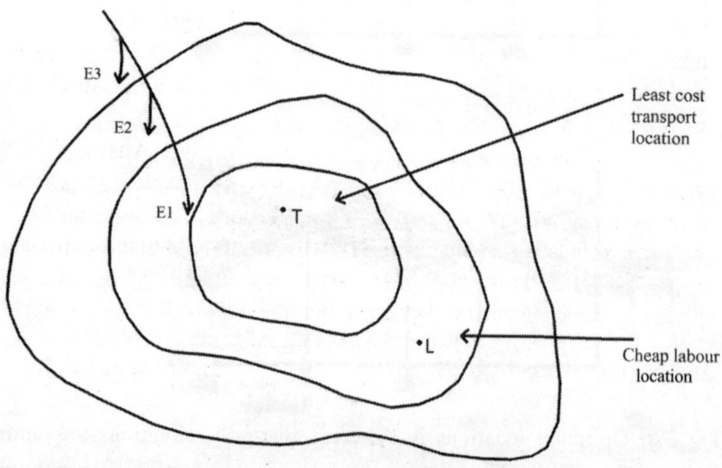

Fig. 3.5: Impact of labour costs on least cost transport location

Labour costs, the second location factor can attract a firm to allocation other than the least transport costs if the savings in labour costs per unit of output are greater than the extra transport costs per unit involved. Weber's contribution of isodapanes provided a technique for the systematic introduction of a new variable (such as labour) into a theoretical scheme. Similarly, a firm may be diverted away from both the least cost transport and labour cost locations if cost economies can be achieved through the third location factor of agglomeration. The advantages of agglomeration might include the development of a pool of skilled labourers and the establishment of specialist services, although, of course, there may be diseconomies such as rising land prices and congestions which may eventually encourage dispersion.

Criticism

Since its publications, Weberian model has been subjected to a great deal of criticisms. Critics have assailed Weber's Theory of Locational Triangle on two major counts: freight rates are not directly proportional to distance and they are not ton for ton the same on finished products as on raw materials. It has been criticized for some of its assumptions, such as constant transport ccsts and production costs and for its disregard of institutional factors such as governmental policy. The model is also very one sided, assuming perfect competition with all fictions having access to unlimited demand. Weber's theory has been criticized by English economists like Prof. S.R. Denison and Prof. P. Sergent Florence. Weber's analysis has stimulated research in the fields of industrial location, but it cannot provide a definite solution to the problem of location in its entirety. Austin Robinson was of opinion that Weber's division of raw materials into ubiquitous and localized was rather vague. Weber ignored the factors of capital and organizing ability. Andreas Predohl pointed out that the distinction between the general and special factors influencing the location of industries was empirical in character and did not follow deductively. Prof. E.A.G. Robinson in his book "Structure of Competitive Industry" showed that the cotton textile industry developed in Lancashire, because the woollen industry was already there and that foreigners were kindly received there. The motor car industry was started by Mr. Ford in Detroit because it was his home town. Hoover elaborated on the Weberian model making far more realistic cost assumption than Weber. Hoover divided costs into transport (procurement and distribution) and production. Transport costs are not directly proportional to distance and weight as Weber assumed, but may vary according to the length and direction of haul and the composition of the goods involved. Hoover also gave more emphasis to institutional factors, such as local taxes which have considerable impact on locational decisions. He also mentioned market areas, but only from an assumed location and his concern was much more with costs than with demand. One of the fundamental weaknesses of the least cost approach is the overemphasis of the input site (cost minimization), and the underemphasis of the output or demand site. But market is a variable and therefore, may be a major location determinant, perhaps overriding the least cost location and its role in industrial location has been analyzed by August Losch in his book "The Economics of Location" (1954). Weberian theory and Loschian theory are complimentary to each other.

Loschian Theory of Profit Maximizing Approach

A. Losch (1906-1945)

Plate No. 3.4

Losch's general theory is an attempt to show how, in given circumstances, all economic activities should be arranged in space. He assumes a broad homogeneous plain with an even distribution of raw materials and uniform transport rates in all directions. The population, engaged in agriculture, is evenly distributed, and all individuals have identical tastes, technical knowledge and economic opportunities. The settlement pattern is one of evenly distributed self-sufficient farmsteads.

Losch attempts to incorporate demand into the theory by considering the optimum size of the market on the basis of the following assumptions:

- No spatial variations in the distribution of factor inputs—raw materials, labour and capital—over a homogeneous plain.
- Uniform population densities and constant tastes.
- No locational interdependence between firms.

If a single farmer decides to produce a surplus of say, beer, for sale, then his sales area will be circular, bounded by a locus of points at which delivered price becomes too high to sell any beer at all. But, if one farmer can produce a surplus so can others, therefore, others enter into this trade. Competition gradually reduces the size of sales area until ultimately they become hexagonal in shape as all space is filled up. Of the geometrical forms that could occupy all space, the hexagon has the highest demand per unit of area and minimizes the total distance from its centre to all points within the market area. As different goods are produced, a system of hexagons will arise for each industry, with the size of market area varying from industry to industry according to nature of the product. Losch then superimposes all of the individual systems so that all have at least one production centre in common. At this centre, where every product is made, there will be a metropolis and at other places where two or more production points coincide there will be towns or cities. Losch asserts that this arrangement has several advantages, the greatest number of location coincides, the maximum number of purchases are made locally, and the sum of the minimum distances between production sites is minimized, so that shipment and transport lines are reduced.

For the analysis, Losch uses and adapts a simple demand curve. At the centre of the market area near the farm (P), the unit price of beer is OP, with demand PQ. Farther from the centre, extra distribution cost results in a higher price, OR, and demand falls to RS. At the far extremities of the market area, extra distribution costs are prohibitive, pushing up the price to OF, and demand is nil. If the shaded quadrant, FPQ, is now rotated around the axis, PQ—P being the farm at the centre of the market, a 'demand cone' is produced. The base of the cone represents the market area, the height represents the quantity sold at anyone point, and the volume represents the total revenue from the market demand. In time, if beer production is profitable, other farmers will develop their own circular market areas, which, according to Losch, will finally adjust into a series of hexagonal market areas covering the entire plain.

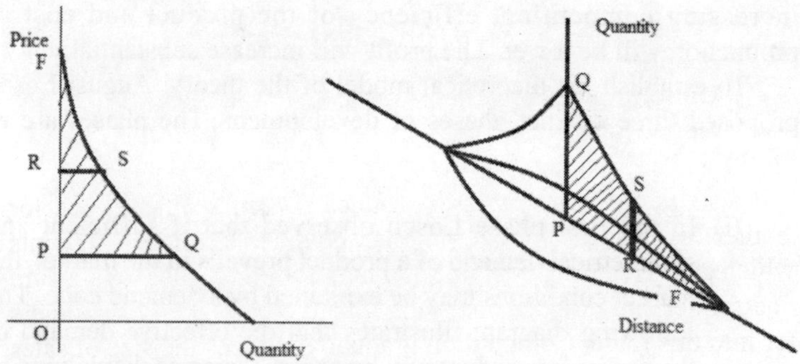

Fig. 3.6: Loschian Demand Curve and Cone

To achieve homogeneity of economy within the region, the theory required some more conditions. These are as follows:

- The entire area should be equally served by the factories. No area should be exempted from the supply; therefore, no new firm would dare to venture in the area.
- There must be conformity in the range and quantum to profit. In case of abnormal profit, new firms may try to establish their own plant.
- The location must satisfy both producer and consumer. The profit of the firm and satisfaction of the consumer must be optimum through the location.
- There must be provisions for consumers to get the products from other adjacent areas.
- The number of consumers, producers and areas should be well defined and not very extensive. Only a limited number of producers within a small area will be able to overcome the complexities and satisfy completely the handful of consumers.

According to Losch, to get the desired result from the location and sustained growth of industry, these conditions are prerequisites.

The major objective of Losch's Location theory is to attain equilibrium in the producing area and the product and the ability of the producer. If a single entrepreneur enters in the production process, within a vast area, the distribution cost will be very high. But when several small producers are engaged in the production process in separate regions, the distribution cost will come down and due to increasing competition, efficiency of the product and cost of production will be lower. The profit will increase substantially.

To establish his theoretical model of the theory, August Losch proposed three distinct phases of development. The phases are as follows:

(i) In the first phase Losch observed that if sufficient and symmetrical demand of a product prevails in the market, the market conditions may be explained by a demand cone. The following diagram illustrates that the effective demand of the particular product will be exactly same as the volume of the cone.

P is producer, and demand curve is lying on QF, P or price line controlled jointly by transport cost and distance. The price increases from P to F along the Y axis or PQ, demand of quantity is measured between PF and QF. When PF is taken as a measure of distance and is rotated about P, the circular market area is formed, bounded by the locus of points F, where the price becomes too high. Total scales are given by the volume of the cone produced by the rotation of PQF. It is clear from the diagram that, away from the centre, with increasing distance, demand of the quantity drops drastically.

(ii) In the second phase, within the vast rounded area, several factories will concentrate. The extensive market area will give a lucrative operational area, but despite the growing competition among the firms to capture larger market areas. There should be some void in the boundary zones and a certain amount of region will remain unserved or poorly served. The circular pattern of the industrial hinterland in phase-II will ultimately decide the future of the industry in that region.

(iii) In the third phase of industrial location, the intermediate space between two market areas will be narrowed. The areas fall vacant between the different market areas become and the target of new enterprises. As new firms set-up within the vacuum, the hinterlands of earlier industries become reduced. The reduction of the market area results in rapid disruption of the early circular pattern. Gradually, the market areas of the industries attain a hexagonal shape. Thus, around the

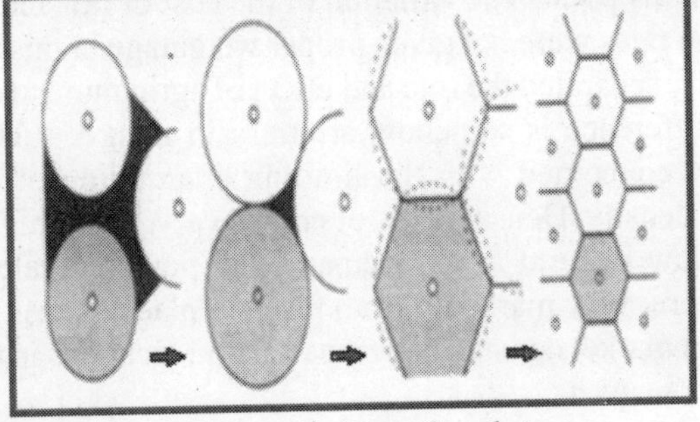

Fig. 3.7: Development of hexagonal shape of market area

nucleus of a city, numerous hexagonal market areas of different commodity will grow.

In this way, industries would concentrate within a region, each having different products. So, all types of minerals including raw materials should be available on that point. Hence, any new industry would get its raw material nearby. Obviously, the total transport cost in that place will be minimum cost. In this way, "equilibrium condition" as stated by Losch may be attained.

Criticism

Losch was the first person to consider the influence of the magnitude of the demand on industrial location. He also emphasizes upon the rate of competition as an important determinant of location analysis. His theory has also a philosophical contribution on the motive of entrepreneur's role. His equilibrium concept is perhaps the greatest contribution among the location theories developed later on.

However, Losch's theory was not entirely flawless. His theory is essentially a simplified model of an ideal condition. In reality, only in a rare occasion, these events may occur. The assumed conditions of homogeneous plain region, equal distribution of raw materials and uniform transport rates never occur in reality. Therefore, according to some critics, this theory is nothing, but an intellectual exercise. Losch even assumed the cultural homogeneity and test of people within the region and idea is quite absurd. He ignored the variation of technological development of different regions. The difference in technical know-how may offset the theoretical model. Political decisions also play an important role in the industrial location. Losch overlooked this point. The variation of the cost of raw materials and labour wage rates were not given proper weightage in this theory. He categorically separated the role and effect of agriculture and industry. But, this difference is somehow arbitrary in nature. Richardson is particularly concerned with the limiting assumption of a uniform population density. Densities do, of course vary, being high in urban areas and low in rural areas. Demand and potential sales revenue will, therefore, vary markedly from place to place. Harris shows the variations in market demand between different locations in the U.S.A.

Chapter 4
Planning and Development

Local, Regional and National Planning

Any national economy is built up of several sectors broadly categorized as, for example, heavy industry, manufacture of goods, production of food, supply of services, tourism etc. All generate wealth in some form and compete for resources in order to do so. A National Economic Development Plan will analyze the country's objectives and priorities in relation to all these sectors in response to well-identified national needs. It will propose and justify an overall plan in which the role of individual sectors, including aquaculture as a source of food, can be seen in context. A well-researched and reasoned policy document is of immense value to a country in the allocation of its scarce resources. It relates the scope and timetable of projects to the resources available and the benefits which will accrue. It enables realistic and achievable decisions to be taken. The private sector looks for a stable and sympathetic environment in which to invest securely and profitably. A national plan provides the evidence to make positive decisions. In developing countries, a national plan also meets the need of the international development banks and donor organizations to make loans or to provide technical assistance to selected national projects with a clear understanding of the benefits, and assured of the government's own wholehearted commitment. Without them, a project has little meaning or purpose. The national plan also enables these different organizations to avoid wasteful overlap and competition by coordinating their respective programmes. Finally, the government which sees fundamentally what must be done to secure its country's prosperity can act purposefully to bring it about. It can take strategic decisions which determine the course of events long into the future. As a component of a National Economic Development Plan, a sector plan for overall development will ensure that the legitimate claim of a share of resources is known and understood. The priorities which dictate selection of sector targets are best described by the framework of needs which an effective industry helps to satisfy. In aquaculture, the principal needs are considered to be four. All countries give highest priority to national food security to supply basic nutrition and to improve diet. As food is not usually distributed evenly, identification of national needs is often by region or possibly a smaller demographic unit. The importance of cultured aquatic foods as development targets for domestic consumption is determined to some degree by government policy, but there is always evidence of consumer trends and import statistics to interpret. For example, the high-protein content of fisheries products and medical support for their wide use in health programmes are undeniable benefits repeatedly in evidence. Low production and distribution costs are prime advantages of nationally produced commodities. These are especially important for cultured products which are trying to establish a share of an existing and often long-established market. Even if production is not viewed primarily as a source of profit, as is the case in some assistance or social projects, those for whom it is intended must be able to pay. There may be persuasive strategic arguments for some high-cost indigenous production to replace cheap imported products. However, the long-term viability of even this investment depends on the reduction of local costs. The potential to achieve reduced costs must exist and be provided for. The existing and forecast balance of trade figures are often used to identify a national need for products which can be exported to earn foreign currency. As with investments for domestic food production or nutritional improvement, the common denominator in every export-based proposal is that investments not adequately rewarded by conventional profit will struggle to survive. The incentive to exploit any accessible resources is to generate corporate profit or, at a lower level, to create income and thereby contribute to an improved standard of living for the producer. This is the most fruitful basis for integrative development, even when the resources may be little more than a natural waterbody or point of water source. Among the rural poor in developing countries, industrial projects which have the profit incentive are a priority. The prospect of profit is self-motivating and attracts ongoing investment for a viable progressive industry. In countries where high levels of long-term unemployment exist, the social implications of sector development may dictate priorities in favour of targets which are labour intensive. At times, some forms of subsidy or investment incentive are necessary, and economic and more appealing targets may have to be sacrificed or postponed as part of the national strategy or plan. Wherever employment opportunities are limited, the major deprived group is often the less educated and unskilled. These untrained resources impose obvious constraints on the types of aquaculture development which will meet this need. The industry, particularly at the level of production, is not labour intensive, although large farms employ significant numbers seasonally for harvest. The post-harvest industries, such as processing and packaging, require higher manning levels. In summary, having established how industries might meet these four principal needs, the purpose of the sector plan is to secure a favourable environment for investment in the broadest sense—knowledge and effort of all kinds, as well as finance. This will be referred to again, but examples are the designation of land and water zones for aquaculture development, and fiscal legislation which encourages more potential investors. The planning for regional development involves identifying the regionalism present, demarcating the region, determining the need of the region, formulating the plan, implementing the plan within the framework of government set-up and reviewing the implementation of the plan (Misra, R.P., 1992). After India gained independence, the Damodar Valley Project was launched in 1948 in the light of Tennessey Valley Authority. This is, however, the first landmark in the history of economic planning and development. The Damodar Valley region once again evolved as an economically viable and physically integrated inter-state planning unit for achieving sustainable development in India. These regions had been of greater importance as far as overall development is concerned.

In 1957, The Dandakaranya Development Project was implemented to rehabilitate the displaced people of East Pakistan (now Bangladesh) in order to promote integrated development of the area with special reference to the tribal and resettled population. This was a project implemented jointly by the then Central Government and three State Governmental agencies like Andhra Pradesh, Madhya Pradesh and Orissa. The aim was not only to facilitate the settlements of the migrants but also to pull up the development of the area, considered to be one of the backward tribal areas of the country.

Indeed the regional development planning and emergence of regional development policies were the key issues from the Third

Five Year Plan onwards. The growing regional disparity within the country itself led to the identification of industrially backward areas in the following Fourth Five Year Plan.

From the human centred perspective of the problem solving process, stage one is very important, because participants can share the ideas under the concept of 'unity from diversity' and shape a common communication base through dialogue. At this stage, information about what participants feel intuitively about regional problems has a high value because it might help in picking up symptoms of emerging problems in the region. This information becomes the seed of a new framework of a regional plan. We have to pay attention to local knowledge instead of central knowledge base at this stage. At this stage, the time schedule control to realize the plan is essential. Main measurement of taking action is efficiency because the goal which each participant has to attain should be well defined at stage six. Mathematical network models like CPM (Critical Path Method) or PERT (Programme Evaluation and Review Technique) are useful tools to support this stage. Actions change the regional circumstances. The result of actions is evaluated in relation to stage five by the general public as well as the specific participants. Evaluation of actions causes next general awareness of the situations. So, this stage is the last stage in the problem solving process, and at the same time, it leads to the first stage of the next problem solving process. The problem solving process is a cyclic process on the time scale.

Regional planning is a category of planning and development that deals with designing and placing infrastructure and other elements across a wide area. Planning zones may include several towns, cities or even parts of different states or regions, each of which could have its own "urban planning" office. The key to regional planning is anticipating the needs of a community or group of communities before those needs arise. Experts in this field might try to predict how and where the population of a region is going to grow over the next decade and recommend the building of roads and other infrastructure to support that growth before it happens. Those involved in the field are often called planning commissioners, and they work with local governments and urban planners within their planning zone to discuss such issues as regional development, land-use, community development, long-range planning, environmental planning, housing, and economic development. Regional planning often walks a fine line between serving the needs of the community, protecting the environment, and taking into account the rights of individual landowners and community members. Depending on the mission statement of the particular planning commission, the group may serve exclusively as an advisory board, as a research arm of the member cities, or as a governmental entity that approves building permits or neighbourhood plans in the region or in unincorporated areas of the region. Commissioners should have sufficient knowledge in many areas, including engineering, the environment, transportation, sociology, and geography. Many colleges and universities now offer degrees in Urban and Regional Planning. Regional planners are key to the thoughtful development of cohesive regions that both serve the needs of the communities within them and keep in mind the environmental impact of large groups of people living together. It is important that they understand how a region is growing and what needs to be done to ensure that growth happens in a logical and reasonable way. Planners are not usually anti-growth; instead, they seek to determine the best way for a community or group of communities to grow for the benefit of all involved.

Regional Spatial Development Planning

The regional spatial development plan seriously breaks with the idea that regional planning manages spatial planning in detail in each municipality. The regional plans created an overview and determined guidelines for spatial development. In the future the state and the municipality will be responsible for ensuring this quality in land-use planning. The regional spatial development plans will be part of this process, but very differently. The regional spatial development plans will not be able to manage in detail and will not have the role of deciding where various functions will be located. If the regional councils, the councillors and employees do not abandon the old way of thinking, the regional spatial development plans will fail and remain sparse documents. But these plans may also become dense. The regional councils have acquired an instrument that can lead the very broad dialogue that is required to create comprehensive spatial development related to the economic future of each administrative region. The regional spatial development plan expresses the regional council's visions for the overall future development of the administrative region across sectors. The regional spatial development

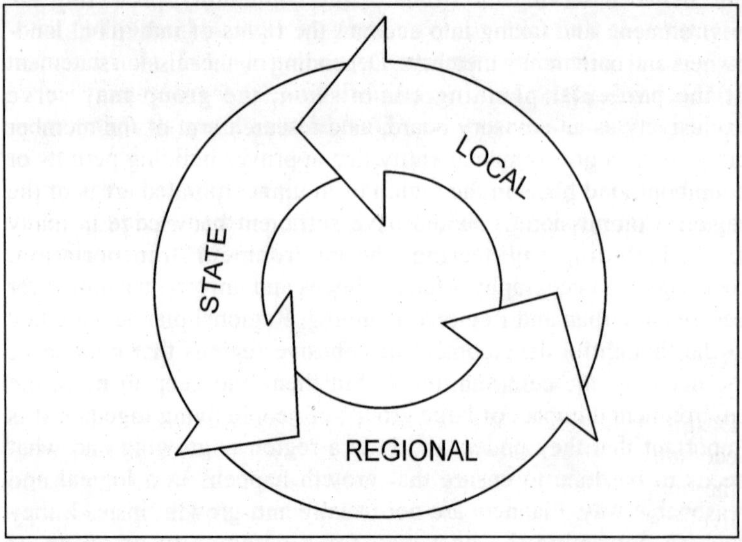

Fig. 4.1:

plan shall provide an overall projection of the administrative region and the territorial structure. Several regional agencies prepare plans and strategies for different sectors. The regional spatial development plan will integrate these plans and strategies and comprehensively portray the overall development of the administrative region.

Chapter 5
Regional Planning and Development

Rural Components of Regional Planning

Despite significant advancement in industrial development, Indian economy is dependent on agro-based activities. Over 70 per cent of the population living in rural areas is dependent on agriculture for livelihood. A majority of these families spend over 90 per cent of their earnings on basic needs such as food, fuel and healthcare. Over 50 per cent of the rural families who are not able to meet even these essential needs fall under the category of the poor. Thus, in an agrarian country like India, for improving the economic status of the population, it is not enough to enhance the per capita GNP, but it is also necessary to ensure prosperity among the poor. Industrial development and adoption of modern technologies are likely to generate additional employment in urban areas and pay rich dividend to elite and rich investors. This in turn might widen the gap between the urban and rural as well as the rich and the poor, with respect to wealth accumulation, resulting in further hardship to the poor. Therefore, we need to address the problems of the poor to ensure social justice and better quality of life.

Rural development also deserves priority for maintaining self-sufficiency in food supply. Our food security is under severe threat because of the growing population. No doubt, India has tripled her food production over the last four decades, to reach the present level of 195 million tons/year. However, with over 1.8 per cent annual birth rate, our growing population is bound to raise the annual demand for food to 250 million tons by 2010 A.D. As food security is a prerequisite for economic progress, agro-based rural development deserves attention.

Fortunately, the Government of India has been giving top priority to rural development. However, in the absence of well planned development programmes and efficient delivery systems, most of these resources do not benefit the target groups. It has been reported that only 18 per cent of the rural development budget reaches the target families, while the rest is wasted due to inefficient delivery systems or drained out. In the process of assisting the poor, a significant portion of the budget is spent on relief and subsidies. Poor families have received sympathy instead of motivation which has resulted in a dependency syndrome. As a result, most of the poor have lost confidence, initiative and entrepreneurship. The inputs and cash distributed for investment in development are being diverted for household consumption. In such a situation, free distribution of inputs may not help the rural poor any more.

The time is now ripe for a change in the strategy. The rural development programme should identify the problems of the poor and address the local needs, instead of forcing them to accept pre-conceived plans. The participating families should take active part in the programme. There should be equal opportunity for the weaker sections of the society and women. The programme should facilitate sustainable management of natural resources and environmental protection and lead to better quality of life. Of late, rural development has assumed global attention especially among the developing nations. It has great significance for a country like India where majority of the population, around 65 per cent of the people, live in rural areas. The present strategy of rural development in India mainly focuses on poverty alleviation, better livelihood opportunities, provision of basic amenities and infrastructure facilities through innovative programmes of wage and self-employment. This chapter overviews the role and function of the Government and its programmes for rural development in India. Science and technological interventions in the field of rural development and efforts being made to document some of the appropriate technologies developed by several research institutes, organizations suitable for application in rural areas are listed. Besides, the actual realization achieved during the Tenth Plan and the proposed target and strategy of the Eleventh Plan have been highlighted to show the recent trend of developmental activities under the Ministry of Rural Development.

Rural Development Strategies and Regional Planning

The Government of India's Twelfth Five Year Plan for the first time has set for itself the goal of faster, sustainable and more inclusive growth. Sustainability has been mainstreamed as a core objective of India's development strategy. The tentative Gross Budgetory Support (GBS) for the Ministry of Rural Development for Twelfth Five Year Plan (2012-17) is 4,43,261 crore, the Ministry of Rural Development's Schemes have an immense potential to contribute to the goal of sustainable poverty reduction and efficient use of natural resources, including improved land-use planning and management practices. For the people in rural areas, particularly the marginalized communities, healthy ecosystems support sustainable agriculture-based livelihoods and essential services such as drinking water, sanitation and healthcare. Investing in natural resources also strengthens adaptation and resilience of communities towards climate change and natural disasters. In specific it looks at:

- Improving quality and carrying of eco-systems including, water in surface bodies, aquifers and soil profile and arresting degradation of natural resources.
- Enabling sustainable livelihoods, based on sustainable use of natural resources.
- Strengthening ecosystem resilience to enable them to recover from extreme weather events and scope with climate change.
- Reducing the ecological footprint of interventions through efficient use of energy, material, natural resources and increased use of renewable materials.

The report recommends measures needed to achieve green, including measuring and tracking, the use incentives and the building of capacities. It also contains a number of case studies showing how green results can be achieved. The Ministry of Rural Development, with continued support from the United Nations Development Programme (UNDP), is keen to take forward the recommendations of this report and make delivery of green results a part of policy considerations and guidelines for its different programmes. I hope that these actions will contribute in large measure to achieve the goals, we have set ourselves, of the Twelfth Five Year Plan and beyond.

Poverty reduction and economic growth can be sustained only if natural resources are managed on a sustainable basis. Greening rural development can stimulate rural economies, create jobs and help maintain critical ecosystem services and strengthen climate resilience of the rural poor. Conversely, environmental challenges can limit the attainment of development goals. The Approach Paper to the Twelfth Five Year Plan notes that "as the economy gains the capacity to grow rapidly, it will come up against the constraint of limitations of natural resources and then need to exploit these in sustainable manner." (see Fig. 4.1) Recognizing the national and global imperatives for regenerating natural resources and conserving ecosystems, the Ministry of Rural Development requested UNDP to examine the environmental implications of its schemes and assess the potential of these schemes to deliver green results. The Report defines 'green' outcomes for major RD schemes, reviews the design and evidence from the field to highlight potential green results and recommends steps to improve green results. In the context of this report, greening rural development refers to five broad green outcomes:

- Improved natural resource conservation;
- Increased efficiency of resource use;
- Reduced negative environmental impacts;
- Strengthened climate resilience of communities; and
- Contribution to climate change mitigation.

These outcomes can be delivered by RD schemes by (a) investing in regenerating natural resources; (b) mobilizing and developing the capacities of community institutions to utilize natural resources in a sustainable manner; and (c) aggregating 'small initiatives' in several locations to improve natural capital on a macro-scale. The rationale for greening rural development emerges from the Twelfth Five Year Plan (2012-17) strategy of faster, sustainable and inclusive growth for poverty alleviation and MoRD's mandate to reduce rural poverty and ensure a better quality of life especially for the poor. The major schemes mentioned above can potentially make a significant contribution to sustaining natural resources and ecosystem services. Some examples are: A vast majority of the works under MGNREGS is linked to water, soil and land. The list of 'permissible' works provide environmental services such as conservation of water, groundwater recharge, reduced soil erosion, increased soil fertility, conservation of biodiversity, reclamation of degraded crop and grazing lands, enhanced leaf manure, fuel wood and non-wood forest products supply among others. The Integrated Watershed Development Programme (IWDP) aims to restore ecological balance in a watershed by harnessing, conserving and developing degraded natural resources such as soil, water and vegetative cover and thereby help provide sustainable livelihoods to the local people. The scheme's potential for green outcomes is also enhanced, if it supports the adoption of "greenagronomy" practices and promotion of use patterns that sustain natural resources including groundwater and soil fertility. Under NRLM, the guidelines for non-timber forest produce-based livelihoods under the Mahila Kisan Sashaktikaran Pariyojana (MKSP) identify regeneration and sustainable harvesting of NTFP species as key objectives; similarly, promotion of organic and low-chemical agriculture and increased soil health and fertility to sustain agriculture-based livelihoods is an objective under the sustainable agriculture component of MKSP; increased availability of green inputs and advisory services to farmers and livestock herders and use of renewable-based energy services for processing activities have immense potential for green outcomes. Under Indira Aawas Yojana (IAY), green results include efficient use of resources, including water, energy and construction material. Further, IAY can encourage greater use of renewable and locally available construction material, and reduced use of water and energy. Nirmal Bharat Abhiyan formerly the Total Sanitation Campaign (TSC)—has recently expanded its scope from eradication of open defecation to comprehensive sanitation in rural areas. Ten per cent of the project funds are earmarked for solid and liquid wastes management. NBA can ensure safe disposal of solid and liquid waste, and prevent untreated wastewater from re-entering the water system. These results can substantially improve the quality of water. The National Rural Drinking Water Programme Guidelines give high priority to water supply source sustainability and water quality. Further, the potential for green outcomes is enhanced by an emphasis on safe disposal of sludge after treatment of contaminated water, and the use of renewable energy for water pumping. The above green results can be achieved through specific measures—(a) at the level of the Ministry, and (b) for each scheme.

To achieve incremental results, the Ministry of Rural Development may identify a key set of green outcomes that are feasible and have high impact; prepare Green Guidelines which will detail how to achieve these desired results. The hallmark of the Green Guidelines will be : (i) a set of non-negotiable principles and goals and (ii) flexibility beyond the non-negotiable so that people and institutions are encouraged to adopt creative and innovative activities.

From a network of support organizations by designating select civil society organizations, technical institutions and academic centres to facilitate the implementation of the Green Guidelines. Establish an Innovations Portal for greening rural development. This portal will encourage innovative ideas, activities, technologies and processes adopted to promote and expand the greening activities. Set-up a Green Innovations Fund to promote and incentivize the development and extension of technologies and social processes to achieve green outcomes and set-up a dedicated Green Cell within the Ministry for guiding the greening agenda and for the implementation of Green Guidelines in the country. The Green Cell will develop procedures to converge actions and funding for greening activities that cut across rural development schemes. The orientation of the schemes will entail specifying rural principles, goals, actions, processes, desired outputs and outcomes, monitoring and evaluation procedures and systems in the scheme guidelines. Unless the green commitment and content are specified in the guidelines, implementation is likely to depend on individual initiative rather than be systemic. While most schemes have included significant green features in their recently revised Guidelines, the results are well below potential. Higher priority to be accorded to the green features, closer monitoring of green results and to strengthen implementation to achieve incremental green results across all schemes. Priority Recommendations for NRLM include as 'essential' outcome in Mahila Kisan Sashaktikaran Pariyojana (MKSP) guidelines, a result each on sustainable harvested produce and sustainable agricultural practices (in addition to current one on soil health) for all initiatives. Develop protocols for sustainable harvest of non-timber forest produce and sustainable agriculture and livestock management, and facilitate their adoption by SHGs. Earmark 2 per cent of overall budget (or 10% of provision for 'infrastructure and marketing') for work at mass level on developing niche markets for sustainable harvested produce and for green input supply chains provide back loaded 'labour subsidy' to SHGs for adoption of sustainable practices to compensate for lower labour productivity (in current guidelines, there is provision only for capital subsidy or revolving funds for SHGs) sustainable basis. India's commitment to planned economic development reflects government's determination to improve the economic condition of its people and an affirmation of the role of the government in bringing about this outcome through a variety of social, economic, and institutional means. India's First

Five Year Plan (1951-56) was aimed at economic stabilization and investment in the agrarian sector. This Plan supported community development aimed at transforming the social and economic conditions of the villages. The Second Five Year Plan initiated structural transformation with an emphasis on heavy industrialization. The first two plans laid the foundation for development planning in India. At the centre of India's current development strategy is raising the rates of economic growth and enabling inclusion. Raising the rates of investment is a key driver to economic growth as well as structural transformation, and investing in infrastructure is expected to remove constraints to growth. Natural capital or environmental resources are an important complement to such planned investment in achieving development goals. The Planning Commission notes in its Approach Paper to the Twelfth Five Year Plan that "economic development will be sustainable only if it is pursued in a manner which protects the environment. With acceleration of economic growth, these pressures are expected to intensify, and we, therefore, need to pay greater attention to the management of water, forests and land. These concerns are reflective of the situation in other countries as well.

In India forest management, reduction of freshwater availability and an extreme biodiversity loss rate does not leave enough time to the environment for recovery and regeneration. Nearly two-thirds of the services provided by nature to humankind are found to be in decline world-wide. Globally, economy-wide policy reforms designed to promote growth and liberalization have been encouraged with little regard to their environmental consequences, presumably on the assumption that these consequences would either take care of themselves or could be dealt with separately. Such policies will limit growth and increase risk to economic activity and human well-being. Given the fundamental uncertainties about the nature of ecosystem dynamics and the dramatic consequences we would face, if we were to guess wrong, it is necessary that we act in a precautionary way so as to maintain the diversity and resilience of ecosystems. It would, however, be incorrect to positive growth and environmental sustainability as mutually incompatible. What matters is the content of growth, i.e. the composition of inputs (including environmental resources) and outputs (including waste products). This content is determined by, among other things, the economic institutions within which human activities are conducted. Sustainable use of environmental resources can contribute to growth and stability. Global debates on green growth draw attention to the contribution of environmental resources to increasing the productivity of investment and to the effectiveness and longevity of infrastructural investment. The elasticity of substitution between natural capital and other inputs is found to be low, which implies that it may be possible to compensate for the loss of natural capital with other capital inputs in the short run but not in the long run. Moreover, while direct economic benefits from environmental policies will accrue mainly over the long term, green policies can also contribute to short-term economic growth. This strengthens the case for paying attention to environmental sustainability. There have been references in the literatures on the contribution of natural capital to sustained and equitable growth.

The UN Secretary General's High Level Panel on Sustainability notes that there exists tremendous opportunity for a dramatic improvement in the lives of the rural poor, even while they move towards more sustainable production models. Resource users will need access to assets, technology and markets. Success will depend, in great part, on investment. Success will also depend on institutions and initiatives with capacity to effectively coordinate efforts in priority areas of agriculture, land management and water. The Schemes of the Ministry of Rural Development are well located to deliver green outcomes, i.e. to restoring and enhancing ecosystem services and natural capital. There have also been extensive discussions in the literature on how to deliver on environmentally sustainable growth. Measures range from the regulatory and institutional to market-based economic instruments. Reliance on market instruments alone will not deliver environmentally sustainable growth, with the market being unable to generate pricing signals and green responses due to issues such as externalities, the 'public-good' nature of environmental assets, information asymmetry and agency problems and missing property rights. In particular, regulating or supporting services provided by ecosystems are difficult to define, measure, value and assign. The characteristics of resources and social interaction may present condition for the evolution of effective self-governing resource institutions which could be based on design principles outlined by the path-breaking work of Elinor Ostrom.

The Ministry of Rural Development (MoRD) spearheads the country's efforts to reduce poverty in the rural areas. Until recently, its work was divided among three departments: (i) Department of

Rural Development, (ii) Department of Land Resources, and (iii) Department of Drinking Water and Sanitation. In July 2011, the Department of Drinking Water and Sanitation was converted into a separate Ministry, the Ministry of Drinking Water & Sanitation. The MoRD website states, "This Ministry's main objective is to alleviate rural poverty and ensure improved quality of life for the rural population especially those below the poverty line." Towards this end, it sponsors scores of development programmes, big and small, influencing "various spheres of rural life and activities, from income generation to environmental replenishment." A small number of programmes of two Ministries—MoRD and MDWS, however, account for a substantial share of the expenditure on rural development. Primarily, these include the following:

(i) *Mahatma Gandhi National Rural Employment Guarantee Scheme (MGNREGS)*: This aims at enhancing the livelihood security of people in rural areas by guaranteeing hundred days of wage employment in a financial year to a rural household whose adult members volunteer to do unskilled manual work (Budgetary allocation in 2012-13: INR 33,000 billion).

(ii) *National Rural Livelihoods Mission (NRLM)*: The basic objective of the National Rural Livelihood Mission is to create efficient and effective institutional platforms of the rural poor that enable them to increase their household incomes through sustainable livelihood enhancements and improved access to financial services. It plans to cover 70 million households living below the poverty line (BPL) in rural India (Budgetary allocation in 2012-13: INR 3,563 billion).

(iii) *Integrated Watershed Development Programme (IWDP)*: The main objectives of the IWDP are to restore ecological balance in a watershed by harnessing, conserving and developing degraded natural resources such as soil, water and vegetative cover, and thereby provide help to sustainable livelihoods to the local people (Budgetary allocation in 2012-13: INR 2,744 billion).

(iv) *Indira Awaas Yojana (IAY)*: This scheme provides financial grants to rural BPL families and the next of kin of defence personnel killed in action for construction of houses and upgradation of existing unserviceable *kutcha* houses (Budgetary allocation in 2012-13: INR 9,966 billion).

(v) *National Rural Drinking Water Programme (NRDWP)*: The goal of this scheme is to provide adequate safe water for domestic uses on a sustainable basis (Budgetary allocation in 2012-13: INR 10,500 billion).

(vi) *Nirmal Bharat Abhiyan (NBA)*: The Total Sanitation Campaign, now renamed as the Nirmal Bharat Abhiyan, assists Gram Panchayats to achieve comprehensive sanitation coverage (Budgetary allocation in 2012-13: INR 3,500 billion).

The Approach Paper to the Twelfth Five-Year Plan notes that "as the economy gains the capacity to grow rapidly, it will come up against the constraint of limitations of natural resources and in the need to exploit these in a sustainable manner." Despite the concerns and the efforts of the Government of India—in the States and at the Centre, of environmentalists, voluntary organizations and communities across the country, the condition of India's environment poses formidable challenges. As the official State of India's Environment Report, *India 2009*, notes, "Land, degradation is taking place through natural and man-made processes, resulting in the loss of invaluable nutrients and lower foodgrain production. Loss of biodiversity is of great concern since many plant and animal species are being threatened. Air quality in cities is deteriorating due to vehicular growth and a sharp increase in air pollution related diseases. The issue of availability of water, which is going to be one of the critical problems in the coming decades, needs to be addressed on priority basis.

At the international level, a quarter century ago, the Brundtland Commission articulated the need for environmentally sustainable development. Today, there is much greater knowledge and awareness of the impacts of rising greenhouse gas emissions on global warming and climate change. In its recent report 'One Planet to Share', the United Nations Development Programme (UNDP) has proposed that governments of the Asia-Pacific region raise rural resilience since rural areas in the region are the main "food suppliers and carbon sinks". Recognizing the national and global imperatives for regenerating natural resources and conserving ecosystems, the Ministry of Rural Development requested UNDP to examine the environmental implications of its schemes and assess the potential of these schemes to deliver green results. UNDP has undertaken this study "Greening Rural Development Programmes in India" in response to this request. Rural Development uses green indicators and metrics for monitoring and evaluation of rural development projects and schemes. In the context of this report, greening rural development refers to six broad "green rural outcomes":

1. *Improved resource conservation*: Rural development schemes especially MGNREGS and IWDP focus on regeneration of natural resources. Conserving and regenerating land and water ressources enhances their productivity, leading to increased agriculture outputs and improved livelihoods derived from agriculture, forests and pastures. These schemes can assist in reducing run-off and soil losses, recharge groundwater, increase vegetative cover and improve biodiversity, and thereby, augment the productivity of natural resources and ecosystems.
2. *Improved resource efficiency*: Rural development schemes can substantially improve the efficiency of natural resource use in rural livelihoods and essential services. Under IWDP, there is opportunity to support farmer groups to adopt practices that improve efficiency of irrigation water. These can be done through appropriate crop choices, farming techniques, drip and sprinkler irrigation systems and improved field irrigation methods. Under NRLM, women's-self-help groups and farmers can be supported on efficient nutrient management by combining chemical inputs with organic inputs.
3. *Reduceed soil erosion:* Under MGNREGS, soil erosion can be reduced leading to lower run-off of chemical fertilizers and higher yields per unit of applied chemical fertilizer.
4. *Reduced negative environmental impacts*: Greening Rural Development Schemes can potentially reduce the negative environmental fall-out of economic development (pollution, waste generation etc.). Solid and liquid waste management in the Nirmal Bharat Abhiyan (formerly the Total Sanitation Campaign) improves local sanitation and hygiene and thereby, the well-being and health of local residents. In the Indira Awaas Yojana, the use of locally available resources such as rice husk ash and fly ash reduces diesel required to

transport manufactured materials over long distances, and thereby, environmental pollution. Organic farming and sustainable harvesting of NTFPs under NRLM and the use of renewable energy for lifting water in NRDWP are other examples.

5. *Strengthened climate resilience of communities*: Greening rural development schemes can potentially enhance the resilience of rural population and production systems, and reduce risks arising from climatic variations and extreme events such as droughts, floods and cyclones. Afforestation, plantations, fodder development and vegetation belts in coastal areas under MGNREGS, IWDP or NRLM build livelihood resilience and improve local communities' coping capacity to potential impacts of climate change. They also increase biodiversity and make the local ecosystems more resilient. Flood control measures under MGNREGS and IWDP enhance resilience in flood-prone areas.
6. *Contribution to climate change mitigation*: Large-scale forestry and soil conservation measures can sequester carbon and reduce greenhouse gas emissions. For example, afforestation, plantations and vegetation belts under MGNREGS and IWDP can help sequester carbon and contribute to national and global efforts to address climate change.

A critical element in meeting the planned target of nine per cent annual GDP growth is to sustain an annual growth rate of four per cent in the agricultural sector. This is important for ensuring that growth is more inclusive. Although agriculture contributes to only 14 per cent of India's GDP, it is the main source of income for 58 per cent of the rural population, particularly small farmers with limited opportunities for migrating to the modern growth sectors. Agriculture also has a strong influence on food security and the prices of food, and therefore, on monetary wages. Further, agriculture has a very strong multiplier effect because of its impact on rural income and demand, and its supply of raw materials to several industrial sectors. While there has been insignificant amerced revival in agricultural growth in India since 2004, for the Eleventh Five-Year Plan as a whole, the growth rate is 3.6 per cent. This is lower than the target for the Twelfth Plan. The year-to-year variability of agricultural growth has been declining, both on irrigated and rainfed land. Yet, the importance of climate-resilient domestic production of foodgrains has been highlighted by the recent spikes in global foodgrain prices. The impact of this variability goes further, with a one per cent decline in agricultural growth pulling back industrial growth and GDP growth by 0.52 per cent.

A vision document prepared by the Central Research Institute for Dry Land Agriculture estimates that there is a large scope for improving productivity in rainfed agriculture ranging from 200 per cent to 500 per cent depending on the crop. It is further estimated that rainfed agriculture requires an investment of only INR 2.7 billion for each additional million tons of food-grain production. The comparative investment for an additional million tons of irrigated food-grain production was estimated at INR 62.4 billion in 2010-2011. Rainfed agriculture's output is, therefore, essential for achieving higher and sustained overall growth in agriculture. Rural development schemes such as MGNREGS, IWDP and NRLM can contribute substantially to sustaining agricultural growth and reducing its variability in rainfed areas. The programmes such as MGNREGS, NRLM and IWDP target the private landholdings of the poor besides common lands. Small-scale water and soil conservation techniques that are applicable at the field level are adopted more easily by poor households. The diversion of even a small amount of water, e.g. even the grey water from the kitchen for a small domestic kitchen garden can make a significant difference to household nutrition. In rural areas, most people depend on their immediate environment for their daily survival—food water, fodder, firewood and shelter. N.S. Jodha's pioneering research a few decades ago showed that the rural poor in particular were heavily dependent on common property resources. This is true even today. Rural development schemes aimed at regenerating and conserving the rural natural resource base improve the well-being of the rural poor in several ways. A major role that public investment plays in a backward economy is to stimulate growth by encouraging and "crowding in" more private investment. Rural development schemes have the potential to play this role in India. Greening rural development can stimulate local growth by providing opportunities for private investment in green businesses: renewable energy generation, organic input chains and advisory services, green product supply chains, production of environment-friendly construction materials (fly ash and rice husk ash cement, fly ash and limestone bricks, Ferro-cement products and filler slabs for roofs). Rural development schemes can help widely disseminate information on green technologies and give an impetus to environment-friendly innovations in agriculture, processing, housing and construction of rural roads. Rural development schemes such as the NRLM and IWDP could include 'new style' interventions to improve the productivity and competitiveness of selected enterprises.

The Planning Commission notes in its Approach Paper to the Twelfth Five-Year Plan that "economic development will be sustainable only if it is pursued in a manner which protects the environment. With acceleration of economic growth, these pressures are expected to intensify, and we, therefore, need to pay greater attention to the management of water, forests and land. The State of India's Environment Report, 2009, supports this by observing that "Land degradation is taking place through natural and man-made processes, resulting in the loss of invaluable nutrients and lower food-grain production. Loss of biodiversity is of great concern since many plant and animal species are being threatened. The issue of availability of water, which is going to be one of the critical problems in the coming decades, needs to be addressed on priority basis." The 2005 Millennium Ecosystem Assessment estimated that 15 out of 24 of major global ecosystem services have already been degraded. If current environmental challenges intensify, the global Human Development Index in 2050 is likely to be 8 per cent lower than in the base case and 12 per cent lower for South Asia and Sub-Saharan Africa. The risks include impact on production in the agriculture and allied sectors, stress induced by rising water scarcity and deteriorating resource quality. Rural development schemes can contribute significantly to conserving water resources, soil quality and biodiversity.

The Report of the Working Group on Sustainable Groundwater Management submitted to the Planning Commission for the Twelfth Plan quoting the Report of the Expert Group on Groundwater Management and Ownership of the Planning Commission (2007), states that, "in 2004, 28 per cent of India's blocks were showing alarmingly high levels of groundwater use. A recent assessment by NASA showed that during 2002 to 2008, India lost about 109 km^3 of water leading to a decline in water-table to the extent of 0.33 metres per annum." With 80 per cent of drinking water for rural India and 60 per cent of irrigation water sourced from groundwater aquifers, this depletion is alarming. Rural Development schemes such as MGNREGS, IWDP and the source sustainability component of NRDWP can help arrest and even reverse the decline in groundwater levels in critical regions. This is particularly useful for hard-rock regions where groundwater depletion is at its most acute. Soil is a primary resource for generation of most renewable natural raw materials for production systems. But a study conducted by the Central Soil Water Conservation Research and Training Institute (CSWCRTI) in Dehradun estimates that India loses about one millimetre of top soil every year due to soil erosion. This amounts to an annual loss of 16.4 tons/ha or a total loss of 5,334 million tons annually. Soil contains enormous quantities of carbon in the form of organic matter. Soil carbon provides nutrients for plant growth. There is an estimated gap of about 10 million tons of nutrients (NPK), to begin with, between the absorption of nutrients by crops and their addition through fertilizers. Soil erosion depletes soil fertility and adds to global warming. Soil conservation works are a large part of MGNREGS and IWDP activities. Soil fertility enhancement is a key objective of the MKSP and sustainable agriculture components of NRLM. Together, these schemes can contribute substantially to addressing the issue of land degradation.

The goal of National Rural Drinking Water Programme (NRDWP) is to ensure that the basic minimum requirements of safe water for all rural household needs and cattle are met on a sustainable basis. The overall objective is to ensure permanent drinking water security in rural India. The Working Group on Rural Domestic Water and Sanitation for the Twelfth Plan has recommended that 55 per cent of the rural households be covered by piped water supply with house connections wherever possible. It also recommended that these systems supply minimum of 55 lpcd. The present NRDWP guidelines give high priority to water supply source sustainability and water quality. An elaborate water quality monitoring and surveillance system has been conceptualized in an attempt to ensure supply of safe drinking water. Due to the dispersed nature of water resources, source sustainability requires a primary role for rural communities in planning, managing and maintaining water resources and systems. For greening NRDWP, therefore, the critical components will include: (i) Regeneration and conservation of the resource base through roof-rain water harvesting; (ii) Renovation of traditional water harvesting structures; (iii) Treatment of the recharge zones of springs, groundwater aquifers and streams; (iv) Water quality monitoring and treatment to minimize contamination and ensure potable drinking water supply; and (v) use of renewable energy sources for pumps and higher resource use efficiencies.

A focus will enable MGNREGS to effectively deliver on its objective of creating durable assets and strengthening the livelihood resource base of the rural poor. By thus, ensuring livelihoods security, MGNREGS will increase labour absorption in natural resource-based livelihoods, and decrease demand for the employment in public works. Livelihoods security for the rural poor will be ensured even while the demand for work under MGNREGS declines. This will limit outlay under MGNREGS in the future. This will result in greater longevity for drinking water supply systems and will reduce the number of 'slipped-back' habitations. The average number of slipped back habitations targeted for coverage each year in the period 2002-8 to 2009-10 under the NRDWP has been more than 1,00,00,035. The NRDWP invests considerable funds in securing drinking water supply for such habitations. This expenditure can be reduced through green outcomes of rural development schemes. Recognizing this, NRDWP has recently increased the allocation for "Sustainability" component from 5 per cent to 20 per cent of its overall budget. This is for implementing the sustainability measures in rural water supply projects by the states. This underscores the importance of green outcomes (source sustainability) in making NRDWP expenditure effective. The MGNREGS and the IWDP can help bridge the gap between irrigation potential created and irrigation potential utilized, for small and micro irrigation projects. These schemes can also help maintain irrigation.

Natural resources such as farmlands, pastures, forests and water sources (surface and groundwater) are subject to degradation and loss of productivity. Satellite data showed that in 2005-2006 about 15 per cent (47.22 mha) of India's land mass were wasted or under-productive lands. Such degradations are important factor in the loss of livelihood assets and income poverty in rural India. The MGNREGA, therefore, proposes large investments in works like soil and water conservation, land development and afforestation that address the causes of chronic rural poverty. It also lays stress on creating durable assets. These key elements of the Act — productivity enhancement and sustainability of the rural natural resource base— strengthen its potential for green outcomes. MGNREGS is the largest rural development programme in the country in terms of its reach and budget. A vast majority of MGNREGS works are 'green' in nature given their focus on the regeneration and conservation of natural resources and ecosystems and their main emphasis being on land (farmlands, forests, pastures and waste lands) and water resources. In fact, since the initiation of MGNREGS more than 50 per cent projects are related to water through implementation of water conservation works, flood control, irrigation, drought proofing, renovation of traditional water bodies and micro-irrigation. Their main developmental consequences are higher crop productivities and production. Drought proofing activities, floods management works and vegetation belts planted in the coastal areas also reduce the potential damage due to extreme weather events. There is ample evidence that even basic MGNREGS works have led to the regeneration of degraded soil, land (farms, forests and pastures) and water resources and the conservation of the assets created. Their green outcomes include reducing soil erosion, improving soil fertility, increasing biodiversity, augmentation of surface and groundwater resources for irrigation and household use and increasing carbon sequestration. A number of such outcomes have been highlighted in many states like Karnataka, Madhya Pradesh, Andhra Pradesh, Rajasthan, Kerala and Maharashtra. Some examples of the impact of basic MGNREGS soil and water works from different parts of the country are: In Sidhi district (M.P.), 55 per cent of 240 respondents said that construction of ponds, tanks and wells and renovation of old structures led to an increase of 372 acres in the cropped area. Thirty-four anicuts (stone bunds) built under MGNREGS in Rajasthan irrigated 26 ha each on an average, enhancing groundwater recharge in nearby wells and raising their water levels between 10-40 feet. Renovation and construction of ponds under MGNREGS in Kerala led to an increase in the availability of irrigation water promoting the cultivation of cash crops like ginger and sugarcane.

There is also emerging evidence that some MGNREGS projects can have global green impacts. Activities, like soil conservation, fodder development, afforestation and drought proofing works, help sequester carbon. It has been estimated that tree planting activities over an area of 2,341 ha in Chitradurga district could lead to sequestration of 93 tons of carbon per ha over a 30-year period. No reliable estimates have been made yet on the amount of carbon sequestered as a result of MGNREGS soil conservation works. There are also several innovative MNREGP projects going beyond the routine activities with significant green results in the country.

National Rural Livelihoods Mission (NRLM) was launched by the Ministry of Rural Development (MoRD), Government of India in June 2011. The Mission aims at creating efficient and effective institutional platforms of the rural poor enabling them to increase household income through sustainable livelihood enhancements and improved access to financial services. The sustainability and green dimensions are reflected in the NRLM document: "Respect for nature and its stewardship to ensure sustainable livelihoods for present as well as future generations" which points out "Environmental stewardship and sustainable harvest/natural resource management are central for ensuring sustainability of livelihoods of rural poor." For the purpose of greening this scheme, the focus has been on three key livelihood components of the NRLM mainly livelihoods based on non-timber forest produce (NTFP), sustainable agriculture and non-farm employment. The NRLM is at its initial stage of deployment and state rural livelihood missions are being operationalized. Already the NRLM has a strong green emphasis. The greening strategies for the key livelihood sub-sectors that are outlined can be taken into account as the national-level activities. Additionally, the institutions of the poor being set-up and strengthened under NRLM offer an excellent platform for introducing and institutionalizing green strategies.

An explicit commitment under NRLM is evident in the 'Sustainable Agriculture for the Small Producers component of NRLM and the Mahila Kisan "Sashaktikaran" Pariyojana (MKSP). Community managed sustainable agriculture is emphasized with a strong focus on empowering women in agriculture. The sustainable agriculture focus of NRLM draws on the successful Community Managed Sustainable Agriculture Programme of Andhra Pradesh (*see* Case Study 3 on this programme) and reflects strong green emphasis as evident:

- A shift away from using chemical inputs in agriculture that will reduce external costs of cultivation and also, help in restoration of natural processes such as replenishment of soil nutrition, higher moisture capture in soils, increase in beneficial insects etc.

- Restoration of soil health (and multiple crop-systems) that can build up soil organic carbon and helping carbon sequestration.
- Intensive knowledge inputs to farmers in closely observing and strengthening natural cycles and farm-level ecologies that will build a 'green perspective' to farming on a large-scale.

For non-farm based livelihoods, an overall strategy is proposed for NRLM which involves developing non-farm based interventions at the block level that can follow a sub-sector approach along with identifying value chains that respond to the agro-ecosystem context and markets. The greening dimension can be introduced as with NTFP-based livelihoods described earlier by looking at greening nodes starting from resource base to exploring green technology options and processes. This is captured in the figure ahead. Further, potential for greening lies in the establishment of a fund to support innovative projects. The innovation fund is meant to support extension of tested livelihoods development innovations that substantially benefit the poor, involve end-to-end solutions, organization of the poor for livelihoods and partnership or consortia-based projects. The document specifically mentions projects that include "small and marginal farmers' ecological and organic farming", livelihoods associated with NTFP collectors, coastal communities, people in ecologically fragile regions and commons. It also supports forward linkages in agriculture and livestock, both of which can be linked. Integrated Watershed Development Programme (IWDP) construction, large amounts of raw materials including natural resources, energy and water are consumed. There is significant potential to green the scheme by encouraging the use of green building materials, construction methods and building environment-friendly designs. The IAY guidelines in fact do emphasize using low-cost, environment-friendly and disaster-safe construction technologies. As greening should be integrated through the entire life-cycle of a building, greening the IAY requires:

1. *Reduction in the amount of manufactured building materials*: The main manufactured building materials used in rural housing are cement, steel and bricks. All of them are produced by processing ores or soil with intensive use of commercial power or energy and the release of pollutants into the

surrounding environment. These can be substituted with naturally available construction materials like mud, stones, timber or bamboo. Mud walls or mud mortar is, however, identified with *kutcha* (weak) structures. With the guidelines emphasizing that the house should be a *pucca* one, mud tends to be ignored in IAY. But, there are options to enhance the durability of mud by adding small amounts of cement or straw. Bamboo poles tied together can make a strong and ductile beam. Resource conservation can also be achieved by using fly ash cement or rice husk ash cement. In both cases, the use of 'waste' products, i.e. fly ash from thermal power stations or rice husk ash from burning the husk reduces the need for lime stone.

2. *Intelligent construction processes for conservation of resources and reduction in the development footprint*: The use of local materials reduces the consumption of fossil fuels that are normally used for transporting manufactured materials to construction sites. Secondly, in a typical IAY house, a solid brick wall can use 480 bricks and 65 kg cement whereas rat trap bonded masonry requires 400 bricks and 6 kg cement. The consequent non-renewable energy embedded in the wall reduces from 486 Mega Joules per cum to 388 Mega Joules/cum in a rat trap wall. The CO_2 emission of solid brick wall is 327 kg/cum against 254 kg in rat-trap bonding. Use of labour instead of machines and less water also help conserve resources. A shift is required in the scheme's emphasis from quantitative to qualitative aspects—from regenerating or augmenting resources to their sustainable use. Thus, the scheme activities must shift focus from soil conservation to soil fertility enhancement, from augmenting water resources to their conservation and sustainable use, from merely planting saplings to their survival rates and species diversity and from unsustainable high external input agriculture to low external inputs sustainable agriculture. Key aspects of a sustainable production system include a nutrient/pest management approach that increases the use of organic or biological inputs, cultivation practices such as minimum tillage, soil mulching, ploughing back crop residue, crop rotation and companion cropping, seed banks, integration of livestock

husbandry with agriculture, and post-harvest storage and processing. These shifts will make the farms more productive, will sustain the natural resource base, increase biodiversity on the commons and the farms, and reduce ecological vulnerabilities and pollution due to agricultural chemicals. All of this entails a revision of the scheme objectives, activities and desired results. As also redesigning the capacity building processes for stakeholders' groups to include greener watershed approaches that are reflected in the new project plans or detailed project reports. The new green results for IWDP will need to include: (i) ecological and economic aspects; (ii) quality of life for the watershed communities; (iii) institutions and their capabilities; (iv) planning and implementation; and (v) convergence of resources. Most rural development water supply systems depend on groundwater sources at a time when there are heavy competing demands from industry and agriculture. Despite impressive figures of coverage of habitations with water supply systems, slippages continue to dog the sector due to drying up of sources, reduction in discharge or contamination. At the same time, the Working Group on Drinking Water and Sanitation for the Twelfth Plan has recommended piped water supply, preferably with house connections to 55 per cent rural households up from 35 per cent at present. The function of the Rural Development Division is primarily to provide overall policy guidance in formulation of plans and programmes for Rural Development. This is the nodal Division for matters relating to poverty eradication, employment generation in rural areas and Land Record Modernization Programme (NLRMP). The following specific activities are undertaken by Division:

(i) To assist in formulation of rural development programmes to be included in Five Year Plans and Annual Plans and to make periodic assessment of progress achieved.

(ii) To maintain liaison with Ministry of Rural Development, National Institute of Rural Development (NIRD) and other allied organizations mainly and participating in the meetings.

(iii) To collect information from various Divisions of the Planning Commission, State Governments and also from the Central Ministries which are implementing various schemes related to rural development.

(iv) To organize Working Group meetings to finalize the Draft Five Year Plan proposals of the State Governments. This involves the preparation of background papers, discussions on *inter se* plan priorities, critical examination of plan proposals in relation to plan objectives and approaches, preparation of Working Group Reports giving, *inter alia,* outlays and physical targets.

(v) Finalization of the Five Year Plan outlays of the Ministry of Rural Development. Finalization of Annual Plans of the Central Ministry of Rural Development and State Governments. This includes assessment of progress both in physical and financial terms, in relation to the approved targets and outlays, scheme-wise examination of proposals and reviewing targets and finalizing allocation for next Annual Plan.

(vi) To provide comments, materials etc. for Public representations, VIP references, Parliament Questions and Agenda items for the meetings of Consultative Committee/Standing Committee for the Planning Commission pertaining to rural development sector are also attended to.

The Rural Development Division looks after the following programmes being implemented by the Ministry of Rural Development (MoRD): Mahatma Gandhi National Rural Employment Guarantee Act (MGNREGA).

The MGNREGA was launched on February 2, 2006 and the first full year of operation was 2006-07 covering 200 districts. The programme was expanded to 330 districts in 2007-08 and covers the whole country from April 1, 2008. The MGNREGA aims at enhancing the livelihood security of the people in rural areas by providing guaranteed wage employment through works that create durable assets and strengthen the livelihood resource base of the rural poor. The choice of works suggested addresses causes of chronic poverty like drought, deforestation and soil erosion etc. The MGNREGA thus provides a social safety net for the vulnerable groups and an opportunity to combine growth with equity. The implementation of Act ensures that local employment is available to every rural household for at least 100 days in a financial year.

Swarnajayanti Gram Swarozgar Yojana (SGSY)/National Rural Livelihood Mission (NRLM)

Swarnajayanti Gram Swarozgar Yojana was launched in April 1999 following the restructuring of the erstwhile Integrated Rural Development Programme (IRDP) and its allied programmes along with Million Wells Scheme (MWS). The objective of SGSY is to bring the poor families (*Swarozgaris*) above the poverty lines by organizing them into Self-Help Groups (SHGs) through the process of social mobilization, their training and capacity-building and provision of income-generating assets through mix of bank credit and government subsidy. The SGSY programme is conceived as a process-oriented programme for the poor with emphasis on social mobilization and formation of SHGs. Funding pattern is 75:25 between Centre and States and 100 per cent central assistance in case of UTs.

The SGSY has been restructured as National Rural Livelihoods Mission (NRLM) renamed as *Aajeevika* to implement it in a mission mode in a phased manner for targeted and time-bound delivery of results. *Aajeevika* will support creations of strong institutions of the rural poor and will also support them in increasing their incomes through improvements in their existing livelihoods and also diversifying into new livelihoods. In order to ensure a holistic approach towards income enhancement of the rural poor, *Aajeevika* will focus on four streams of livelihoods which would be as follows:

- Coping with vulnerabilities—debt bondage, food insecurity, migration, health shocks.
- Existing livelihoods—stabilizing and expanding, making them sustainable.
- Self-employment—micro-enterprise development.
- Skilled wage employment—opportunities in growing sectors of the economy.

Key Features of *Aajeevika* include Universal Social Mobilization, Promotion of Institutions of the Poor, Training, Capacity Building and Skill Building, Revolving Fund and Capital Subsidy, Universal Financial Inclusion, Provision of Interest Subsidy, Infrastructure Creation and Marketing Support and Skills and Placement Projects.

Indira Awaas Yojana (IAY)

The Indira Awaas Yojana (IAY) is a flagship scheme of the Ministry of Rural Development to provide houses to below the poverty line (BPL) families in the rural areas. It has been in operation since 1985-86.

The funding of IAY is shared between the Centre and States in the ratio of 75:25. In the case of UTs, entire funds of IAY are provided by the Centre. However, in the case of NE States, the funding pattern has been changed and at present is in the ratio of 90:10. The ceiling on construction assistance under IAY is Rs. 70,000 per unit in the plain areas and Rs. 75,000 in hilly/difficult areas. In addition, all nationalized banks have been instructed to include the IAY houses under the Differential Rate of Interest (DRI) Scheme for lending up to Rs. 20,000 per housing unit at interest rate of 4 per cent for SC/ST beneficiaries. For upgradation of *kutcha* houses, the financial assistance is Rs. 15,000 per unit.

National Social Assistance Programme (NSAP)

NSAP was launched by Government of India on 15th August, 1995 with the aim to provide social assistance benefit to poor households in the case of old age, widows, disabled and death of primary breadwinner of the BPL households. The programme supplements the efforts of the State Governments with the objective of ensuring minimum national levels of well-being and the Central Assistance is an addition to the benefit that the States are already providing on Social Protection Scheme. With a view to ensure better linkage with nutrition and national population control programmes, the maternity benefit component of the NSAP was transferred to the Department of Family Welfare, Ministry of Health and Family Welfare from the year 2001-02. NSAP, at present, comprises of Indira Gandhi National Old Age Pension Scheme (IGNOAPS), Indira Gandhi National Widow Pension Scheme (IGNWPS), Indira Gandhi National

Disability Pension Scheme (IGNDPS), National Family Benefit Scheme (NFBS) and Annapurna Scheme. The funds under NSAP were released as Additional Central Assistance (ACA) till 2013-14 by the Ministry of Finance on the recommendation of Ministry of Rural Development (MoRD), as NSAP has been transferred to State Plan, w.e.f. 2002-03. From 2014-15, NSAP is a Centrally Sponsored Scheme under Ministry of Rural Development and funds are routed through the consolidated fund of State.

The Components and Scale of Central Assistance under NSAP is as follows:

- *Indira Gandhi National Old Age Pension Scheme (IGNOAPS)*: Rs. 200 per month per beneficiary to BPL persons who are in the age group of 60-79 years and Rs. 500 per month to 80 years and above.
- *Indira Gandhi National Widow Pension Schemes (IGNWPS)*: Rs. 300 per month per beneficiary who are BPL and in the age group of 40-79 years.
- *Indira Gandhi National Disability Pension Scheme (IGNDPS)*: Rs. 300 per month per beneficiary who are in the age group of 18-79 years.
- *National Family Benefit Scheme*: Rs. 20,000 to the bereaved household in case of the death of primary bread winner of the family. The eligibility criteria are BPL person who is primary bread winner of the family and in the age group of 18-59 years.
- *Annapurna Scheme*: 10 kg of foodgrain (wheat or rice) per month per beneficiary to those who are not covered under IGNOAPS.

National Land Records Modernization Programme (NLRMP)

For modernization of land records system in the country, a modified programme, *viz*. the National Land Records Modernization Programme (NLRMP) has been formulated by merging two Centrally sponsored schemes of Computerization of Land Records (CLR) and Strengthening of Revenue Administration and Updating of Land Records (SRA & ULR) in the Department of Land Resources (DoLR), Ministry of Rural Development. The NLRMP was approved by the Cabinet on August 21, 2008.

The integrated programme would modernize management of land records, minimize scope of land/property disputes, enhance transparency in the land records maintenance system, and facilitate moving eventually towards guaranteed conclusive titles to immovable properties in the country. The major components of the programme are computerization of all land records including mutations, digitization of maps and integration of textual and spatial data, survey/re-survey and updating of all survey and settlement records including creation of original cadastral records wherever necessary, computerization of registration and its integration with the land records maintenance system, development of core Geospatial Information System (GIS) and capacity building. Detailed Guidelines and Technical Manual for better implementation of the NLRMP Manuals have been prepared after obtaining inputs from the leading technical agencies as well as from the field experience of States.

The main objective of the NLRMP is to develop a modern, comprehensive and transparent land records management system in the country with the aim to implement the conclusive land-titling system with title guarantee, which will be based on four basic principles, i.e. (i) a single window to handle land records (including the maintenance and updating of textual records, maps, survey and settlement operations and registration of immovable property); (ii) the mirror principle, which refers to the fact that cadastral records mirror the ground reality; (iii) the curtain principle which indicates that the record of title is a true depiction of the ownership status, mutation is automated and automatic following registration and the reference to past records is not necessary; and (iv) title insurance, which guarantees the title for its correctness and indemnifies the title holder against loss arising on account of any defect therein.

1. Community Development is the method and Rural Extension the agency through which the Five Year Plan seeks to initiate a process of transformation of the social and economic life of the villages. The Plan provides Rs. 90 crore for community projects and proposes the establishment of over a period of about ten years a network of extension workers throughout the country. The object of this chapter is to indicate briefly the significance of the two programmes and their place in national reconstruction.

2. For some three decades rural development work has been undertaken by different branches of the administration in the States. Until a few years ago, the expenditure on development was meagre and rural development work was thought of largely in terms of particular items of improvement in village life and in agricultural practice, and special attention was given, for instance, to the number of wells sunk or repaired, for the supply of irrigation or drinking water, the supply of seeds or fertilizers, or the number of manure pits dug. Starting of rural credit societies etc. These are essential items in any rural programme, but there was no coordinated approach to village life as a whole.

3. If one goes back to the study of the efforts made before Second World War in individual Provinces and States and considers the experience gained in later years in Sevagram in Madhya Pradesh, in the Firka Development Scheme (1947) in Tamil Nadu, (Formely Madras State) in the Sarvodaya centres in Mumbai (Formely Bombay), in Etawah and Gorakhpur in Uttar Pradesh and other centres which are perhaps less well known, certain broad conclusions emerge. These are:

(i) When different departments of the Government approach, the villager, each from the aspect of its own work, the effect on the villager is apt to be confusing and no permanent impression is created. The peasant's life is not cut into segments in the way the Government's activities are apt to be; the approach to the villager has, therefore, to be a coordinated one and has to comprehend his whole life. Such an approach has to be made, not through a multiplicity of departmental officials, but through an agent common at least to the principal departments engaged in rural work, which it is now customary to describe as the village level worker.

(ii) Programmes which have been built on the cooperation of the people have more chances of abiding success than those which are forced down on them.

(iii) While the official machinery has to guide and assist, the principal responsibility for improving their own condition must rest with the people themselves. Unless they feel that a programme is theirs and value it as a practical contribution to their own welfare, no substantial results will be gained.

(iv) Programmes largely dependent on expenditure by the Government, in which the elements of self-help and mutual cooperation on the part of villagers are present only in a nominal degree are shortlived. The essential idea should be the reduction of chronic unemployment which is a feature of rural life—through the practice of scientific agriculture and cottage and small-scale industries.

(v) Advice and precept are of no avail unless they are backed by practical aids—supplies of seed and fertilizer.

Community Development Programme

1. These lessons from the experience of the past have been brought together in the conception and concrete formulation of the Community Development Programme, which has been launched during 1952. While the concept is not a new one, progress has in the past been hampered by insufficiency of available funds.

Size of the Unit

2. For each community project, as at present planned, there will be approximately 300 villages with a total area of about 450 to 500 square miles, a cultivated area of about 1,50,000 acres and a population of about 2,00,000. The project area is conceived as being divided into 3 Development Blocks, each consisting of about 100 villages and a population of about 60,000 to 70,000. The Development Block is, in turn, divided into groups of 5 villages each, each group being the field of operation for a village level worker.

Location of Units

3. The initial programme has been started with approximately 55 projects of rural development located in select areas in the several States of India. A certain degree of flexibility is allowed in the actual allotment of projects. Thus, while many are complete projects of about 300 villages each, some are also independent development blocks of about 100 villages each, depending upon the needs and conditions of the particular areas chosen for development.

4. As increased agricultural production is the most urgent objective, one of the basic criteria in the selection of this first set of project areas has been the existence of irrigation facilities or assured rainfall. In assessing irrigation facilities and the possibilities of development, irrigation from river valley projects, from tube-wells, as well as from minor irrigation works have been taken into account. In States like

West Bengal and Punjab, with a large population of displaced persons, the selection of project areas aims also at helping the resettlement of these persons. Seven areas have been selected on the ground of their being inhabited predominantly by scheduled tribes. In every field of activity, whether social or economic, urban and rural developments are complementary, for, neither towns nor villages can advance alone. Where the existing urban facilities are inadequate or where large numbers of displaced persons have to be rehabilitated, the intention is that the urban development should take the form of new townships. Six such projects have been proposed to be taken up under the current programme.

Under such rural-CMW-urban development, new towns will come into existence to serve as centres which will draw sustenance from the surrounding countryside and, in return, carry to it new amenities and the spirit of a developing and changing economy. The creation of new centres of small-scale industrial production, closely coordinated with rural development is fundamental to national development, for in no other way can the present occupational imbalance between agriculture and industry, between village and town, be corrected. With the development of power resources and of communications and the growth of basic industries, the scope for establishing such centres will steadily increase and, as the economy develops, this programme will gain in importance. During the first few years, however, it is inevitable that by far the greatest stress in community development, as indeed in national planning, should be on rural areas. The intensive development of agriculture, the extension of irrigation, rural electrification and the revival of village industries, wherever possible, with the help of improved techniques, accompanied by land reform and a revitalized cooperative movement, are programmes closely related to one another, and together calculated to change the face of the rural economy.

Main Lines of Activity

5. The main lines of activity which will be undertaken in a community project, can be briefly divided into the following Agriculture and related matters—Irrigation, Communications, Education, Health, Supplementary Employment, Housing, Training, and Social Welfare.

Agriculture and Related Matters

6. The programme includes reclamation of available virgin and waste land; provision of commercial fertilizers and improved seeds; the promotion of fruit and vegetable cultivation, improved agricultural technique and land utilization; supply of technical information, improved agricultural implements, improved marketing and credit facilities, provision of soil surveys and prevention of soil erosion, encouragement of the use of natural and compost manures and improvement of livestock, the principal emphasis here being on the establishment of key villages for breeding pedigree stock and the provision of veterinary aid, as well as artificial insemination centres. For attaining this objective, agricultural extension service will be provided at the rate of one agricultural extension worker for every five villages.

One of the important functions of the agricultural extension worker will be to encourage the growth of a healthy cooperative movement. The aim will be to see that there is at least one multi-purpose society in every village or group of villages on which practically every agriculturist family is represented.

It is expected "that the cooperative principle, in its infinitely varying forms, will be capable of adaptation for finding a solution to all problems of rural life." Multi-purpose societies will, therefore, have to be used for practically every development activity in the community project area, including the encouragement of rural arts and crafts.

Irrigation

7. The programme visualizes provision of water for agriculture through minor irrigation works, e.g. tanks, canals, surface wells, tube-wells etc., the intention being that at least half of the agricultural land, if possible, be served with irrigation facilities.

Communications

8. The road system on the country side is to be so developed as to link every village within the Project area up to a maximum distance of half a mile from the village, the latter distance being connected by feeder roads through voluntary labour of the villagers themselves, only the main roads being provided for and maintained by the State or other public agencies.

Education

9. It has been realized that the full development of a community cannot be achieved without a strong educational base, alike for men and women. The community projects have been planned to provide for social education, expansion and improvement of primary and secondary education and its gradual conversion to basic type, provision of educational facilities for working children and promotion of youth welfare. Vocational and technical training will be emphasized in all the stages of the educational programme. Training facilities will be provided for imparting improved techniques to existing artisans and technicians, both in urban and rural areas. Training centres which already exist in any area, will be strengthened and developed, and new ones established to meet the requirements of the project area.

Health

10. The Health Organization of the Project area will consist of three primary health units in the Development Blocks and a secondary health unit equipped with a hospital and a mobile dispensary at the headquarters of the Project area and serving the area as a whole. It would aim at the improvement of environmental hygiene, including provision and protection of water supply; proper disposal of human and animal wastes; control of epidemic diseases such as Malaria, Cholera, Small-pox, Tuberculosis, etc. Provision of medical aid along with appropriate preventive measures, and education of the population in hygienic living and in improved nutrition.

Supplementary Employment

11. The unemployed and the underemployed persons in the village community will be provided with gainful employment to such an extent as is possible, by the development of cottage and small-scale industries, construction of brick kilns, saw mills and encouragement of employment through participation in the tertiary sector of the economy.

Housing

12. Apart from the provision of housing for community projects personnel, steps will be taken, wherever possible, to provide demonstration and training in improved techniques and designs for rural housing. In congested villages, action in the direction of development of new sites, opening of village parks and playgrounds and assistance in the supply of building materials, may also be necessary.

Training

13. The training of village level workers, project supervisors and other personnel for the Community Development Programme will be carried out in 30 training centres, which have been set-up with the assistance of the Ford Foundation of America. Each training centre will have facilities for about 70 trainees. Each centre will have double training staff so that the trainees can be divided into two groups. One group will be getting practical and supervisory work experience, while the other group will be utilizing the centres' facilities for lectures, demonstrations and discussions. In view of the great demand on the training centres to turn out people quickly for the opening of new projects, the training period will, in the first instance, be limited to six months. In addition to the training of village level workers and supervisors, the agricultural extension service workers in the Project areas will take steps for the training of the agriculturists, panchayats and village leaders.

Social Welfare

14. There will be provision for audio-visual aid for instruction and recreation, for organizations of community entertainment, sports activities and *Melas*.

Organisation

15. *Centre*—For the implementation of the Community Development Programme as indicated above, the Central Organization will consist of a Central Committee (the Planning Commission has been designated as the Central Committee) to lay down the broad policies and provide general supervision, and an Administrator of Community Projects under the Central Committee. The Administrator will be responsible for planning, directing and coordinating the Community Projects throughout India under the general supervision of the Central Committee and in consultation with appropriate authorities in the various States. He will be assisted by a highly qualified executive staff to advise him on administration, finance personnel, community planning and other matters.

16. *State*—At the State level, there will be a State Development Committee or a similar body consisting of the Chief Minister and such other Ministers as he may consider necessary. There will also be a State Development Commissioner or a similar official who will act as the Secretary to the State Development Committee and will be responsible for directing community projects in the State. Where the work justifies it, there may, in addition, be a Deputy Development Commissioner specifically in charge of community projects.

17. *District*—At the District level, there will be, wherever necessary, a District Development Officer responsible for the Community Development Programme in the district. This officer will have the status of an Additional Collector and will operate under the directions of the Development Commissioner. He will be advised by a District Development Board consisting of the officers of the various departments concerned with Community Development, with the Collector as Chairman and the District Development Officer as executive Secretary.

18. *Project*—At the Project level, each individual project unit (consisting of a full project or one or more Development Blocks where there is not a full project) will be in charge of a Project Executive Officer. In the selection of Project Executive Officers, special regard will be paid to experience, general outlook, understanding of the needs and methods of Community Development, capacity for leadership and ability to secure both official and non-official cooperation. Each Project Executive Officer in charge of a full project, will have on his staff approximately 125 supervisors and village level workers, who will be responsible for the successful operation of all activities at the Project Level. This organizational pattern will be adapted to suit local conditions and needs as may be deemed necessary by the Administrator and the respective State Governments.

People's Participation—the Crux of the Programme

19. While on the subject of organization, it is necessary to stress the importance of ensuring, right from the start, the people's participation, not merely in the execution of the Community Development Project but also in its planning. This, in fact, is the very essence of the programme.

20. The Community Development Programme aims at the establishment of a suitable organ to ensure participation of the villagers at the planning stage. It contains provisions for the setting up of a Project Advisory Committee. It is intended that the Project Advisory Committee should be as representative as possible of all the non-official elements within the project area. In securing participation of the villagers in the execution of the programme, the Community Projects Organization will avail of all non-official local voluntary organizations and especially the Bharat Sevak Samaj, which is likely to be set-up in the project area on the lines indicated in the pamphlet recently circulated by the Planning Commission.

Villager's Contribution to the Programme

21. The pattern of the project as drawn up includes major items of works normally implemented through Government agencies. This is bound to involve higher expenditure through elaborate administrative staff, middlemen's fees and possibly in certain cases, questionable practices. If the people are to be trained to be the builders of the future, the works have to be entrusted, even at certain risks, to the people themselves through their representative agencies, the Governmental organization furnishing the technical assistance and the essential finance. It is intended that a qualifying scale of voluntary contribution, either in the form of money or of labour, should be laid down and this contribution will be a condition precedent to development schemes being undertaken under the Community Development Programme. In all these cases, contributions may be in the form, either of voluntary labour or of cash. In respect of backward areas and areas predominantly populated by scheduled castes and scheduled tribes, it may not be possible for the villagers to make any financial contribution. In these areas, the villagers should be asked to contribute by way of labour effort required for executing the works programme under various heads. The agency of the Bharat Sevak

Samaj is hoped to become a major avenue for the organization of the voluntary effort on the part of the villagers.

22. The estimated expenditure on a basic type of a rural community project varies according to size, issue and place.

In order to enable expansion of the programme in future years, the Central Committee felt that some reduction in the estimated cost of a rural community project, basic type, should be made and, after examination of the question, has now decided that oil community projects should be operated on the basis of a reduced total of Rs. 45 lakh per project. So far as the existing projects are concerned, this would mean that the area of operations under each project on a population basis of 2 lakh per project should be so revised or adjusted as to conform to the new expenditure pattern.

The Community Development Programme imposes financial obligations on the Centre as well as on the State Governments. Broadly, the proportions which have been fixed are 75 per cent for the Centre and 25 per cent for the State in respect of non-recurring expenditure, and 50 per cent each for Centre and States in respect of recurring expenditure. This applies to 'grants-in-aid'. Loan amount is totally found by the Centre. After the three-year period, the Community Project areas are intended to become Development Blocks on the lines recommended for adoption in Chapter VI of the Grow More Food Enquiry Committee's Report. It is expected that in so far as the Community Project areas are concerned, the expenses of such development blocks will be borne entirely by State Governments after the third year. The expenditure, mostly recurring, is likely to be about Rs. 3 lakh per project.

Supporting Projects

23. The Community Development Programme is related to and supported in part by most of the other projects under the Indo-American Technical Cooperation Programme. The fertilizer required by the Community Development Programmes will be acquired and distributed in accordance with the Operational Agreement No. 1 who deals with the "Project for Acquisition and Distribution of Fertilizer." Similarly, the iron and steel needed for farm implements and tools will be acquired and distributed in accordance with the "Project for the Acquisition and Distribution of Iron and Steel for Agricultural purposes." The tube-wells to be constructed in the project areas will be allocated from the "Project for Ground Water Irrigation." Information and services with respect to soils and fertilizer application will be made available from the "Project for distribution of soil fertility and fertiliser use." Assistance in Malaria control in the project areas will be forthcoming from the "Project for malaria control planned under the Technical Cooperation Programme." The training of Village Level Workers and Project Supervisors will be carried out under the "Village Workers Training Programme."

Evaluation

24. A systematic evaluation of the methods and results of the Community Development Programme will, no doubt, make a significant contribution by pointing up those methods which are proving effective, and those which are not; and furnishing an insight into the impact of the Community Development Programme upon the economy and culture of India. In order that it may be useful to those administering the Community Development Projects and serve as a basis for informed public opinion regarding the programme, the evaluation work is being arranged to be conducted by the Planning Commission in close cooperation with the Ford Foundation and the Technical Cooperation Administration.

National Extension Service

In setting out our proposals on the subject of administration of district development programmes, we have already attempted to analyze the organizational features of extension work in the district. The entire subject has been carefully reviewed recently by the Grow More Food Enquiry Committee. After examining the results of the campaign for increased food production, which has been in progress for several years, the Committee states the problem which extension workers have to meet in the following words:

1. "No plan can have any chance of success unless the millions of small farmers in the country accept its objective, share in its making, regard it as their own, and are prepared to make the sacrifices necessary for implementing it. The integrated production programme has failed to arouse enthusiasm for the reasons we have given. The food problem is a much wider one than mere elimination of food imports. It is the problem of bringing about such a large expansion of agricultural production as will assure to an increasing population progressively rising levels of nutrition. In other words, the campaign for food production should be conceived as part of a plan for the most efficient use of land resources by the application of modern scientific research and the evolution of a diversified economy. In its turn, agricultural improvement is an integral part of the much wider problem of raising the level of rural life. The economic aspects of village life cannot be detached from the broader social aspects; and agricultural improvement is inextricably linked up with a whole set of social problems. The lesson to be derived from the working of the G.M.F. programmes thus confirms the experience of States and private agencies engaged in village development. It is that all aspects of rural life are interrelated and that no lasting results can be achieved, if individual aspects of it are dealt with in isolation. This does not mean that particular problems should not be given prominence but the plans for them should form parts of, and be integrated with, those for achieving the wider aims. It is only by placing this ideal—of bringing about an appreciable improvement in the standards of rural life and making it fuller and richer—before the country and ensuring that the energies of the entire administrative machinery of the States and the best non-official leadership are directed to plans for its realization that we can awaken mass enthusiasm and enlist the active interest and support of the millions of families living in the countryside in the immense task of bettering their own condition."

2. This analysis led to the Committee to propose the establishment of a national extension organization for intensive rural work which could reach every farmer and assist in the coordinated development of rural life as a whole. The detailed proposals of the Committee on the organization of the extension network at various levels have been described earlier. The programme envisaged by the Committee, for which the necessary provision has been made in the Plan, is that the Central Government should assist State Governments in establishing extension organizations so as to bring their entire area under extensive development within a period of about ten years. During the period of the Plan, about 1,20,000 villages are to be brought within the operations of the extension, that is, nearly one-fourth of the rural population. The Central and the various State Governments are expected in the near future to frame detailed programmes for reorganizing the existing extension services, arranging for further recruitment and preparing training programmes.

In drawing up these programmes, the Central and State Governments will have to examine the necessity for providing the basic training in agriculture and animal husbandry to the village level workers and the various supervisory subject matter specialists. Where existing facilities are inadequate, steps will have to be taken to augment them with a view to ensuring an adequate supply of extension workers for each major linguistic region. There is little doubt that the implementation of these proposals can give a new and powerful momentum to all rural work and, in particular, to the programme for increased agricultural production.

3. The organization of extension services with the object of securing increased production and raising the standard of village life is a new undertaking. Extension is a continuous process designed to make the rural people aware of their problems, and indicating to them ways and means by which they can solve them. It thus involves not only education of the rural people in determining their problems and the methods of solving them, but also inspiring them towards positive action in doing so. It is, therefore, of the highest importance that for this task, personnel of the right type should be obtained who will take to their work with zeal and enthusiasm. The qualities required are not only the ability to acquire knowledge but also dedication to the task of serving the rural people and the development of a will to find solutions for their problems. People from village surroundings with experience of practical farming are likely to prove of special value as extension workers.

4. The training of extension workers requires the closest attention and must be related to the services that they will have to perform. They have to understand rural problems, the psychology of the farmer, and other solutions to his various difficulties. They have to try and find out the felt needs of the people, and the solutions that they offer must be demonstrated by acting in close cooperation with the farmers. They should be able to discover leadership and stimulate it to action. Their success will depend on the extent to which they gain the confidence of the farmers. Their duties have thus to be educative and demonstrative. Their training will thus have many facets. Periods spent in gaining a thorough training will be a good investment. If the period of extension training is to be shortened, so as to be able to cover a larger area than may be otherwise possible, care should be taken to see that it is preceded by adequate opportunities for basic training in all aspects of rural development. Their conditions of service should also be such as are calculated to keep up their zeal and enthusiasm and ensure the continuous maintenance of high standard of performance. There should be considerable scope for promotion for men who start at the bottom. In order to develop the true extension approach much might be gained if all extension workers, whether graduates or field level workers, were to start at the field level and only those who proved their worth, received promotions to higher positions. A fair proportion of these positions should also be open to village workers who display the necessary qualities of leadership and ability. For this purpose, courses should be provided at different levels to enable the promising extension workers who start at the field level to reach positions of greater responsibility.

5. It is important to secure that the extension service retains its character of continued utility to the rural areas which they serve. This factor should, therefore, be particularly borne in mind in judging the work of officials who man this service. Local opinion on the extent to which an extension worker has made himself useful should be an important criterion in assessing his ability.

6. The confidence of the villager is gained with difficulty and lost easily. It is, therefore, of the essence of extension that the initial start is made with items whose usefulness to the cultivator in increasing agricultural production has been well established. It is only after sufficient confidence is gained that comparatively untried measures can be put forward, and even these should be held out as experiments until the people have found the answer for themselves.

7. The immediate effect of the first impact of an extension organization is to increase the demands of the cultivator for credit, supplies and implements. The satisfaction of these demands is a necessary consequence of extension activities and they will succeed to the extent this responsibility is handled efficiently. Extension activities will be adversely affected if arrangements cannot be made for supplying the needs which they generate.

8. Finally, it may be pointed out that extension workers have to be supported effectively by research workers to whom they can bring their problems and whose results they carry to the people. Special arrangements are, therefore, needed to ensure the closest cooperation between extension and research.

• • •

As appropriate form for the future city has not yet emerged, but serious attention has been directed to the nature of the modern urban settlement in two major areas: the redevelopment of internal urban structure and planned decentralization of the city population into the New Towns. The results have not been conclusive in either of these areas, but our present consideration of the New Towns may serve as important examples in shaping our vision of the city of tomorrow. Studies on urbanization and urban development in Western Europe and North America have led to the formulation of a number of theories of urban growth. Scholars in Western Europe including the British Isles have discussed the more formal regions within a city in relation to broad morphological characteristics. For instance Dickinson in his study of West European Cities observed their common tendencies to grow in concentric zone of distinctive build and character. American scholars on the other hand have generalized the land-use pattern for American cities as influenced by the ecological processes. These have resulted into the formulation of Concentric Zone Theory by Burgess and Sector Theory of Residential Neighbourhoods by Hoyt. The objective here is to critically examining the land-use development of any city, a historic city and an emerging Indian Metropolis in the light of these Western theories of urban growth. In a general discussion, Indian Cities can be cited as examples. The chapter highlights that any developing country like India has also experienced the concentration of investments and higher order administrative and political functions in few large urban centres. Sir W. Arthur Lewis articulated: "Agriculture has been the weakest link in the development chain."

Michel Lipton firmly asserts, "I do not believe that poor countries should 'stay agriculture' in order to develop, let alone instead of developing. The argument that neither the carrying capacity of the land, nor the market for farm products, is such as to permit the masses in poor countries to reach high levels of livings without a major shift to non-farm activities seems conclusive" (Meier, 1995). Recent economic reform in India has delivered growth in India, but economic growth has not delivered poverty reduction, what M.S. Swaminathan very aptly calls it "joyless growth". On the contrary, poverty reduction of the 1980s could be attributed to the "push" factor of rural migration of peasants to many complementary but subsistence oriented informal RNFSs (Rural Non-Farm Sectors) and relatively a minor one in comparison with China. Value-added potential of these informal off-farm employment generating stations is comparatively higher than the Farm Sector (FS).

In the chapter of Regional Planning: Functional and Nodal, Prof. Alam brings out the inherent differences between two types of territorial systems—the functional organization of a region which is based on the homogeneity and specialization of functions in an area on the one hand and integrative nodal regions on the other. Finally, in the face of the growing social and economic problems associated with urban expansion, it is increasingly realized that the network of rural non-farm activities could play an important role in checking the large scale rural-urban migration. Thus, through localizing employment in rural areas themselves, the rural non-farm activities would contribute towards casing of urban congestion and reducing the pressure of scarce urban infrastructural facilities (e.g. housing, transport, education etc.). Undoubtedly, labour exodus from rural areas which is the main breeding ground for urban slums and a host of socio-economic problems would get intercepted. Hence, the potential role for rural non-crop activities, particularly rural industries have to be seen in the context of the facts mentioned above. It is clear that expansion of rural non-farm activities will have to play a crucial role in overcoming rural poverty and underemployment. Apart from the employment consideration, the advocates of agriculture-led growth theories also visualized important rates for the rural non-farm sector in stimulating agricultural growth through inter-sectoral linkages. Moreover, there is comprehensive evidence of an inverse relationship between non-farm employments on the one hand and farm size and total income opportunities the rural poor world is even worse-off and the income distribution even more skewed (Saith, 1992).

When it comes to local transport external to the farm, the story is the substitution of bicycles, motor-bicycles, cars and trucks for the most primitive methods has meant, or promises to mean, a substantial decline in the relative cost of transport. But, it is not sufficient to consider merely the relationship of a settlement to its lands, since only an entirely self-sufficient community has no need of regular friendly external contacts. Most people have friendly contacts of one kind or another with their neighbours and are a cogent consideration in the choice of a location: certainly, it has become increasingly important with the passage of time, as the degree of local self-sufficiency has declined but felt extremely needed for urban sustainability.

Traditionally, the main link with other communities was through the travelling of persons and the interchange of goods, which render location on or near lines of communication as advantage. The principle can be applied fairly easily to settlements that are part of a hierarchical system, as is normally the case in Europe and as is envisaged in most theoretical studies of settlement organization as postulated by Christaller (1966) and Losch (1954). In this sense, such locations may still be viewed in terms of the Weberian system, for Weber considered both the assembly of raw materials for manufacture and the distribution of the goods to the respective markets. In a hierarchical system, trade transactions take place in a well defined manner between settlements of higher and lower orders so that the directions and nature of the trade links can be established with some degree of precision.

Experience in India is instructive. Agarwal in 1971 selected two groups of villages, one in which consolidation had occurred (like Project Village) and another control group in which it had not. Dispersal of the rural population does raise some awkward problems under two headings: (a) the costs of providing roads and public utilities such as electricity and water which are greater than where everyone lives in compact settlement; and (b) the loneliness which often characterizes life on isolated farms, which may be specially burdensome for those accustomed to the society of village life. Therefore, it is essential to find compromising solutions to be attempted and a discussion of these occupies major focus of regional planning. There remains huge advantage concerning dispersal of population from existing nucleated settlements but dispersal is not the universal trend. Under conditions in which the population is increasing, satellite settlements which are occupied seasonally may come to be permanently inhabited and to possess a complete economy of their own, independent of the village from which they sprang.

Urban Components of Regional Planning

Socio-economic development is inextricably linked with the current as well as past land-use. In fact, land-use pattern and access to land determine the socio-economic development of vast stretches of rural agricultural practices. For socio-economic development an integrated approach is recommended for sectorial planning and management of land and its resources. The driving forces of historical as well as present land-use changes, which transformed many societies and socio-economic, biophysical and land management themes. These forces include use of labour in the past history, national and international policies that is access to credit, taxes, subsidies, conventions and agreements, market forces, national and global demographic and social changes, environment, climate, pests and diseases, technological changes in transportation systems and mechanization, subdivision, land values, agricultural diversifications, urbanization, industrialization, changing cropping patterns, use of wetlands, waste generation, disposal and landfills.

Urban dynamics is the study of land transformations occurring in any urban areas through time. Urban areas in the developing countries face the growing problems of haphazard growth, loss of vegetation, decline in arable lands and also decline in wildlife habitat. Most of the problems are attributed to the growing population pressure. In fact, the impact of metropolization on urbanized villages has thrown challenging questions about land-uses and its dynamics, besides water facilities and sanitation. Urban expansion mostly engulfs its surroundings and acts as the facilitator of drastic changes in land-use of its vicinity. Conventional ground methods of land-use mapping are labour intensive, time consuming and relatively infrequent. In recent years, satellite remote sensing techniques have been developed, which has proved to be of immense value for preparing accurate land-use or land-cover maps and monitoring changes at regular intervals of time. The planet earth is unique in several respects supporting lives, structurally complex rich in resources diversified into several subtypes and highly productive in terms of energy. There is now immense awareness of land concerning the importance of natural resources, initially natural ecosystems and their functioning were guiding factors for human activities in the biosphere.

Urbanization in Regional Planning

In broadest terms, urban and regional planning is the process by which communities attempt to control and/or design change and development in their physical environments. It has been practised under many names: town planning, city planning, community planning, land-use planning, and physical environment planning. The object of planning is the "physical environment", which is taken to mean land and all its uses, along with everything that has tangible existence on or beneath the land surface. Planning also includes the manner and style by which buildings are laid out in a city, and the design of public places.

Physical environments are partly natural and partly man-made. A satisfying man-made or "built" environment is the ultimate goal of planning, but relations between natural and built environments, and interactions between people and their environments, are also of vital concern. Human activities can have negative impacts upon the natural environment, just as certain natural conditions are hazardous to human well-being. Planners are equally concerned to protect natural environments from the adverse effects of human use (e.g. water pollution), and to protect people from adverse natural circumstances (e.g. flood zones).

To plan the physical environment means to impose some deliberate order upon it, with the aim of achieving a desired standard of environmental quality. Environmental quality is the heart of planning practice, although there is no universal agreement about the characteristics of a "good" or well-ordered environment. Different cultures have tended to value environmental qualities differently and to organize their environments in different ways. Many factors influence the choice of qualities that are most desired at a particular time and place. Each community, through social and political processes, must set its own standards of a good physical environment. Also, people's needs, tastes and economic circumstances influence the quality of environments that are planned and built.

A variety of issues fall within the scope of urban and regional planning, depending partly on the geographical scale of the planning area. Regional planners will be concerned with such matters as the protection of farmland or other valued resource sites (e.g., forests, mineral deposits, seashores, lakeshores); the preservation of unique natural or historical features; the locations of highways and other transport facilities, such as pipelines or airports; and the growth prospects of communities located throughout the region. If the region is organized around a large city, the planners must also take account of the problems caused by the city's expansion, and its impact upon the surrounding countryside and nearby towns.

For cities and towns, planning issues are of two general kinds. First, there is a need to think ahead to accommodate the city's growth—deciding which lands should be built on and when, and whether they should be used for residential development, for industry or for some more specialized function, such as a shopping centre or playing fields. Eventually, more detailed plans will also be required to determine the layout of every piece of land. The street network has to be designed; sites have to be reserved for schools and parks, shops, public buildings and religious institutions; provision has to be made for transit services and utilities; and development standards have to be set and design ideas have to be tested to ensure that the desired environmental quality is achieved.

A second group of issues concerns those parts of the community that are already developed. Planners will distinguish between areas where change is not desired and those where change is either unavoidable or judged to be needed. In the former case, the concern is for maintaining the built environment at its existing quality, regardless of pressures for change. This applies particularly to inner-city neighbourhoods which face pressures for apartment redevelopment or for streets to be widened to permit through traffic. In the latter case, the problem is to facilitate the changes that are considered most desirable. In one situation this may mean that a deteriorating area has to be upgraded; in another it may mean that buildings have to be demolished to allow their sites to be used in a new and different way. The problems of rapidly changing downtowns, of outdated industrial and warehousing districts, and of inner-city neighbourhoods experiencing a complex mix of social and physical changes all have to be dealt with by planners and public authorities. So, too, must special issues such as heritage conservation, the relocation of railway tracks, the provision of rapid-transit facilities, and the special housing needs of different groups of people.

Urban environments continue to change. As cities age, it becomes more difficult and more expensive to maintain environmental quality. People's needs and desires change as well, and the built environment must be constantly adapted. Special restoration or revitalization programmes may be undertaken to try to draw business back to declining shopping districts and stimulate the local economy. Yet investment funds, both public and private, are in shorter supply than in times of economic growth. The download of services from the higher levels of governments to the municipal level also competes for municipal funds.

Social and Political Foundations of Urban Planning

Like all types of planning (e.g. Regional Development Planning; National Capital Commission; Urban Design), planning cities and regions find its rationale in the belief that a controllable future offers more promise than an uncontrolled one, and that a planned environment provides better opportunities for all people to enjoy their community setting. Urban and regional planning is but one of many approaches adopted by society for achieving the security, comfort and long-term betterment of its members. This does not mean that all plans are prepared by governments, or that all planners are public servants, but it does mean that planning systems are usually designed to ensure that the needs of the entire community are properly considered. Plans come from many sources—from individuals, private corporations and public agencies—all of which have special ends or interests to pursue. In the "planned" community a higher level of forethought and public control is imposed, not to prevent these individual plans from being realized but to ensure that they harmonize with one another and with the overall needs of the community.

It is rarely possible to demonstrate that an action taken in anticipation of the future will benefit an entire community. It is also difficult to show that a single public interest can be served. More commonly, planning is a matter of trying to decide which of many competing interests is more deserving, while also trying to treat everyone in a fair and lawful manner. Should a city council allow a shopping centre to be built in a residential area? An issue like this raises questions about personal rights and freedoms, and about the powers and obligations of public authorities. Hence, the ultimate planning decisions are political decisions, since politics is society's way of settling the conflicts that arise within a community.

Planning, then, is a way by which communities determine how they would like their environment to be. What kinds of benefit can they then look forward to? Official definitions in Canada have generally responded to this question by describing planning as a type of conservation. It is aimed at the wise use and management of community resources, a critical one being land. The idea that land is both a private commodity and a community resource is controversial, but Canadian law has established that there is a legitimate community interest in the development of any land. Large amounts of public money have to be spent on such things as transport facilities, water treatment plants, schools and parks.

The community assumes most of the responsibilities for ensuring that land is developed in ways that will allow these public services to function efficiently. This is taken to mean that the development of land should yield the greatest possible public benefit for the lowest possible public cost. Yet the measurement of benefits and costs is no easy matter. For example, deciding upon the best use of land on the outskirts of a city depends on estimating what values to attach to such benefits as an increase in the supply of new houses or an attractive residential environment, and how to weigh these benefits against a different set of costs, such as long journeys to work or the loss of prime agricultural land. Actions change the regional circumstances. The result of actions is evaluated in relation to stage five by the general public as well as the specific participants. Evaluation of actions causes next general awareness of the situations. So, this stage is the last stage in the problem solving process, and at the same time, it leads to the first stage of the next problem solving process. The problem solving process is a cyclic process on the time scale.

Metropolitan Concept

Lewis Mumford defined the Metropolitan City as the mother city, where more than 70 per cent urban population live. They are the centres of administration, political and military establishments and commercial hub with a concentration of non-agricultural workers. A Metropolis has a defined area with crowded population who has been agglomerated due to the centripetal forces and couple of push-pull forces of migration. Most previous studies of Indian Urban structure have lacked inter-city flow data on a conceptual basis. The problem remains acute for physical planning of towns and cities. A metropolis is a large city or urban area which is a significant economic, political, and cultural centre for a country or region, and an important hub for regional or international connections, commerce, and communications. The term is Greek and means the "mother city" of a colony (in the ancient sense), that is, the city which sent out settlers. This was later generalized to a city regarded as a centre of a specified activity, or any large, important city in a nation. Big cities belonging to a larger urban agglomeration, but which are not the core of that agglomeration, are not generally considered a metropolis but a part of it. The plural of the word metopolis is most commonly *metropolises*.

A metropolitan area, sometimes, referred to as a metro area or just metro, is a region consisting of a densely populated urban core and its less-populated surrounding territories, sharing industry, infrastructure, and housing. A metropolitan area usually comprises multiple jurisdictions and municipalities: neighbourhoods, townships, cities, counties, districts, states, and even nations like the eurodistricts. As social, economic and political institutions have changed, metropolitan areas have become key economic and political regions. Metropolitan areas include one or more urban areas, as well as satellite cities, towns and intervening rural areas that are socio-economically tied to the urban core, typically measured by commuting patterns. For urban centres outside metropolitan areas, that generate a similar attraction at smaller scale for their region, the concept of the regionopolis and respectively *regiopolitan area or regio* was introduced by German professors in 2006. A metropolitan area combines an urban agglomeration (the contiguous, built-up area) with zones not necessarily urban in character, but closely bound to the centre by employment or other commerce. These outlying zones are sometimes known as a commuter belt, and may extend well beyond the urban zone, to other political entities. For example, El Monte, California is considered part of the Los Angeles' metro area in the United States.

In practice, the parameters of metropolitan areas, in both official and unofficial usage, are not consistent. Sometimes, they are little different from an urban area, and in other cases they cover broad regions that have little relation to a single urban settlement; comparative statistics for metropolitan area should take this into account. Population figures given for one metro area can vary by millions. There has been no significant change in the basic concept of metropolitan areas since its adoption in 1950, although significant changes in geographic distributions have occurred since then, and more are expected. Because of the fluidity of the term "metropolitan statistical area", the term used colloquially is more often "metro service area", "metro area", or "MSA" taken to include not only a city, but also surrounding suburban, exurban and sometimes rural areas, all which it is presumed to influence. A polycentric metropolitan area is one not connected by continuous development or conurbation, which requires urban contiguity. In defining a metropolitan area, it is sufficient that a city or cities form a nucleus that other areas have a high degree of integration with a major city together with its suburbs and nearby cities and towns, over which the major city exercises a commanding economic and social influence. Literally construed metropolis from the Greek means "mother city", and by implication there are progeny or dependents scattered about the core area. Sometimes, there may be two or more major cities, as in the Tokyo-Yokohama Metropolitan Area (Japan) or an agglomeration of metropolitan boroughs as in Greater London (England). The U.S. Census employs a unit called a metropolitan statistical area (MSA) which includes either (i) a city with a population of at least 50,000 or (ii) an urbanized area of at least 50,000 population with a total metropolitan population of at least 1,00,000 (75,000 in New England). An urbanized area is defined as having a population of at least 50,000, and a population density of at least 1,000 per square mile.

Metropolitan Planning in India

The concept of planning as a deliberate and organized process is still anathema to many: programmes emerging from plans are considered irksome or impracticable and are resented and opposed as restrictions on individual freedom. The position is still acute for physical plans of towns and cities, as problems are not clearly set out, an overall perspective is lacking, interests of individuals appear to clash with those of groups and of different groups with the urban community as a whole. Most states in India have town planning Acts, and the other states are taking active measures to enact them. Even in those states where proper town planning schemes do not exist; there is other legislation under which city planning can be undertaken. By and large, some enabling legislation does exist under which plans can be prepared for almost all cities of any significance, but of course with many alterations to suit the respective needs.

Indian planning is an open process. Much of the controversy and the debates that accompany the preparation of the plans are public. The initial aggregate calculations and assumptions are either explicitly stated or readily deducible and the makers of the plans are not only sensitive, but responsive to criticism and suggestions from a wide variety of national and international sources. From original formulation through successive modifications to parliamentary presentation, plan making in India has evolved as are responsive democratic political process. The wide political participation in the preparation of the plan is understandable, if one realizes that the plan is not only intended as a set of prescriptions for economic behaviour, but represents the diverse aspirations of a nation for social avancement. Yet, the nation is not a homogeneous political entity; it is composed of a variety of regional, linguistic, economic, cultural and political groups. The many particular and frequently contradictory interests of each of these groups have to be recognized and to the degree it is possible, accommodated within the framework of the plans. The political process which leads to the formulation of the final document is undoubtedly an impressive manifestation of the workings of an open society.

By its very nature it generates many problems from the point of view of mapping an optimal strategy for economic development. Though there has been a considerable amount of debate over the plans, there has been relatively little explicit attention given to alternative strategies or paths of economic growth and development. In fact, the political discussions have been only tangentially concerned with questions of alternative compositions of national targets and much more with the capacity for saving and taxation, problems of direct controls and price stability. The latter are, of course, directly related to social-economic goals and to the mapping of the paths leading towards them. However, the relationships have not been spelled out, and the significance of the plan targets for current and future welfare has been left implicit. Although participation in the debates which accompany the preparation of the plans is widespread, unfortunately, it has not been well informed either on the welfare implications of the plan goals or on many other plan implications. Planning efforts have been absorbed in attempting to make a single plan whose goals, resource requirements and resource availabilities were consistent. Alternative policies have received only limited consideration in part because the alternatives remain relatively unknown. Plausible and consistent alternative plans are difficult to prepare and the enormous amount of information needed for their formulation is not readily available to individuals and organizations outside the Central Government. Hence, in order to arrange alternatives, the Planning Commission and the concerned Ministries would have had to prepare them, and this has not been done. The preparation of alternative plans and the comparison of their implications is not advocated as a service to potential critics. It is an essential part of the planning process, for only in this way can the full implications of any single plan be appreciated. This criticism of Indian planning must be seen in proper perspective. No conceptually satisfactory techniques of planning or more generally of making economic policy for development were readily at hand when the Indian plan was first made.

Regional Planning attempts to analyze the territorial systems which are based on the functionally homogeneous characteristics or are organized around settlement nodes which command exchange regions of heterogeneous characters. These two basic types of territorial systems are not mutually exclusive, but Indian scholars have tended to treat them separately and consequently there are few studies which have analyzed a territorial system in terms of both its functional specialization and nodal exchange characters. Of the two territorial systems, Indian scholars have paid greater attention to the functionally homogeneous regions without discussing the integrated role of urban centres. Initially, the regional approach to planning was not accepted by the Planning Commission and consequently, we find scarce reference to it in the first two Five Year Plans. The concept of regional planning and balanced regional development as understood by the Commission merely implied a judicious location of new industrial units with due emphasis on balanced regional development as a vital step in the direction of wider diffusion of employment opportunities. It is in the Third Five Year Plan period 1961-66, that the Planning Commission approved the regional approach to planning and commended this approach to the planning of large industries which will serve as focal points of development for areas far beyond their immediate environs. It also stresses upon the need of strengthening economic interdependence between towns and surrounding rural areas too.

In the Third Five Year Plan period, the key role of urbanization was played by stimulating social and economic transformation has been realized and the needs to plan the urban centres were felt. Consequent upon the increasing emphasis on urban development Master Plans have been prepared for 322 towns or cities and their immediate regions in the country as a whole. These Master Plans have been prepared by the Departments of Town and Country Planning Authorities of the respective States. Even at the state level an integrated approach for a coordinate development of these states remain still absent. While the need for regional planning and metropolitan planning too have been greatly emphasized in the Fourth Five Year Plan, it is the Fifth Five Year Plan which examines the problem in the national perspective and suggests the formulation of a national policy of urbanization to minimize the pressure of urbanization on metropolitan cities by promoting the development of smaller and medium sized towns. This focus on urbanization at the national level has led to the formulation and enunciation of a national urbanization policy by the Government of India. In general, regional planning includes following activities:

- Evolving a spatial pattern of economic development based on regional planning and location of a hierarchy of human settlements.
- Securing the optimum distribution of population between rural and urban settlements within each region and also among the towns of various sizes.
- Securing the distribution of economic activities in small and medium towns and in new growth centres to achieve the desired population distribution and maximum economic growth.
- Controlling and where necessary, arresting the further growth of economic activities by dispersal of economic activities, legislative measures and establishments of new counter magnets in the region.
- Providing minimum level of services for improving the quality of life in rural and urban areas and gradually reducing differences between the rural and urban life.

Development Planning at National Levels

National Development Planning is the result of a demanding effort of synthesizing proposals and bringing together divergent priorities, while covering a multifaceted approach that touches on the comprehensive developmental choices of the economy and society of the country, the directions of the European Union, financial circumstances and the objective capacities for the effective and efficient implementation of a project. A very well attended public consultation session took place in the context of the preparatory procedures, with the aim of achieving the greatest possible participation and consent to the formulation of the strategic choices that would lead to the adoption of a long term developmental vision for the country.

The phrasing of the proposal of the National Strategic Reference Framework (ESPA) for period 2007-2013 and the coordination of the procedures fall within the competence of the Ministry of Economy and Finance. ESPA was formulated in cooperation with the competent Ministries, the Regional and Local Authorities, and in consultation with the European Commission, in the framework of a strengthened partnership, which was based on the principle of transparency. The major milestones in the framework of the consultation process and development planning was the dispatch of the 1st Circular, the determination of ESPA instruments and qualification levels, the 2nd Circular, the submission of 34 detailed proposals by Ministries and Regions citing their primary development priorities, special thematic meetings with the Ministries, Regions and economic and social partners, the Regional Conventions on Development, the 3rd Circular specializing the principles governing the structure and content of the Operational Programmes, the specialized Technical Guideline outlining the structure, content and methodology for preparing the OP, the 4th Circular and the National Conventions on Development. Throughout this period there was ongoing cooperation with stakeholders, in regard to the planning, as well as with bodies and partners, whose proposals were taken into consideration in the preparation of ESPA. Representatives of the Secretariats of the European Commission, with whom unofficial individual working meetings were also periodically organized, attended the majority of aforementioned activities, in the capacity of observer or spokesperson.

The concept of regional development is based on the development of specific regions. It is generally undertaken where regional differences exist and where a particular region is to be developed. Regional Development is carried through the regional planning which is a technique to evaluate the potential of sub-natural areas and to develop them to the best advantages of the nation as a whole.

To further enhance the critical role of the U.S. in global trade, it is essential to create partnerships across boundaries that produce economic benefits that extend beyond anyone metropolitan area. As a consequence, transportation planners and project managers are looking for opportunities to collaborate across jurisdictional and geographic boundaries to identify opportunities to fund transportation infrastructure investments through related plans and programmes.

Working on the scale of larger regions, or even mega-regions, can increase the economic competitiveness of metropolitan and non-metropolitan areas along major corridors identified as important for current and future freight and passenger flows. This report will focus on mega-regions planning and the role of rural areas in supporting transportation planning that benefits the larger region. Mega regions are defined as networks of metropolitan centres and their connecting land areas linked by economy, culture, history, growth patterns, and natural resources. Researchers have further identified a national set of major mega-regions based on population, demographic, and economic data. While many corridors and regions may be important scales for transportation planning, this white paper focuses on the major mega-regions significant opportunities for increased economic and other benefits through transportation planning. As more regions plan their transportation for global competitiveness, planners will increasingly need to incorporate rural areas in their large-scale planning efforts. Rural areas are a critical part of the identities, economies, and infrastructure of mega-regions. These areas may be both recipients of the benefits derived from this scale of planning as well as contributors to advancing the larger goals of the region. Rural Planning Organizations (RPOs), which serve as the designated transportation planners for many rural areas, are part of the transportation networks and economies of surrounding metropolitan and non-metropolitan regions. However, RPOs may not be active participants in mega-regions initiatives due to organizational constraints. New transportation legislation defines and provides the option for States to designate Regional Transportation Planning Organizations (RTPOs), encompassing transportation roles filled by other types of rural organizations. This research examines how RPOs and rural interests are integral partners in transportation planning efforts for mega-regions and explores methods for their participation. It expands on on-going initiatives by the Federal Highway Administration (FHWA), Office of Planning, including research by Georgia Tech, the USDOT's Volpe National Transportation Systems Centre (Volpe Centre) and others on the important potential contribution planning can make to meet the transportation needs of mega-regions. This includes a companion white paper on best practices in participation by Metropolitan Planning Organizations (MPOs) in Planning for mega-regions.

While the Census provides a definition of "rural", this white paper applies a working definition of "rural areas" as all population, housing, and territory not included within a Census-designated urban area. Other characteristics of rural areas include a low population density and small settlements, or they may be agricultural or wilderness lands. For transportation planning purposes rural areas can be discussed by applying three types of attributes:

1. Destination areas that feature natural amenities (e.g. mountains, lakes, or beaches) and attract Seasonal residents, retirees, and tourists in support of a recreational or leisure culture;
2. Production communities outside of urbanized settings that tend to be focused on a single Industry such as agriculture, manufacturing, or mining;
3. Ex-urban areas that are outside the MPO planning boundaries but which rely on the urbanized area, rather than a local economy, due to convenience transportation access; and
4. MPOs are responsible for conducting multi-modal transportation planning for Census-designated urbanized areas. Larger areas (generally those with 2,00,000 or more residents) are classified as Transportation Management Areas (TMAs). Smaller urbanized areas (with populations between 50,000 and 2,00,000) are often referred to as "non-TMAs". Rural areas, including those within MPO planning boundaries, serve critical functions within larger economic and transportation corridors, as they may contain the following:
   (i) Transportation infrastructure that connects to metropolitan regions;
   (ii) Centres of economic production (specifically industrial, recreational, and agricultural) that may be integrated with the adjacent urban area;
   (iii) Environmental resources that serve ecological health, self-sustainability, and quality of life; and
   (iv) Federal Highway Administration (FHWA) and Federal Transit Administration (FTA), 2012.

"Mega Regions Planning for MPOs and Partners: A Transportation Planning Capacity Building Peer Exchange." Accessed 24 April, 2014:

Planning area boundaries of MPOs often include small cities, towns, and rural areas, as well as the Census-designated urbanized areas. Federal statute does not require MPOs to conduct transportation planning for areas outside their planning boundaries, so State Departments of Transportation (DOTs) or regional organizations typically conduct transportation planning for rural areas. There is no one organization, or type of organization, responsible for transportation planning across all rural areas, which means that many parties with an interest in rural transportation may participate and that local jurisdictions that have an interest in rural transportation planning policy and strategy still need to be consulted. Rural areas actively help define their mega-regions through housing economic production centres and transportation infrastructure, providing ecosystem services, and contributing to the social and environmental character of the region. Rural areas both contribute benefits to the larger mega-region and derive benefits from large-scale planning and activities that include metropolitan areas. The research team considers rural areas to be a critical part of the mega-region, not secondary to the metropolitan areas around which mega-regions are sometimes defined. For the purposes of this report, mega-regions are defined as networks of metropolitan centres and surrounding areas connected through physical features, geographic, cultural, ecological, and economic characteristics as well as major infrastructure. The definition is meant to be flexible to recognize the diversity of organizations engaged in rural transportation planning and active in interregional and mega-regions-scale partnerships. This report specifically looks at how rural areas are critical to transportation planning for these larger scale transportation systems can be used as tools to achieve regional goals. The first type of rural region has stable or declining population levels—people in these areas look to transportation to induce growth. The second has a growing population—local leaders in these areas seek transportation and land-use policies to manage growth while preserving rural character and livability. Rural regions, therefore, can value transportation as a means to both facilitate growth and control its pace and patterns of development. Although many rural regions lack the formal transportation planning processes and multidisciplinary capacities, they still need transportation planning to help their regions realize common goals. Transportation in rural areas can also help regions meet mobility and economic development goals. Since the resources for infrastructure are increasingly limited, rural transportation must be versatile and serve a continuum of needs. The same infrastructure must accommodate the production-oriented resource-based economies and dispersed development patterns of rural areas as well as the mixed-use, consumption-oriented markets of the urban fringe and urban cores. 14 Rural transportation systems should be multimodal and flexible to accommodate the diverse needs of rural regions on limited infrastructure. The formal planning has evolved over time. "A State may establish and designate regional planning organizations to enhance the planning, coordination, and implement of statewide strategic long-range planning. While these rules and the subsequent legislation set a baseline for States to involve rural people in planning, many States exceed the requirements and engage in innovative ways with rural people, as described. Special districts or public authorities play a major role in the provision of public services and making long term capital investment decisions with some isolation from State Government such as maintaining bridges and highways and operating mass transit systems. Local governments are also the implementing agencies for county- and city-owned transportation infrastructure. Finally, local governments and especially local elected officials have a vested interest in improving the economies and infrastructure of their municipalities for the good of their citizens. This interest ties them closely to the outcomes of regional and local transportation planning processes.

Framework Development remains important on the foundation of previous research into mega-regions transportation planning and the needs of rural areas, this research seeks to demonstrate how the participation of rural areas can strengthen transportation planning for mega-regions and extend benefits in the areas of economic development, freight, natural resources, and transportation system operations across the larger region. Through interviews with key stakeholders in rural areas that currently participate in large-scale transportation planning, the research team developed a framework for conceptualizing improved rural involvement in mega-regions.

The Inputs describe the factors that influence planning initiatives within their mega-regions. There are basic overlapping interests between rural areas and mega-regions, most frequently in the areas of economic growth and freight that may motivate RPOs to participate. The RPOs must tailor their activities to fit within their existing relationships with State and metropolitan partners, the policies and regulations that dictate their responsibilities, and of course, the limited staff and financial resources at their disposal. Shaped by these inputs, the Processes describe the ways RPOs can and do participate in interregional planning and partnerships. These are activities, such as attending forums or reviewing corridor plans, and roles that articulate how the RPO fits within the larger institution of a mega-region. Timing is also important to the processes component, as it affects when RPOs can best add value. Timing is closely related to activities and roles, and the previous section describes multiple points for RPO contribution. Finally, the Benefits of RPO partnership in mega-regions initiatives extend to rural, urban, regional, statewide, and Federal organizations. These benefits are a direct outcome of the varied processes for RPO participation. As evidenced in the case studies and background research, non-rural stakeholders cite significant benefits of rural stakeholder's participation, which can include influence on plans and projects.

Case studies support the development of this framework and provide evidence of the inputs, processes, and benefits derived from people's participation in broader transportation planning. This framework provides a flexible model for mega-regions, leaders, State DOTs, and rural stakeholders to consider the mechanisms for and benefits of rural participation in mega-regions, transportation planning. The framework can provide a lens to read the following case studies and the framework may provide them future opportunities for involvement. As with other findings, this framework is meant to open discussion on rural participation and to offer flexibility to all stakeholders, while considering the centrality of rural areas as part of the larger mega-region.

Chapter 6

Case Studies in Indian Context

Modern Planning Processes and RS and GIS

Modern planning laws started developing from the beginning of the Twentieth Century in England and other countries. Now, it is specialized subject practised by people trained in both urban planning and laws. Planning laws are enacted by State Governments in conformance with the Constitution of the country and address the following:

- Defines the planning functions or intent of planning;
- Defines the perimeters of planning;
- Provides legal authorities to planning agencies to regulate land development;
- Provides for constitution of the Planning Agencies; and
- Provides funding provisions.

In fact, it is a local government's responsibility to prepare the city plan and the citizens should have input in it. Therefore, the functioning of the planning agency and exercise of rule making power is within the governmental structure of self-government. Thus, developmentalism is a battleground, where contention rages among bureaucratic economists, Marxist revolutionists, environmental activists, feminists, critics, postmodern skeptics, and radical democrats. Theories of development reach deeply into culture for explanatory and persuasive power, while the end products of such deep thinking, together with the dedicative practices of millions of well meaning people, are political tools with mass people. Regional planning deals with the efficient placement of land-use activities, infrastructure, and settlement growth across a larger area of land than an individual city or town. The related field of urban planning deals with the specific issues of city planning. Both concepts are encapsulated in planning. This idea proposes statutory alternatives for the formation and organizational structure of regional planning agencies. The model legislation describes a full range of functions and duties for such agencies. It details the contents of regional comprehensive and functional plans (such as those for housing and transportation) and procedures for their adoption. C.R. Pathak argues that the urban fringe areas emerge as the spatial counter-part of the urbanization and suburbanization processes. In the earlier stages of such processes, urban places grow through rural-urban migration to the central part of the urban places. They grow in population and urban functions. They grow vertically through the processes of concentration while horizontal process remains haphazard. The development of cities in the developing nations adheres to any contiguous land-use patterns giving rise to infrastructural problems.

Indeed economic component is the crux of regionalism. It is a common knowledge that India is developing economically, in spite of the many achievements registered since Independence. The resources are scarce and demands disproportionately heavy and ever growing on account of continued population explosion there is thus acute competition among individuals, groups and regions within a state. Harrison Selig has thus described the process: As the population mounts, densely populated regions cry Lebensraum or a territory which a state believes is needed for its natural development; living space at their neighbour's. Urban Planning can be a function of the state patterns of planning government or of the local government. There are advantages and disadvantages in both organizational pattern of the planning agency and its structure. There are many options for organizing and structuring a planning agency. The state planning law may require a State Planning Organization to prepare plans for different cities within the State. The advantage of the State Government as planning agency is that local governments are relieved from the financial burden of preparing the plan. The State Government can mobilize the planning staff from one town to another. It is advantageous for small towns and cities. But the disadvantages are many, the Planners and Planning Advisory Council members are transferable and have no permanent interest on Planning and Implementation. There is not much public participation in the State Agency Planning Process. The detail planning such as zoning maps, community development projects, and capital improvement projects are left to the development. The role of the city's council in making the plan and implantation is ignored. The organizational structure may vary according to city-size and political make-up of the city. In fact, Metropolitan Cities will need a sophisticated planning agency structure. Functions of the Planning Agency must be grouped and detailed. Responsibilities are delegated according to different units of the Planning Agency. Staffing the agency with professional, trained, competent and dedicated persons is another matter of importance and success in planning. A very close coordination among the departments or more than one division is involved. A local planning programme may be classified into six functions or categories. To establish community development objectives following issues are required:

- To conduct research on the growth and development of the city;
- To make development plans and programmes;
- To increase public understandings and acceptance of planning;
- To provide technical services to other governmental agencies and private groups;
- To co-ordinate development activities effecting city growth; and
- To administer land-use controls, zoning and sub-division regulations.

Capital improvements mean construction of roads, water supply, sewer system, drainage, landfills, parks, playgrounds, electricity, schools, urban renewal. Projects should be identified and priorities established based on public needs, costs and benefits, make detail plans, cost estimates and time needed to complete. The obvious goal is execution of the capital projects. In addition to already mentioned issue of data access, there are a number of other legal issues that provide the use of GI technologies and data in the practice of urban and regional planning. These other issues include: liability, copyright, cost recovery, and public access. While the general framework on all of the issues with regard to government and private sector data and practices has been established, the applicability to digital geographic information is debated. The legal environment in which GI is produced and used is highly uncertain and often discouraging to creative GI-related activities and developments. The current legal structures are subjected to numerous interpretations and new rules and procedures established locally and by state. A well articulated legal framework would help private and public sector organizations and individuals define their roles and responsibilities with respect to spatial data and would help stabilize their practices and relationships.

Planning and GIS

Planners have always sought tools to enhance their analytical, problem-solving, and decision-making capability (Mandelbaum, 1996). From the late 1950s, planners started to develop and use computerized models, planning information systems and decision support systems to improve performance (Brail, 1987; Klosterman 1990). Adoption of Geographic Information Systems (GIS) is a more recent manifestation of the same effort to incorporate new tools and technologies. Planning departments have been on the forefront of GIS use among local government agencies (French and Wiggins, 1990; Juhl, 1993; French and Skiles, 1996; Warnecke *et al.*, 1998). The planners' interest in GIS derives from the spatial nature of urban phenomena and from the inter-disciplinary nature of urban planning.

Ultimately, the GIS Science as applied in the field of urban and regional planning should contribute to the following goals of urban and regional planning practice:

- Better quality (livable, safe, and aesthetically pleasing) of urban environments;
- Environmentally and socially sustainable communities;
- Effective spatial organization of urban activities (work, residence, commerce, and recreation);
- "Smart growth" of urban areas;
- Efficient communication between various urban functions;
- Revitalization of deteriorated areas;
- Variety of housing options;
- Employment opportunities and economic development; and
- Democratization of the planning and policy-making process.

Planners can apply geographic information technologies in all aspects of the planning process, including: data collection and storage, data analysis and presentation, plan and/or policy making, communication with the public and decision-makers, and plan and/or policy implementation and administration. GIS technology is the most commonly used for comprehensive planning, zoning, land-use inventories, site suitability assessments, and socio-demographic analysis, and generally for mapping purposes (Budic, 1993, 1994; Warnecke *et al.*, 1998). Planners use GIS primarily for mapping activities. The value of maps in understanding and communicating planning issues is well recognized and appreciated. The more sophisticated analytical applications, which contribute to other aspects of the planning process, are less developed. Past research confirms that the GI-based tools developed by vendors and/or academics are for various reasons underutilized and unsuitable for planning (Harris, 1989; Harris and Batty, 1993; Holmberg, 1994; Klosterman, 1997). In their study of parcel-based GIS for land supply and capacity monitoring, Vernez-Moudon and Hubner (forthcoming) attribute this underutilization of GIS technology to the inadequate capacity and structure of planning institutions, which remain unsuited to the new forms and processes required for effective utilization of planning and decision support systems. This same problem has persisted from the early attempts at computerization of land supply monitoring in the 1980s (Godschalk *et al.*, 1985; Bollens and Godschalk, 1987). The additional reasons for underutilization of GIS in planning include, but are not limited to the complexity of technology, lack of trained staff, scarce organizational resources, and incompatibility of mostly generic GI products with the tasks and functions performed by urban and regional planners. The ability to incorporate urban models and to more directly support the decision and policy-making processes are two main deficiencies of the current spatial technologies and tools.

GI science would contribute to better urban planning, if it addresses the following challenges:

- Building tools that meet the needs of planning practice for policy and decision support and for visualization;
- Strategic information resource management through incorporation and institutionalization of technological developments into the planning process; and
- Diffusion and capacity-building by transferring the technology to the participants in the planning process and/or enabling them to build their own tools.

Planning theory is based on two types of rationality that are relevant for understanding the role of geographic information science and technology in urban and regional planning. These are instrumental and communicative rationality. Instrumental (functional) rationality is based on a positivist ideal, which puts information gathering and scientific analysis at the core of planning. It assumes a direct relationship between the information available and quality of decisions based on this information. Communicative (substantive or procedural) rationality focuses on open and inclusive planning process, public participation, dialogue, consensus building, and conflict resolution (Innes, 1996; Godschalk *et al*., 1994). While the two theoretical instances are often viewed as competing (Mannheim, 1940; Sager, 1990; Yifachel, 1999), the role of information is relevant to both of them (and not restricted to instrumental rationality as the more traditional view would hold). Participants in the planning process rely on many types of "information", including both the formal analytic reports and quantitative measures and the understandings and meanings attached to planning issues and activities (Innes, 1998). Indeed, geographic information science and technology have started to contribute to the planning practice, and in some areas the developments transcend the "communicate *versus* calculate" dichotomy.

Following is a review of the main areas of geographic information research that carry the potential of being the most useful for urban and regional planning practice. These areas are:

- GIS database developments for planning-related analysis;
- Integration of GI technologies with urban models;
- Building of planning support systems;
- Facilitating discourse and participation in the planning process; and
- Evaluation of planning practice and technological impact.

GIS Database Developments for Planning-related Analysis

Data collection takes up a considerable proportion of planners' resources. In fact, the effort put into database development is sometimes so immense that leaves little time for analysis and for creative activities in designing plans and/or policies (Arbeit, 1993). GIS database development must be based on clear understanding of planning problems, process, and context (le Clercq, 1990).

Furthermore, since planning databases are usually derived by compiling data from multiple sources and of varying quality and scales, the rules of interoperability and integration are necessary to apply (Devogele *et al.*, 1998). Integration of readily available datasets is one way to reduce database development and maintenance time. For example, remote sensing data acquired *via* satellites or airborne cameras (Mesev, 1997; Tellez and Servigne, 1997), have proved very useful, particularly in mapping land-use change (Lo and Shipman 1990; Logsdon *et al.*, 1996), population density (Sutton, 1997), and human activities and their outcomes (Schweik and Green, 1999). Finally, incorporation of data at several points in time is often useful, but requires system designers to be familiar with building dynamic GIS (Asproth *et al.*, 1995).

In the positivistic vain, GIS databases are most frequently used for performing planning-related analysis and scientific inquiries (Wellar *et al.*, 1994). Webster (1993, 1994) matches the scientific input required to the various stages of the planning process:

(a) Problem identification requires description and prediction;
(b) Goal setting, plan generation, evaluation of alternatives, and choice of solution requires prescription;
(c) Implementation requires description, prediction, and prescription; and, finally,
(d) Monitoring requires description and prediction.

The author claims a limited value of GIS technology for predictive analysis, which is crucial for understanding the consequences resulting from future planning actions. While the GI-based tools have proved useful for understanding physical and environmental processes, the socio-economic dynamics are still hard to model and/or simulate. To address this shortcoming, extensions towards enabling statistical analysis within the GIS environment have been attempted (Zhang and Griffith, 1997; Luc Anselin, Space Stat Web Site).

Integration of Geographic Information Technologies with Urban Models

To enable prediction of urban phenomena and processes, GIS software must allow for modelling procedures to run within its environment. This is, incidentally, one of the most frequently cited deficiencies of

GIS (Harris and Batty, 1993). Predictive modelling is usually performed outside GIS and loosely coupled to the system *via* programming procedures. Embedding of urban models within GIS has been attempted in advanced research projects (Batty and Xie, 1994), but has not become part of commercial GIS software. Landis' (1994, 1995) California Urban Futures Model, Landis *et al.*, (1998) California Urban and Biodiversity Analysis, and Klosterman's (1999) "What if?" are probably the three most comprehensive attempts to date in simulating land-use scenarios resulting from given demographic and economic trends, environmental constraints, and urban development policies. The progress in modelling land-use change in particular is impressive (Matheny *et al.*, 1999), but yet to gain usability and acceptance in planning agencies at various levels of government.

Building of Planning Support Systems

Planning Support Systems (PSSs) aid the planning process *via* integrated developments usually based on multiple technologies and common interface. PSSs are expected to facilitate data management, analysis, problem-solving, design, decision-making, and communication activities. Hopkins (1999), for instance, conceives of PSS to provide "views and tools for sketch planning, model building, scenario building, evaluation, lineage tracking, and plan-based action" (p. 333). He finds, however, that GIS mapping concepts are insufficient for building PSS. Despite the limited value, GIS have become a useful component and an integral part of PSS, which tend to incorporate one or more of the following features: modelling procedures (Harris, 1999; Kammeier, 1999), expert systems (Edamura and Tsuchida, 1999; Shi and Yeh, 1999), databases, decision trees, computer aided design or CAD (Alley, 1993; Schuur, 1994; Ranzinger and Gleixner, 1997), hypertext (George, 1997), mapping (Singh, 1999), user interfaces for public participation (Shiffer, 1992), virtual reality, and World Wide Web (Doyle *et al.*, 1998; Heikkila, 1998).

Planning support systems have evolved along with planning practice as (Klosterman, 1997): (a) applied science in 1960s; (b) politics in the 1970s; and (c) communication in the 1980s. Corresponding to this evolution is the information science concern with data, information, and knowledge, respectively. Intelligence and collective design are the *modus operandi* of urban planning. In line of increasingly recognized collective nature of planning analysis, design, communication, and decision-making, the 1990s have witnessed development of collaborative planning systems, planning groupware, and cooperative work systems (Jones, 1998). Laurini (1998) defines groupware as a "set of computer- and network-based technologies allows several users, located at different sites and using different work-practices, to work together towards the same goal" (p. 315). Referring to a group planning situation, Shiffer (1992) discusses group cognition, access to media, and access to computerized analysis tools as components of a holistic planning process. He built several prototype systems to integrate and test these concepts in the planning context.

Development of group support systems technology (Coleman and Khanna, 1995), including group decision support systems (DeSanctis and Gallupe, 1987, Hwang and Lin, 1987), as well as theoretical and empirical studies of its use (Jessup and Valacich, 1993, Chun and Park, 1998), have been carried out in the management and decision sciences for over ten years. More recently, information technologies such as Geographic Information Systems (GIS) (Godschalk *et al.*, 1992, Faber *et al.*, 1994, 1995, 1996), their offspring Spatial Decision Support Systems (SDSS) (Armstrong, 1993, Densham, 1991, Heywood, Oliver, Tomlinson, 1995, Jankowski *et al.*, 1997, Nyerges *et al.*, 1998b, Reitsma, 1996), and Spatial Understanding (and decision) Support Systems (SUSS/SUDSS) (Couclelis and Monmonier, 1995, Jankowski and Stasik, 1997) are being suggested as information technology aids to facilitate geographical problem understanding and decision making for groups, including groups embroiled in locational conflict. Clearly, research concerning collaborative decision making for geographically-oriented public policy problems continues to gain momentum (Couclelis and Monmonier, 1995, Densham, Armstrong and Kemp, 1995, Faber *et al.*, 1994, 1995, 1996, Godschalk *et al.,* 1992, Golay and Nyerges, 1995, Jankowski *et al.*, 1997, Nyerges and Jankowski, 1997, Nyerges *et al.*, 1998a, Nyerges *et al.*, 1998b, Reitsma, 1996, Reitsma *et al.*, 1996, Shiffer, 1992).

Facilitating Discourse and Participation in the Planning Process

Similar to other technologies, GIS is socially constructed *via* negotiations between various social groups (Harvey and

Chrisman, 1998). In the case of planning, those groups include professional staff, decision-makers, developers, special interest groups, citizens, and other stakeholders. GIS technology promises to improve public access to information and facilitate public participation in the planning and policy-making process. Contrary to the expectation that GIS will enhance democracy and empower disadvantaged groups, Clark (1998) warns about the creation of GIS technocratic elite. In her study of Virginia Planning Agencies Nedovic-Budic (1998) finds little evidence about improvements in public access to data. Sieber (1998) reports the difficulties experienced by non-profit organizations in obtaining GIS data. Meanwhile, there is an increasing trend towards empowering communities to plan through provision of integrated GIS software and planning databases. HUD's new Community 2020 CD ROM package, made available to local governments on a national basis, Bundles Caliper's Maptitude with an extensive database of geographic, demographic, and programmatic information. Seattle's Neighbourhood Data Viewer, provided to its neighbourhood planning groups, includes ArcView and a comprehensive database of maps on land-use, crime, and other planning information. Several authors offer examples of the positive effect of GIS and other technologies on community participation in the planning process (Sawicki and Craig, 1996; Craig, 1998; Sarjakoski, 1998; Schon *et al.*, 1999). New developments which strive to include in GI-based systems the subjective information on citizens' perceptions, views, and ideas, promise to enhance even further the potential of GI technology and tools to aid public participation in the planning process (Al-Khodmany, 1999, Talen, 1999).

Evaluation of Planning Practice and Technological Impact

Evaluation research is pursued in two venues: one is GIS-aided evaluation of the quality of urban communities and of planning practice; the other is evaluation of GIS impact on planning process, practice, and outcomes. With respect to planning practice, Talen (1998) applies GIS to examine the equity in distribution of public services to various segments of the community, and to search for areas that have not received adequate planning attention and have not been allocated their fair share of public resources. In an earlier study, Talen (1996) uses GIS to assess achievement of open space goals by comparing the planned and implemented projects. Knaap *et al*. (1998) have used GIS in their evaluation of the relevance and outcomes of planning. They ask if planning matters, and to answer this question they model the land development process as interaction between local government policies and land market participants to measure the effect of planning as a change in social welfare. Finally, the Urban Institute has initiated a project to explore a feasibility of creating national system of indicators to be used for evaluating the quality of life at the neighbourhood level (Sawicki and Flynn, 1996).

The other research venue has to do with finding out if the employments of GI technologies and tools have made any difference in planning practice. Planners have always been on the forefront of GIS diffusion, but the benefits to them are not yet well documented. To understand the impact of GIS and apply that information in designing systems that will suit planning practice, Nedovic-Budic (1998, 1999) reviews the evaluation frameworks, methods, and empirical studies. The evaluation dimensions include: system quality, information quality, information use, user satisfaction, individual impact, organizational performance (i.e., efficiency and effectiveness), and societal impact. The author finds that information processing is still perceived as the main GIS benefit, while the enhancement in decision-making and empowerment is yet to be achieved. Montagu (1999) examines the benefit between GIS technology and the natural resource planning process in the context of Papua New Guinea's State Government. He finds "little impact on the planned outcomes of environmental management across the country" and argues that the "domination of the prevailing political economy of environmental management in the planning process" is the reason for inadequate utilization of well-designed and custom-developed GIS. Obviously, the experiences and insights into building successful GIS in planning organizations at various levels, different mandates, and diverse settings, will provide useful information for many current and prospective users. GIS-based research in planning spans all five contribution areas (listed above) and a variety of planning subfields, including urban growth management, land-use planning, zoning, housing, community and economic development, transportation planning, environmental issues, provision of community parks and open space, and supply of public utilities and amenities. This includes,

- Spatial Data Acquisition and Integration;
- Distributed Computing;

- Extensions to Geographic Representations;
- Cognition of Geographic Information;
- Interoperability of Geographic Information;
- Scale;
- Spatial Analysis in a GIS Environment;
- The Future of Spatial Information Infrastructure;
- Uncertainty in Geographic Data and GIS-Based Analyses; and
- GIS and Society.

Remote Sensing (RS) and Geographical Information System (GIS) research priorities are all applicable to the field of urban and regional planning. Data collection and integration are the most time consuming planning activities and GIS is a prominent tool to aid in data-related activities. The data-related understanding between planners and engineers is probably the one that needs improvement the most. Two-way exchange, with planners appreciating and taking advantage of the engineering precision and accuracy, and with engineers' ability to utilize more uncertain and generalized planning data, is still a challenge to overcome. If the traditional planners' connectivity to engineering and many other public and private organisations is to be realized by computer-based networking, distributed computing, interoperability, and scale issues are essential for enabling exchange of data between many specialized local agencies. Planners need to understand the quality of data and analyses they rely upon for plan and policy-making. Better analytical capabilities embedded in GIS software would also be useful extension of existing tools.

Advancements in the NSDI and Web tools hold the potential to improve the public access to planning information and the democratic and participatory requirements in the planning process. Understanding the cognitive aspects of GI-based tools will enhance planners' effectiveness in using these tools to communicate with decision-makers and the public. This understanding will also lead to development of tools that match the cognitive structures of various groups involved in the planning process. Finally, having the society as a reference for evaluating the impact of technology is compatible with public nature of most urban and regional planning activities, which strive for increasing community welfare and quality of life.

Urban and regional planning applications will certainly benefit from the research in the priority areas listed above. These priorities, however, promise to extend on the generic aspects of GI tools, but do not address the specific needs of planning practice. The most critical areas that are focused on urban and regional planning needs include:

- Development of planning support systems;
- Linking of tool developments with planning organizations, process, theory, and methods;
- Understanding the impact on planning process and outcomes; and
- Visualization of spatial processes and phenomena.

Development of planning support systems include integration of GI with other technologies (hypertext, groupware, audio/visuals, multimedia, models, simulations, expert systems etc.). Although the strides have been made in that direction (as evidenced in the most recent issue of Environment and Planning—1999, 26/3), many challenges are still ahead. Current developments of customized GI and other tools only partially respond to analytical, design, administrative, communicative, and decision-making support needed. Integration of those modules into a functional planning support system and their customization to various planning institutions is yet to be achieved.

Similarly, most of the collaborative decision-making support systems research is about GIS development rather than about GIS use, without a strong theoretical link between the two. Consequently, broadening and deepening the conceptual underpinnings about GIS-supported collaborative decision-making is a major research goal. To advance the GI science and to be useful in urban and regional planning practice, this broadening has to take the perspective of geographic information use. Evaluation of impact of GI technologies and tools is probably the most direct way of providing a link between the science and planning practice. Theoretically, founded and systematic evaluation provides knowledge that can inform GI diffusion, and can be applied in strategies for achieving effective implementation of GI technologies and tools. Once the planning tools are developed, they have to be effectively introduced into planning organizational settings. Technology transfer and incorporation of technology in the planning process is, therefore, a challenge related to building of PSS. This process usually implies a major organizational change and re-structuring to create new organizational forms, processes, procedures, information flows, and responsibilities. The organizational change implies mutual adjustment between the technology and the organization (Nedovic-Budic, 1997). While the knowledge base about GIS implementation process has started to consolidate during the past decade (Innes and Simpson, 1993; Budic and Godschalk, 1994; Campbell and Masser, 1995; Huxhold and Levinsohn, 1995; Nedovic-Budic and Godschalk, 1996; Tulloch *et al.*, 1996; Brown, 1997; Azad, 1998), the lessons learned are generic and not directly applicable to the planning context. Better understanding of planning organizational contexts and processes is crucial for effective embedding of planning support systems.

Understanding the relationship between planning theory and methods and GI technology is crucial for building and implementing tools that are suitable to planning practice. Esnard and MacDougall (1997) maintain that there is a common ground for integrating planning theory and GIS in data creation, analysis, and presentation. They suggest this integration as part of an educational experience. Guhathakurta (1999) also finds that urban modelling and decision support tools can be developed to serve practice and to link to its theoretical underpinnings. The author refers to a new form of rationality, which encompasses both positivist and interpretative epistemiology, promises to provide framework for development of planning technologies and tools.

In addition to the rational theory, social theory and post-modernism form vital cornerstones to planning theory. These theories provide a critique of the use of technology in the planning process and the rejection of a single narrative discourse usually pursued *via* the information technology (despite the technological capability to handle multiple narratives and views). Both theories relate to economic restructuring and globalization—topics well-covered in planning and geography, and, certainly assisted by spatial technologies. Without establishing these linkages between planning theory and practice, the technological developments would operate in a vacuum and end up being driven by immediate short-term concerns rather than overarching mission and purpose of planning action.

Finally, visualization of existing urban-related processes and phenomena and simulation of outcomes of proposed plans and policies is in the core of planning practice. Further developments in 3D modelling, virtual reality, incorporation of images, easy graphical manipulation of various urban components, movement through space, changing perspectives, link with planning and policy documentation and descriptive statements, annotation tools for dialogue and commentary, will all enhance the communication capacity of urban planners. As in the case of all applicable technologies, to make the visualization tools useful for planning practice, their customization and integration into the planning process will be a necessary aspect of the development. They also include the following:

- Emerging Technologies for Delivering GIS Science Education;
- Supporting Infrastructure;
- Access and Equity;
- Alternative Designs for Curriculum Content and Evaluation;
- Professional GIS Education Programmes;
- Research-based Graduate GIS Education;
- Learning with GIS; and
- Accreditation and Certification.

The RS and GIS education priorities listed above are all applicable to the field of urban and regional planning. GIS is described as "another quiet revolution" in the planning practice, and GIS courses have been introduced as an important component in the undergraduate and graduate planning curricula. GIS-related capabilities, techniques, and methods contribute to several skill areas of professional planners, including: analytical/research, communication, and data processing (Godschalk and McMahon, 1992; Friedmann and Kuester, 1994; Kaufman and Simons, 1995). Infrastructure for teaching is crucial, but difficult to secure and make fully accessible in planning schools and departments. The demand for continuing education and training of planning professionals in emerging geographic information technologies also has to be met. The educational materials, however, for both regular programmes and continuing education need to be tailored to the disciplinary framework of urban and regional planning by providing examples from planning practice and using methods that are common to planners.

As suggested in the list of educational priorities, securing exposure to GIS through research is a desired educational practice among planning programmes. Finally, with regard to certification, the American Institute of Certified Planners (AICP) and American Planning Association (APA), which have both began to recognize GIS training as one of the professional requirements, are for now unlikely to pursue any GIS-related certification, although the future may be different. However, other organizations, like the Urban and Regional Information Systems Association (URISA), have started to seriously discuss the issues of professional education and certification (http://www.urisa.org/certific.htm). The area where professional planning associations may assume a stronger role is in the programme accreditation process. For example, Planning Accreditation Board (PAB) may start to look close into the programmes' provision for education in GI-based computerized technologies and tools.

Closely related to the professional accreditation and certification is the question of ethics. This question is subsumed under the RS and GIS research priority GIS and Society, which states that it is important to "lessen the likelihood that geographic information technologies will be misused, or their products misinterpreted, or inappropriate decisions be made based on their products." Practicing ethical behaviour and possibly developing and adhering to a professional code of ethics, is, however, in the realm of education and certification.

Esnard (1998) alerts us that the codes of ethics and ethics in general are so critical and need to be a high priority for educators who prepare the next generation of professional planners. The author asks how do we seriously think of constructing guidelines that can serve as simple common language of ethical behaviour—guidelines that are easy to remember and build upon. Should the multidisciplinary GIS community have a common code for all GIS users and if so, what happens to our own professional codes, in case of planners—the American Institute of Certified Planners (AICP) and the American Planning Association (APA)—AICP/APA Ethical Principles in Planning. Esnard finds the current provisions addressing data analysis and information to be outdated and sometimes contradictory. She calls for both studying the questionable uses of information technology to understand their ethical and legal implications and impacts, and using the examples of misuse as the source of education. Defining a framework that would help GIS practitioners delineate the behavioural boundaries and make judgements about their responsibilities and actions is of utmost priority.

In summary, the following are educational priorities that would respond more closely to the needs of urban and regional planning:

- Development of training materials to suit the planning professionals;
- Obtaining support for RS and GIS technology for teaching and research; and
- Developing a code of ethics for RS and GIS development and use.

The policies that would help advance the application of GI technologies and tools in urban and regional planning practice are in the areas of standardization, database development, access to data, tool building and integration, technology transfer, and legal framework. Each of the areas is briefly discussed below:

Support for Development and Maintenance of Local Databases

One of the most time consuming and difficult task performed by planners is data collection in support of particular project and/or agency function. In addition to collecting primary data, planners draw on numerous secondary data sources, including other agencies and government censuses, to acquire data and integrate them into a useful database. External support in developing local databases, for example on properties, streets, utilities, and detailed neighbourhood characteristics, would be of great value to local planners. This support could come in form of technical assistance, staffing, and/or financing options, and would not necessarily have to be managed within planning agencies, as long as the planners' have access to other databases developed by public funds.

Standardization

While integrating data from a variety of sources, planners deal with issues of data format and quality on daily basis. Standardization of data, formats, and metadata would help alleviate some of the difficulties in physically integrating the data, and would promote common terminology and contents in describing data. As in the case of database development and maintenance, the focus should be at the local level, where it is most difficult to establish and adhere to common features that would be acceptable to multitude of local data providers and users. Awareness about the existing standards and standardization efforts is the first step in preparing the local GIS communities to consider and accept standardization of GI technologies and products.

Access to Data

Similar to standardization, access has its technical and non-technical aspect. Technically, the tools for accessing data of various formats and proprietary codes are yet to be developed. The non-technical issue has to do with legal right to access government generate data and records, as well as with organizational motivation and willingness to provide open access to their data holdings. The easier it is to import and convert various geographic and attribute data formats, and the more open the database owners are towards free access to their databases, the more firm will be the foundation for building the National Spatial Data Infrastructure.

Tool Building and Integration

Planning support systems are applied in a unique organizational and social environment and under specific circumstances. Most of the planning support systems would be employed in local government settings where the nature, intensity, and impact of urban development and re-development are contested on daily bases between various public and private stakeholders and decision makers. While generic research in decision support systems provides relevant frameworks, concepts, and tools to be applied in planning practice, only the research in the planning specific context would secure achievements that are useful to planning practice and would hopefully enhance it. Therefore, funding by the major funding agencies in the US and abroad should be encouraged to explicitly address the needs of local planning. This research is very broad in scope to include tool integration, decision systems, simulation, visualization, and modelling in planning specific settings.

Education and Technology Transfer

Education is one way of preparing people for future use of GI technologies and tools. Encouraging such GI-focused educational programmes throughout the college experience and later during professional continuing education, is an important step in raising awareness about the existing technological potential and in providing skills for operating and developing GI technologies and tools. To aid the actual diffusion of GI technologies and tools, the inventors of new planning support tools should be required to disseminate their products in the real organizational/user settings. While commercial GI products generally find their way quickly to the market, the developments from academia which are often more sophisticated and potentially more useful, tend to remain buried in research reports and articles and seldom reach the wide range of professional and voluntary groups, which could benefit from those developments.

CASE STUDY

The area of study covers the southern districts of West Bengal, namely North and South 24-Parganas, Howrah, Hugli, Purba Medinipur and Paschim Medinipur and industrial use of land monitoring through Remote Sensing and Geographical Information System has been carried out in this study. The present project work is confined to sample study areas of Kharagpur, Paschim Medinipur, Falta, South 24-Parganas and Dankuni, Hugli districts. Spatial indicators to trace the use of land have been selected as follows: (a) Built-up areas, (b)Water Bodies, (c) Areas covered by crops, vegetation or forests, and (d) Wet land, waste land, vacant land, fallows etc. which are preferred by industries. Observation of these indicators can be broadly traced and distinctly understood by RS and GIS data. Analysis of digital Remote Sensing data and fieldwork is quite obvious.

The present study is an explanatory one and endeavours to explain and interpret interrelations between various aspects of industrial and urban development in the southern districts of West Bengal in a geographical context. Fieldwork and sample survey were followed by compilation and analysis of data as well as their presentation through maps and diagrams using techniques of RS and GIS supported by interpretation. The research work aims at exploring the causes and effects of changing uses of land and it attempts to provide a geo-economic analysis of the same.

Objectives: The study includes Image interpretation for delineating the prospective industrial area in the above selected specified study area and its surroundings.

Background: Various data set of the area were used for interpreting and unifying them within GIS and Image Processing environment and analysing the given data for identifying and delineating the prospective industrial area within the abovementioned selected study areas.

Data available: The following data were used for this project work:

(a) Scanned topographical sheet.
(b) Landsat satellite image having 28.5 m spatial resolution.

(c) IRS cartosat multi-spectral satellite image having 5 m spatial resolution.
(d) Google Earth image for additional assistance.

Software used: TNTmips V7.4 and V2009 were used in the present project study.

Case Study I: Application of RS and GIS in Delineating Kharagpur and its Neighbourhood for Planning Purpose

Few case studies have been incorporated from various research projects (conducted by author) which are given below for presentation:

At present the techniques in relation to RS-GIS are widely utilized for the delineation of areal units or regions for planning purposes. Various data sets of the area are often used for interpreting and unifying them within GIS and Image Processing environment and analyzing the given data for identifying and delineating the prospective area (that may be industrial, agricultural, urban etc.) within the selected study area. The study includes image interpretation for delineating current area under industry and the prospective industrial site(s) in the selected specified study area and its surroundings in Kharagpur, Paschim Medinipur district, West Bengal. The study area covers approximately 68.45 square kilometres. The following data were used to work upon by the tool of GIS, the area of study, delineated for planning purposes:

- Sets of scanned topographical sheets.
- Landsat satellite image having 28.5m spatial resolution for the identification of land-use components.
- IRS Cartosat multi-spectral satellite image having 5m spatial resolution.
- Google Earth image for additional assistance.

By using TNT mips Version 7.4, the given set of data was analysed and while using the given data, the following process flows were followed for unifying and interpreting the data:

(a) The topographical sheet was imported in a project file.
(b) The Topographical sheet was geo-referenced using Geographic and World Geodetic System 1984 (WGS 84) Datum.

(c) The given area extends from 22° 18′ N to 22° 21′ 36″ N and 87° 15′ E to 87° 21′ E. The area of interest is shown below:

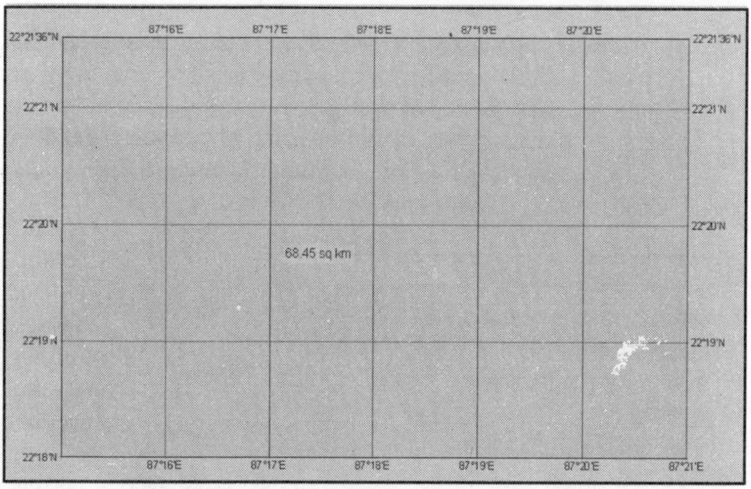

Fig. 6.1: Location of Kharagpur Study Area

(d) Landsat satellite image was imported in the same project file.

(e) The image was georeferenced using image to image geo-

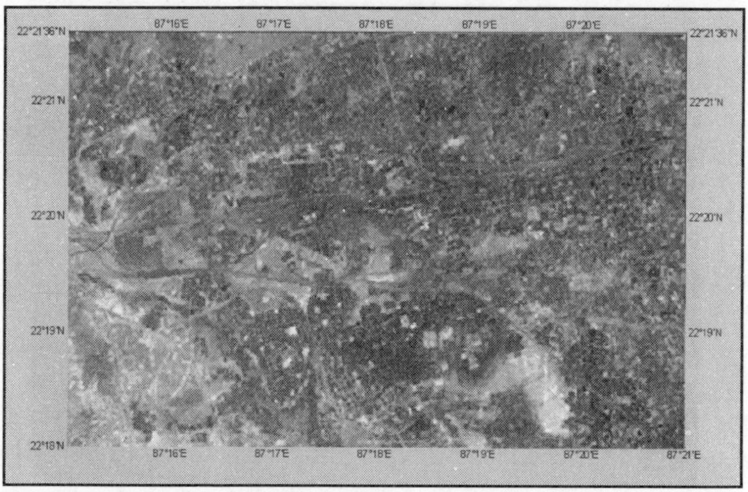

Fig. 6.2: Landsat imagery of the study area in standard FCC

referencing method, where the reference image was the topographical sheet.

(f) For standard FCC Band-4 (NIR), Band-3 (Red) and Band-2 (Green) were used.

(g) Necessary enhancement methods were implied for individual band to get the multi-spectral view. The study area in multi-spectral view is shown in Fig. 6.2.

(h) Landsat imagery was classified using Maximum Likelihood supervised Classification method to identify different land-use classes. Classes area are shown below:

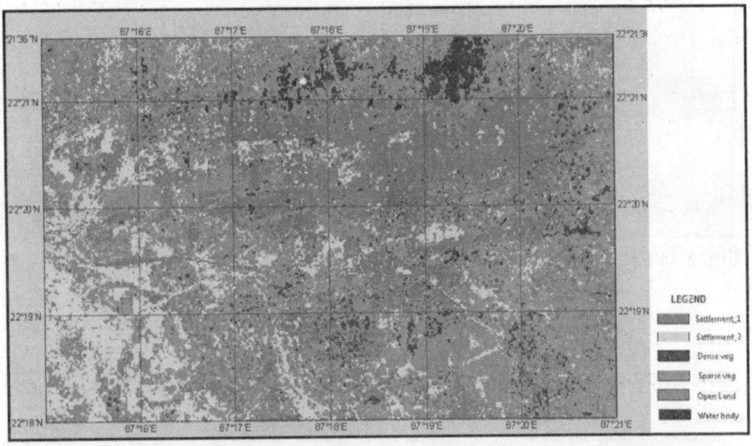

Fig. 6.3: Settlement and Broad Land-use

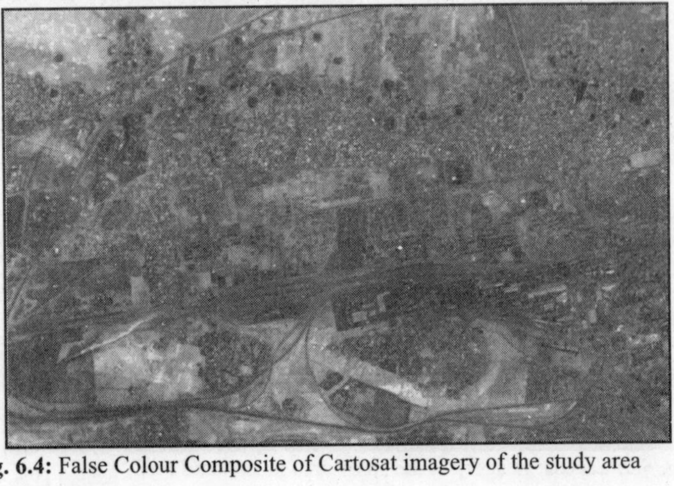

Fig. 6.4: False Colour Composite of Cartosat imagery of the study area

(i) IRS Cartosat multi-spectral satellite image was imported in the same project file.

(j) The image was geo-referenced using image to image geo-referencing method; here also the reference image was the topographical sheet.

(k) Classified land-use layout was cross-checked with Cartosat multi-spectral imagery.

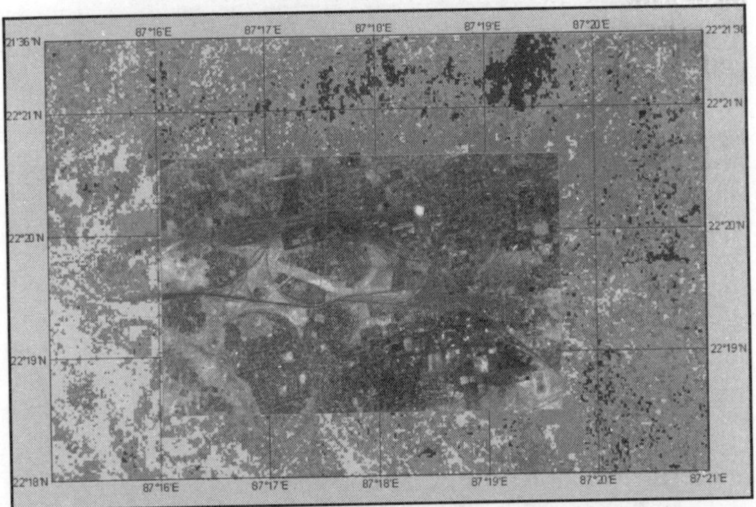

Fig. 6.5: Superimposition of Different Data Sets

(l) Google Earth image was collected and imported in the same project file.

(m) Google Earth image was referenced using image to image geo-referencing method for proper superimposition on the existing Topographical sheet, Landsat image and Cartosat imagery.

(n) Proper matching was checked.

(o) With the implementation of visual and digital image interpretation technique, the regions with prospective industrial possibility have been delineated.

Following factors were taken into consideration for delineating the zones of interest:

- Facilities for communication and transportation.

Fig. 6.6: Data from Google

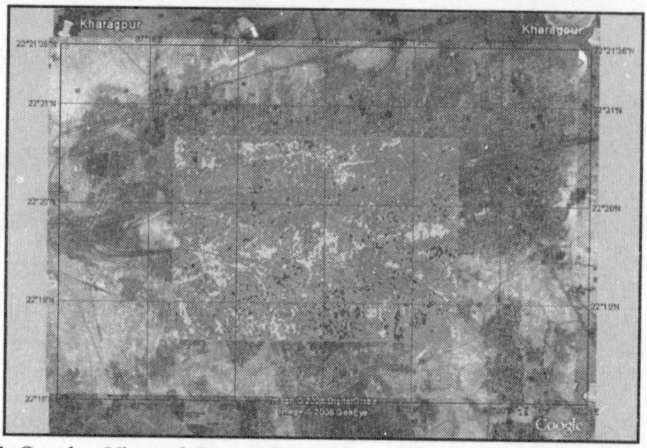

Fig. 6.7: Overlay View of Google Earth, Cartosat and Classified Landsat Image

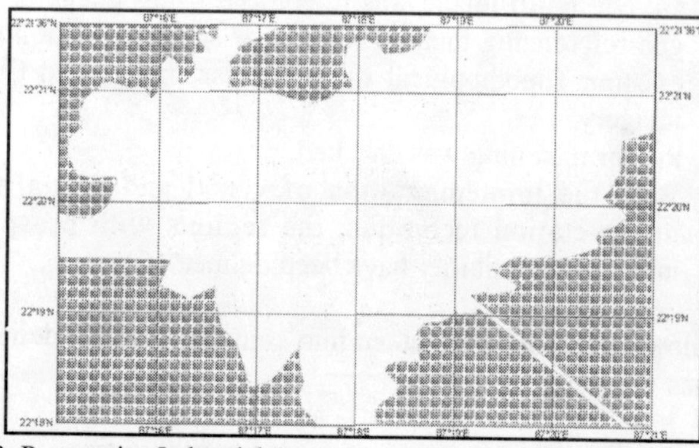

Fig. 6.8: Prospective Industrial Area

- During image classification for land-use type settlement areas were differentiated into two types, as in this study area dense and scattered type of settlement are available. South Western zone and South-eastern zone are demarcated for prospective industrial zones as these areas having scattered settlement and other facilities meet the conditions for the same.

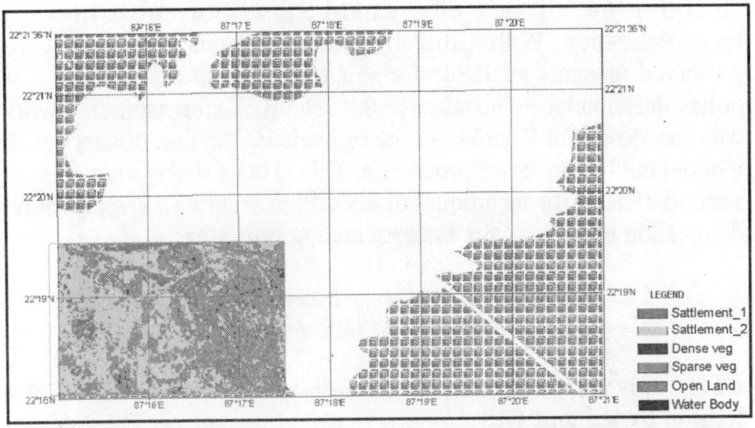

Fig. 6.9: Identification of Settlements

- Rest of the areas is demarcated with open land of sparse vegetation.

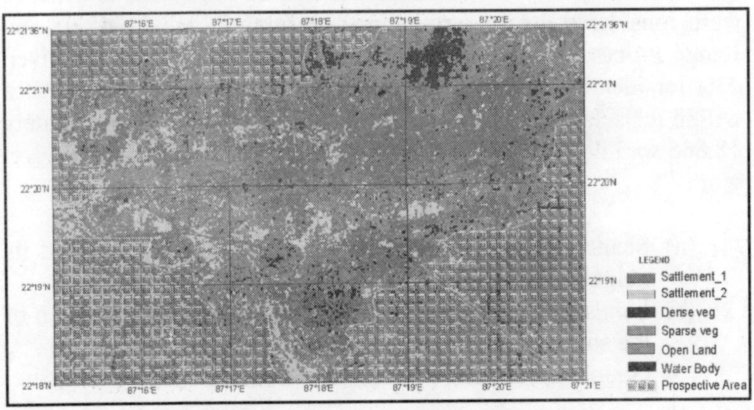

Fig. 6.10: Land-use and Prospective area for Industries

In the present status of study all the parameters related to the process of delineation of regions for industrial suitability could be well accomplished. The zones, with this approach can be easily and of course authentically delineated as prospective industrial regions. Hence, it may be stated that the delineated zones are the probable prospective areas for industrial use. Obviously, the roads and railways emerging out of this city would draw more attention for industrialization. Within the city, the open lands are either to be preserved or made available for small and household industries. A policy decision has to be taken in this regard. An intensive fieldwork was carried out in Kharagpur site to evaluate the preliminary result worked out by the above procedure. This gives a strong viewpoint in support of using the techniques of RS-GIS in accurate and meaningful delineation of regions for future planning purposes.

Source: Chatterjee, K. 2011, UGC Major Research Project on "Industrial area use of land monitoring through RS and GIS"

Case Study II: Identifying the Potential Industrial Areas at Falta Region by RS and GIS

Following the process of delineation of potential region for establishing industries in Kharagpur, another area, namely Falta had been chosen for identifying its potential pockets of development on the basis of industries. Likewise, sets of data in relation to the area were considered for interpreting and unifying them within GIS and Image Processing environment. This helps in analyzing the given data for identifying and delineating the prospective industrial area within the selected study area. The study area covers approximately 18.865 sq. kilometres. The following data were used for this project work:

(a) Scanned Topographical Sheet in relation to Falta and its neighbourhood.
(b) Landsat satellite image having 28.5 m spatial resolution of the study area.
(c) Google Earth image for further assistances.

The software package TNTmips V 2009 were used in order to identify the region of potential industrial sites and the study was completed in 42 days. Using the given data, the following process flow were followed for unifying and interpreting the data:

(a) The topographical sheet was imported in a Project file.

(b) The Topographical sheet was geo-referenced using Geographic and World Geodetic System 1984 (WGS 84) Datum.

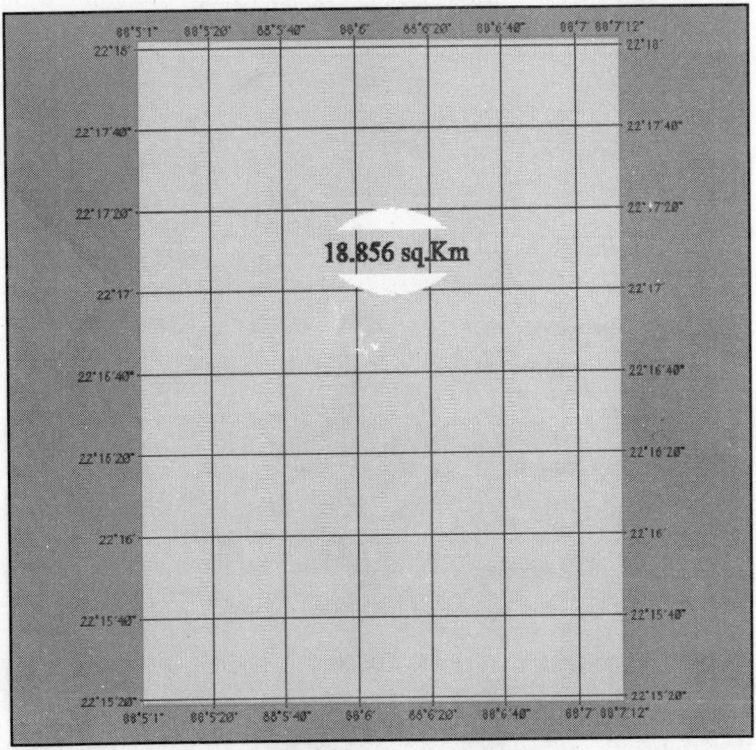

Fig. 6.11: Location of Falta Study Area

(c) The given area extends from 22° 15' 18" N to 22° 18' N and 88° 05' E to 88° 07' 12" E.

(d) Landsat satellite image was imported in the same project file.

(e) The image was geo-referenced using image to image geo-referencing methodologies, where the reference image was the topographical sheet.

(f) For standard FCC Band-4(NIR), Band-3(Red) and Band-2 (Green) were used.

(g) Necessary enhancement methods were implied for individual band to get the multi-spectral view. With this various land-use components may be truly separated. The study area in multi-spectral view is shown in Fig. 6.12.

(h) Landsat imagery was classified using Maximum Likelihood Supervised Classification method to identify different land-use classes. Classes area are shown below:

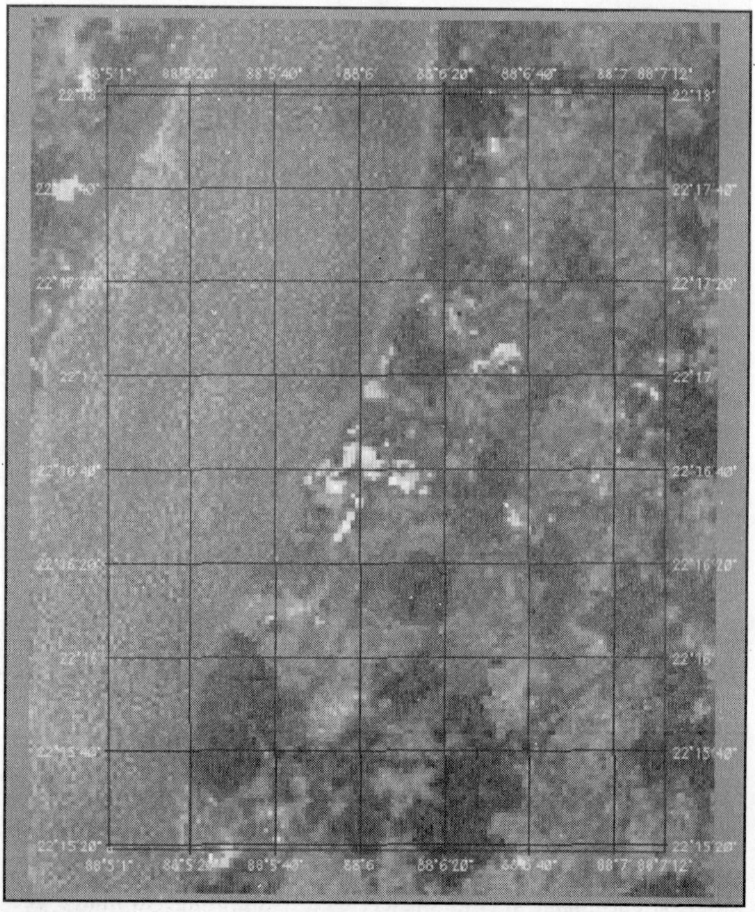

Fig. 6.12: Landsat Imagery of the Study Area in Standard FCC

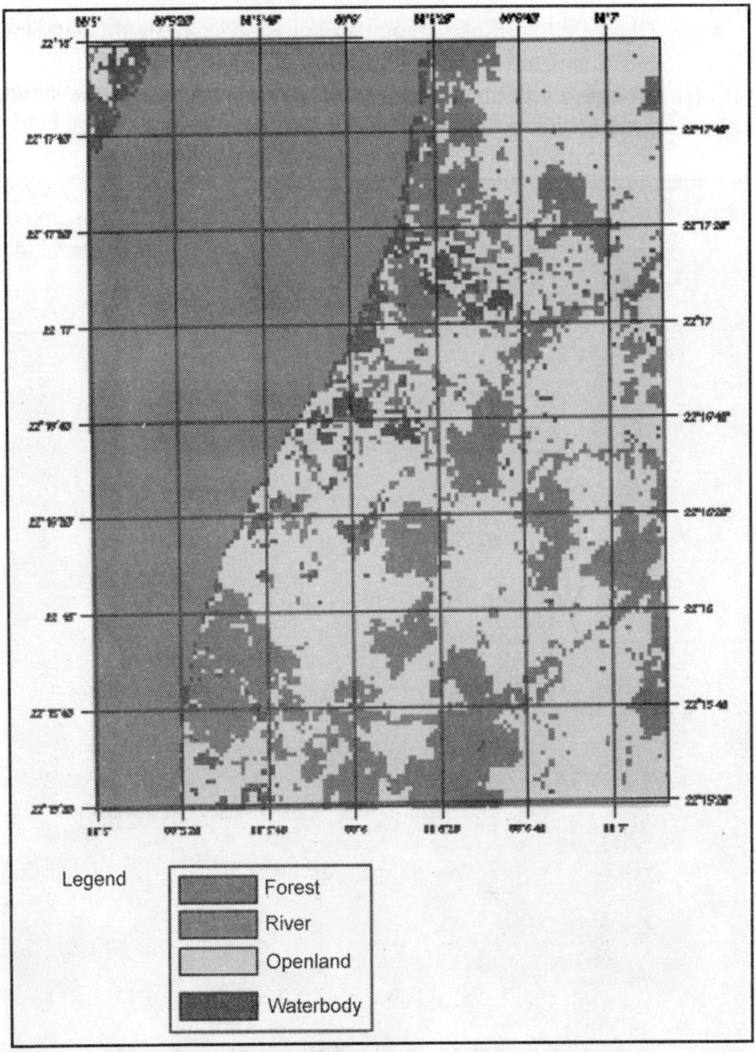

Fig. 6.13: Land-use Map of the Study Area

Open land and sparse vegetation area merged as a single class using raster combination algorithm because in the current scope of work we are trying to find out the area which can be identified as prospective industrial zone where land availability is an important parameter.

(i) Classified land-use layout was cross-checked with Landsat multi-spectral imagery.

(j) Google Earth image was collected and imported in the same project file.

Fig. 6.14: Landsat in FCC and Land-use Overlay View of Study Area

(k) Google Earth image was referenced using image to image geo-referencing method for proper superimposition on existing topographical sheet, Landsat image and Cartosat imagery.

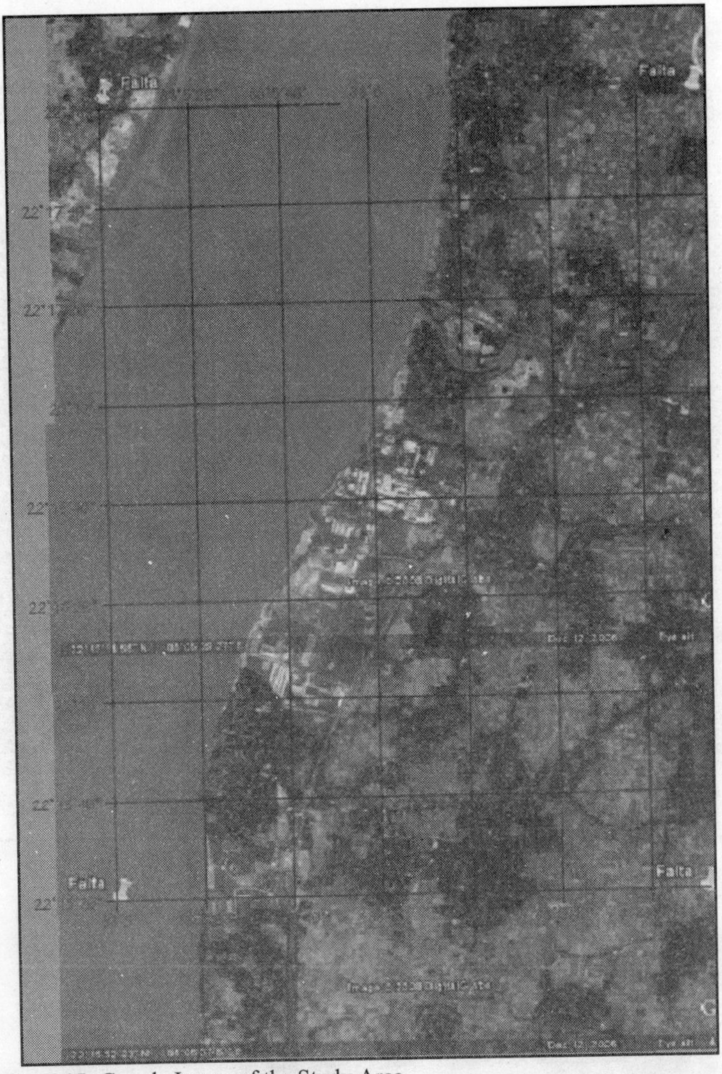

Fig. 6.15: Google Image of the Study Area

(l) Landuse Classified map was cross checked to predict the accuracy level.

(m) With the implementation of visual and digital image interpretation technique, the areas having prospective industrial possibility have been delineated which are shown below:

Fig. 6.16: Overlay View of Google Image and Classified Land-use Map

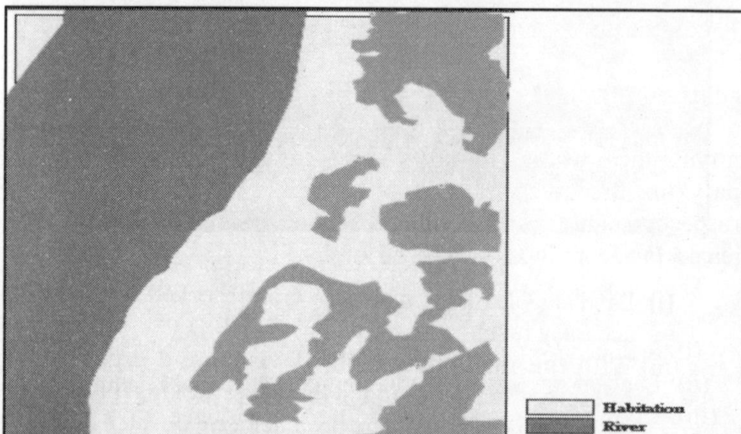

Fig. 6.17: Prospective Industrial Area

Following factors were taken into consideration for delineating the zones of interest:

- Facilities for communication and transportation.
- During image classification for land-use type sparse vegetation and open land areas have been merged into a single category as in this scope of study we are trying to demarcate the land which can be acquired for industrial uses. South-east zone is demarcated for prospective industrial zone as this area having scattered settlement coverage, open land (including waste and wet land) and other facilities meet the conditions for the same.

In the present status of study all the parameters related to industrial suitability were considered. The zones, which have been delineated as prospective areas, have been verified using the field data. So, the delineated zones are the probable prospective areas. An intensive fieldwork was carried out in Falta site to evaluate the preliminary result worked out by the above procedure.

Source: Chatterjee, K. 2011, UGC Major Research Project on "Industrial area use of land monitoring through RS and GIS."

Case Study III: Identification of Prospective Industrial Zone at Dankuni, West Bengal by RS and GIS.

The study includes Image interpretation for delineating the prospective industrial area and industrial site in the selected specified study area and its surroundings in Dankuni, Hugli district, West Bengal.

Various data sets of the area were used for interpreting and unifying them within GIS and Image Processing environment and analyzing the given data for identifying and delineating the prospective industrial area within the selected study area. The study area covers approximately 4.53 sq.kms.

The following data were used for this project work:

(i) Scanned Topographical Sheet.
(ii) Landsat satellite image having 28.5m spatial resolution.
(iii) Google Earth image for additional assistance.

TNTmips V 2010 were used in this project. This project work took 25 days for compilation, calculation etc. Using the given data, the following process flows were followed for unifying and interpreting the data:

(a) The topographical sheet was imported in a Project file.
(b) The Topographical sheet was geo-referenced using Geographic and World Geodetic System 1984 (WGS 84) Datum.
(c) The given area extends from 22° 40' 09" N to 22° 38' 49" N and 88° 17' 09" E to 88° 18' E. The area of interest is shown in Fig. 6.18.

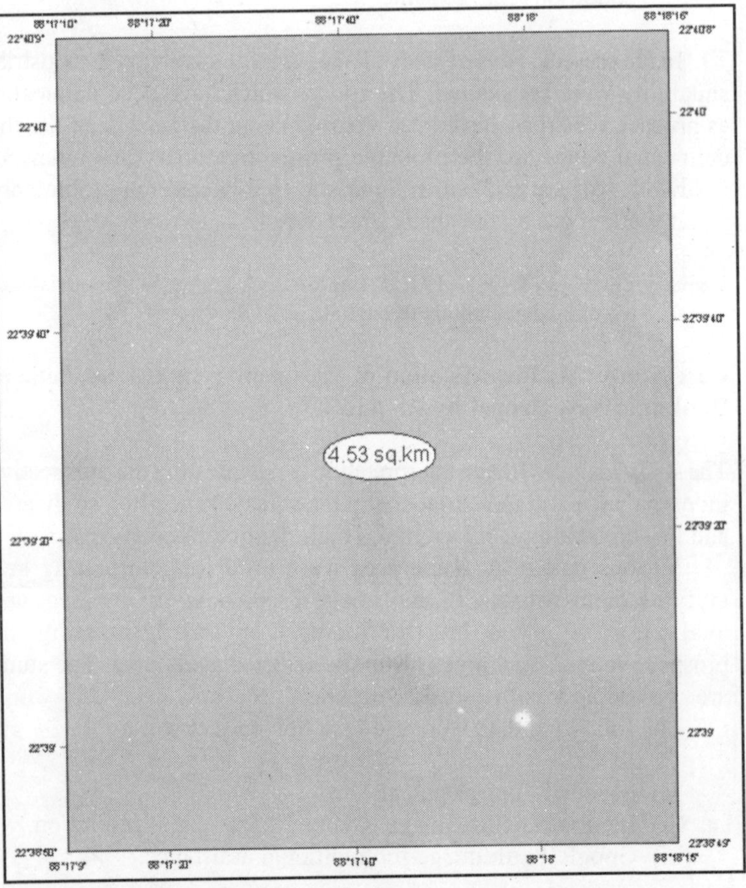

Fig. 6.18: Location of Dankuni Study Area

(d) Landsat satellite image was imported in the same project file.

(e) The image was geo-referenced using image to image geo-referencing method, where the reference image was the topographical sheet.

(f) For standard FCC Band-4 (NIR), Band-3 (Red) and Band-2 (Green) were used.

(g) Necessary enhancement methods were implied for individual band to get the multi-spectral view. The study area is shown in Fig. 6.19.

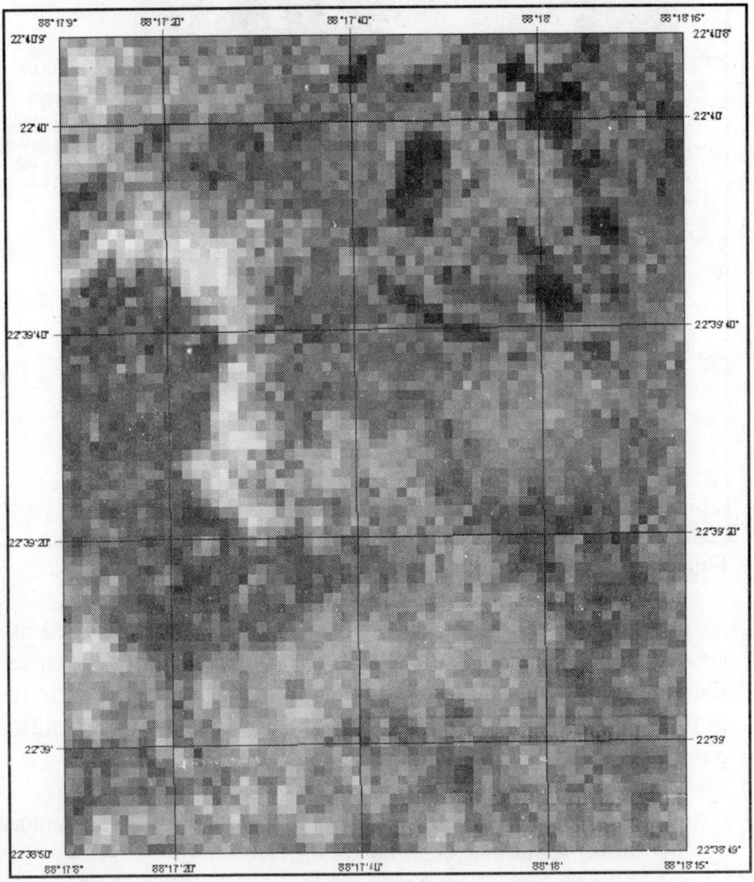

Fig. 6.19: Landsat Imagery of the Study Area in Standard FCC

(h) Landsat imagery was classified using Maximum Likelihood Supervised Classification method to identify different landuse classes. Classes area are shown in Fig.6.20.

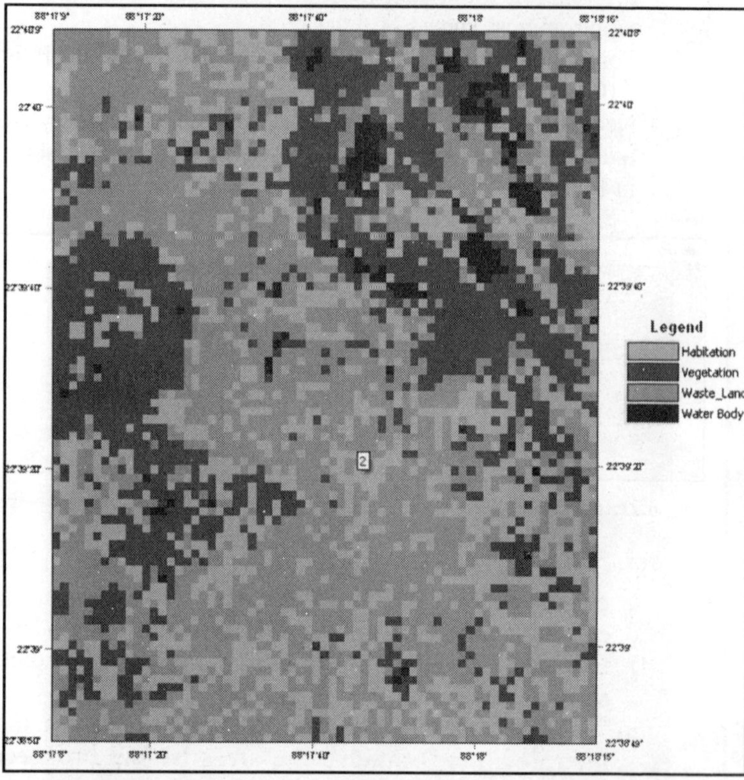

Fig. 6.20: Land-use Map of the Study Area

Waste land and sparse vegetation area have been merged as a single class using raster combination algorithm because in the current scope of work we are trying to find out the area which can be identified as prospective industrial zone where land availability is an important parameter:

(i) Classified land-use layout was cross-checked with Landsat multi-spectral imagery. (Fig.6.21)

(j) Google Earth image was collected and imported in the same project file. (Fig.6.22)

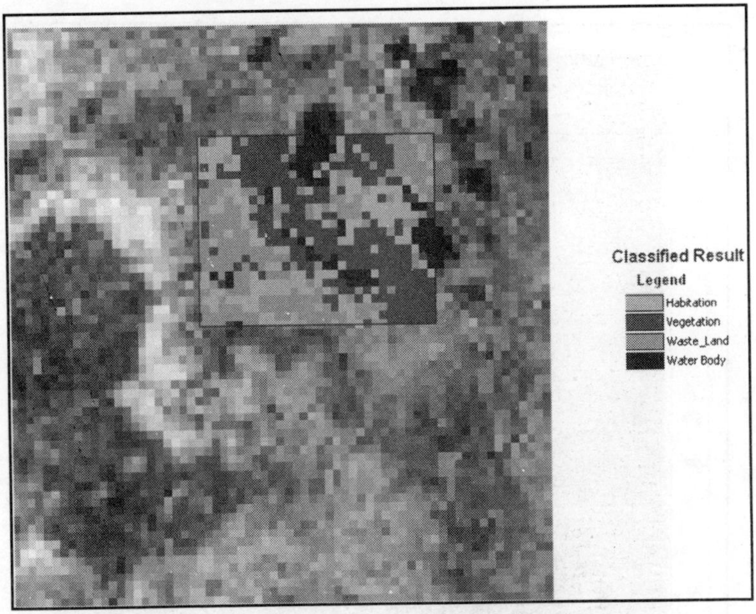

Fig. 6.21: Landsat in FCC and Land-use Superimposed View of Study Area

(k) Google Earth image was referenced using image to image geo-referencing method for proper superimposed on the existing topographical sheet, Landsat image. (Fig.6.23)

(l) Land-use Classified map was cross-checked to predict the accuracy level.

(m) With the implementation of visual and digital image interpretation technique the areas having prospective industrialization possibility have been delineated which are shown in Fig. 6.24.

Following factors were taken into consideration for delineating the zones of interest:

- Facilities for communication and transportation.
- During image classification for land-use type sparse vegetation and open land areas have been merged into a single category as in this scope of study we are trying to demarcate the land which can be acquired for industrial uses.

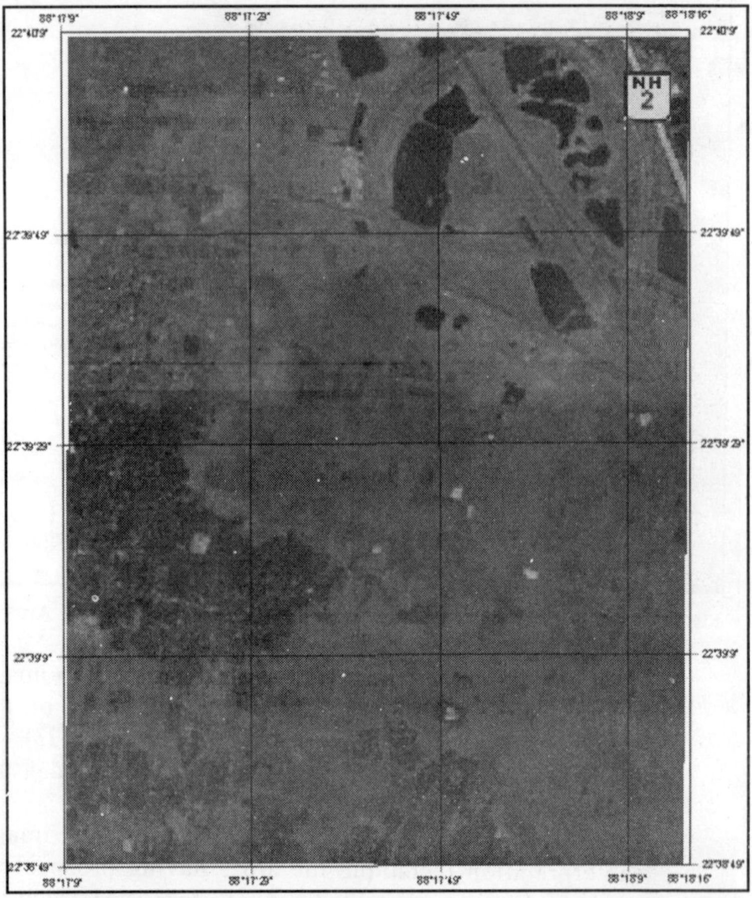

Fig. 6.22: Google Image of the Study Area

- From the observation of study area, Highway and Rail track are passing through the North-East portion, which is a healthy condition for industrial suitability study. It requires a buffer zone as per the Railway and Highway Authority. Considering this condition 50m buffer zone have been used to segregate that portion from the enter study area as shown in Fig. 6.25.

Considering all these factors, the actual suggested area for industrialization is shown in Fig. 6.26.

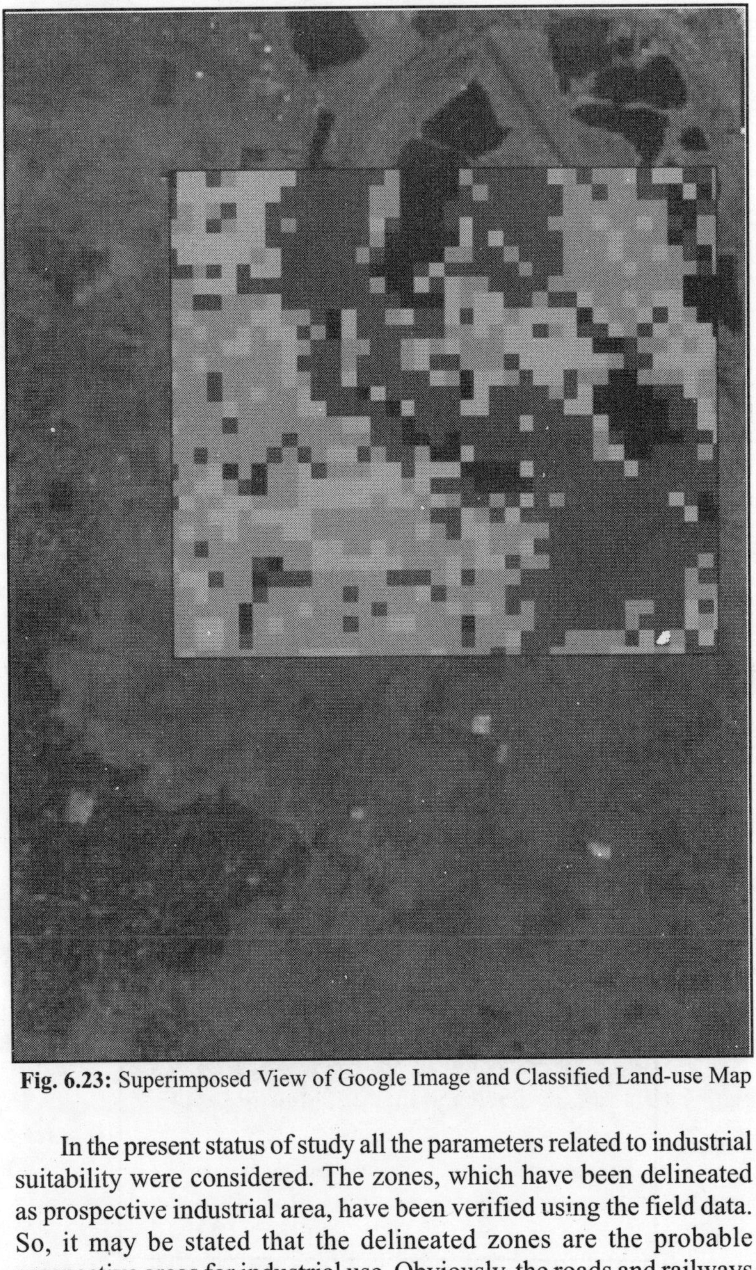

Fig. 6.23: Superimposed View of Google Image and Classified Land-use Map

In the present status of study all the parameters related to industrial suitability were considered. The zones, which have been delineated as prospective industrial area, have been verified using the field data. So, it may be stated that the delineated zones are the probable prospective areas for industrial use. Obviously, the roads and railways

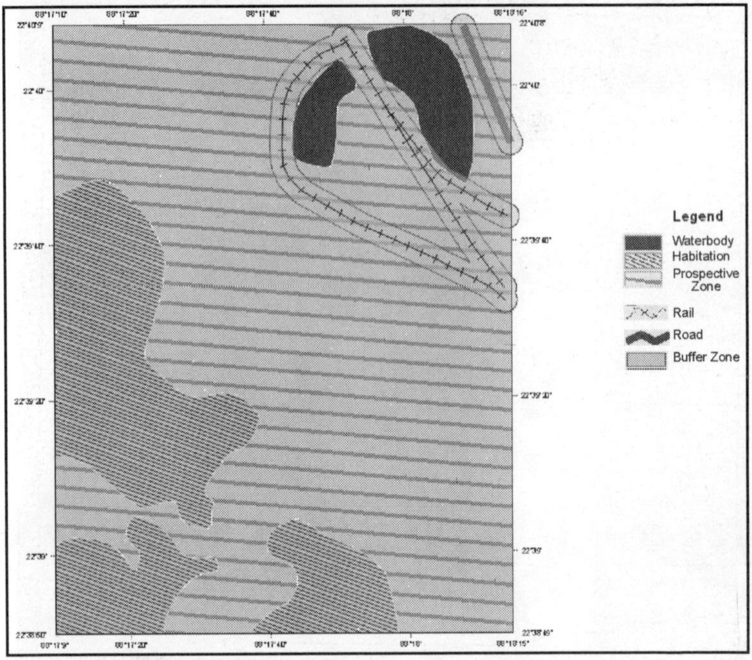

Fig. 6.24: Prospective Industrial Area

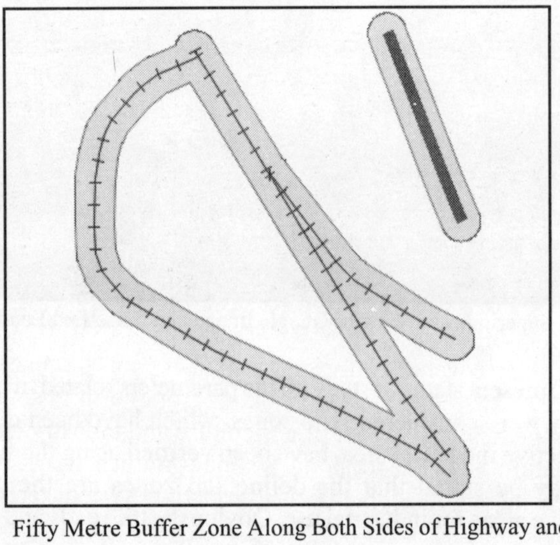

Fig. 6.25: Fifty Metre Buffer Zone Along Both Sides of Highway and Railway Track

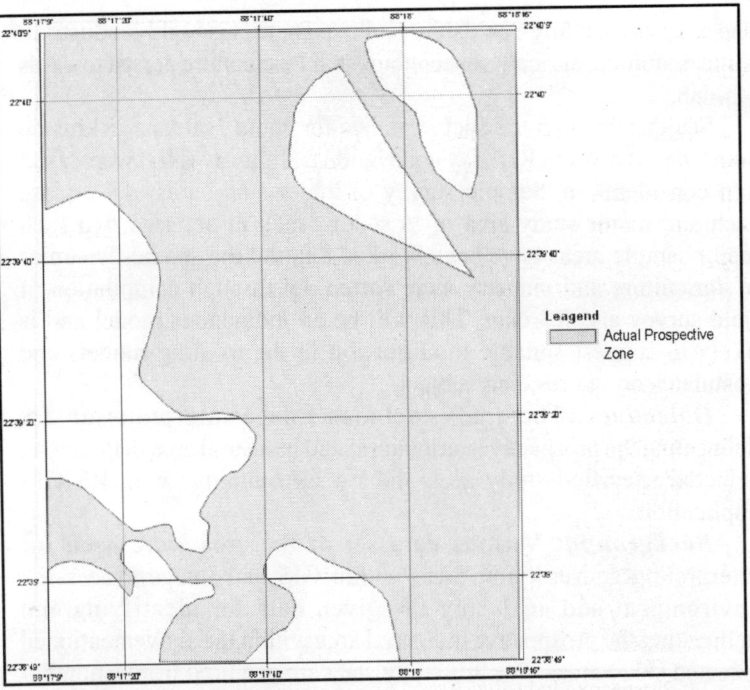

Fig. 6.26: Prospective Industrial Area

will draw more attention for industrialization. Within the city, the open lands have either to be preserved or made available for small and household industries. A policy decision has to be taken in this regard.

Source: Chatterjee, K. 2011, UGC Major Research Project on "Industrial area use of land monitoring through RS and GIS."

CASE STUDY

The area of study covers the districts of Maldah, Murshidabad, Nadia, North and South 24-Parganas and Kolkata from north to south. The spatial arrangement and layout of agriculture and industry and their dynamic nature were made along Sealdah-Maldah transact using Remote Sensing and Geographical Information System techniques.

The area surrounding Sealdah in Kolkata District is highly industrial, while traditional agricultural economy and Pisciculture persist towards Maldah.

Sealdah-Maldah transact stretches for about 300 kms. 5 kms on both sides of Eastern Railway and National Highway (NH) were taken into consideration. Sample survey of major study area of 1 sq.km. each and minor study area of ¼ sq.km. each in between two such major sample areas have been worked out and the spatial dynamics of agriculture and industry were sorted out through compilation of field survey and RS data. This will be an indigenous model and is likely to suggest suitable modification in the existing models and postulates on the restated subject.

Objectives: The study includes Image interpretation for delineating the prospective agricultural and industrial area in the above selected specified study area and its surroundings with RS GIS application.

Background: Various data set of the area were used for interpreting and unifying them within GIS and Image Processing environment and analysing the given data for identifying and delineating the prospective industrial area within the abovementioned selected study areas. For this study, data are acquired from a number of sources. Since, the nature of land-cover monitoring requires images of different time period, and that change detection analysis is carried out most effectively with not less than 3 images of the study area, three Landsat ETM Satellite images of Oyo State are acquired. 1993, 2003 and 2013 with spatial resolution of 1000 m. Other ancillary data like topographical map are also used.

Data available: The following data were used for this project work:

(a) Scanned topographical sheet.
(b) Landsat satellite image having 28.5 m spatial resolution.
(c) IRS cartosat multi-spectral satellite image having 5 m spatial resolution.
(d) Google earth image for additional assistance.

Software Used: Quantum GIS (1.8.0), TNTmips V 7.4 and Arc View 3.2a are used in the project study.

Case Study IV: RS and GIS Application on Spatial Dynamics of Sealdah and its Surrounding Areas, West Bengal

Economic development and population growth have triggered rapid changes to Earth's land-cover over the last two centuries, and there is every indication that the pace of these changes will accelerate in the future. The present study shows the utility of remote sensing techniques integrated with GIS to study the spatial dynamics of Agriculture and Industry in the selected specified study area and its surroundings in Sealdah, Kolkata District. Various satellite image data were analyzed within a digital image processing system to provide up-to-date information of the whole area. The extracted information from remotely sensed data was then integrated with visually interpreted information and field inputs in a GIS to create a comprehensive spatial database. This permitted the integration of several layers of information with the remotely sensed data in both temporal and spatial dimensions.

Remote sensing technology has been recognized as a useful means of supplying up-to-date information and have the potential to respond to the growing and urgent demand for timely and accurate land-cover information over large areas. In the recent past, land-cover mapping from satellites has come of age, through research on various issues regarding data pre-processing, classification and accuracy assessment, new and unique data/land-cover products are being generated which could not be produced by earlier techniques. Various data set of the area were used for interpreting and unifying them within GIS and Image Processing environment for analysis and interpretation.

The following data were used for this project work:

- Landsat satellite image having 28.5 m spatial resolution.
- IRS Cartosat multi-spectral satellite image having 5m spatial resolution.
- Digital Globe high resolution image (0.5 m) from Open Source Google.
- Earth repository for Visual interpretation and as a supplementary data for interpretation.

TNTmips Pro 2014, the integrated GIS and Image Processing platform were used in the present study.

Workflow

- Satellite Images were imported in a project file within TNTmips Pro platform.
- The Images were geometrically rectified with the GCP by using Geographic coordinate system and World Geodetic System 1984 (WGS 84) as Datum. Affine transformation model has been deliberately selected for this sampling area to maintain the geometric area and shape accuracy.
- The sampling location extends from North 22°33' 50.720″ to North 22°34' 23.234″ and East 88°22'04.958″ to East 88° 22'39.968″.
- As per the present scope of study to meet the temporal data requisite two different year data has been collected.
- Image preprocessing was implemented on both the images to improve the quality and interpretability.
- Extraction model was implemented on the scenes to get the 1 sq.km sampling area as decided to process with in the buffer zone of 5 kilometre both of the railway track from Sealdah to Maldah at the location of Sealdah station to get the surrounding bird's eyeview. (Fig. 6.27)

Fig. 6.27: Google Image 1 sq.km

Once, we have the processed image for both the years, the remarkable change between reflectance values were quite obvious. Study through this factor is highly dependent on the solar illumination

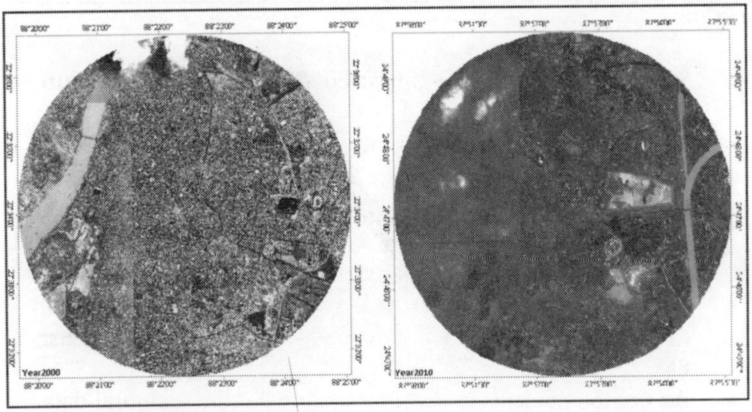

Fig. 6.27(a): Google Image 78.51 sq.km

of that particular time and date. Here is a comparative diagram of those values of particular location. (Fig. 6.28)

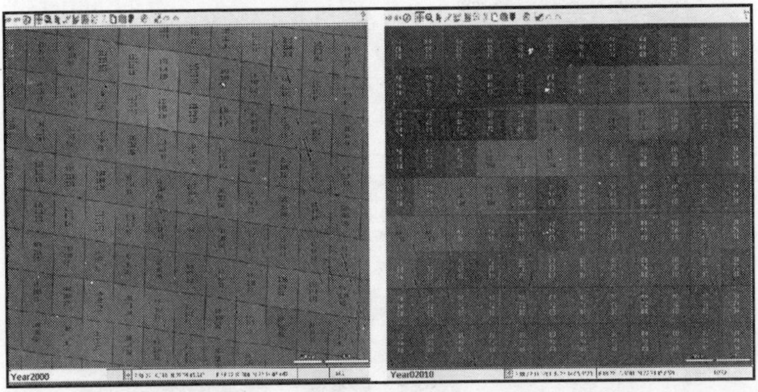

Fig. 6.28: RGB Values

As a part of visual interpretation the important land-cover patterns have been delineated by using manual vectorization followed by building of topology between the spatial feature. The platform used throughout the process flow is a topology in-built system, where we have achieved the optimum vector statistics for further comparison with digital interpreted result.

The implementation of the visual image interpretation technique, the areas having proper land-use differentiation had been delineated. Areas are shown in Fig. 6.29.

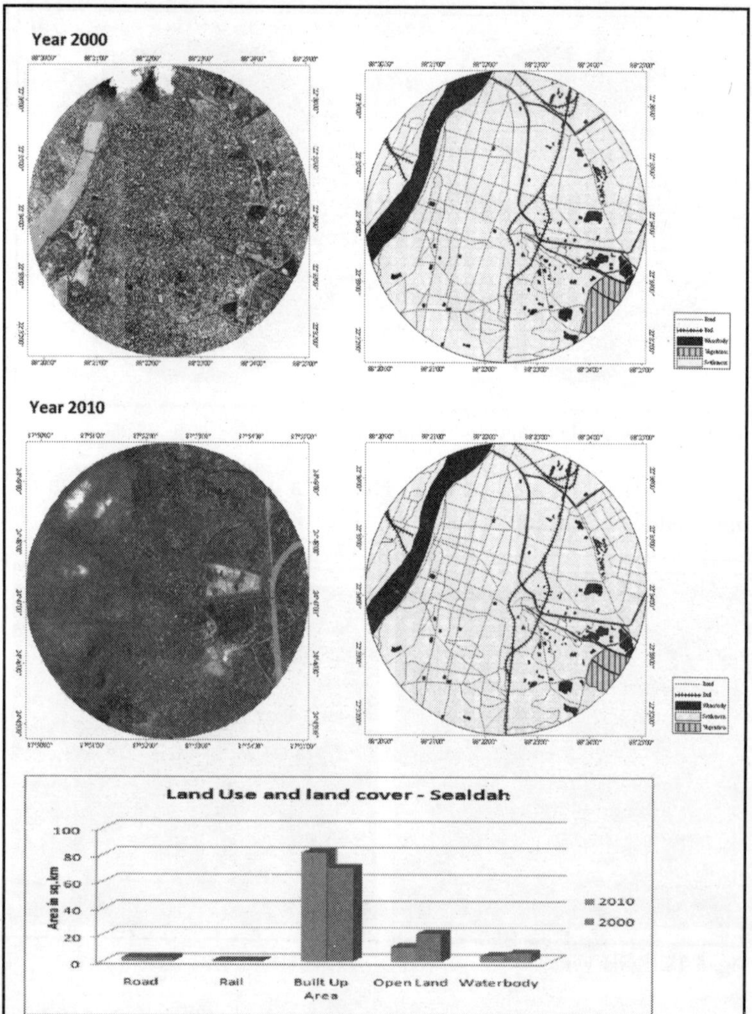

Fig. 6.29: Google Image 78.51 sq.km Land-use and Land-cover Map

Factors Considered: Following factors were taken into consideration for delineating the zones of interest:

- In order to create a balanced and sustainable industrial growth in any zone and maximize use of uncultivable land in any area, it is felt that some parts of this zone can be identified as industrial growth poles, because of such factors such as availability of non-agricultural land, historical industrial presence and availability of good infrastructure. This will mean optimal use of the existing industrial infrastructure and upgradation of infrastructure where required and create new industrial infrastructure for project in backward areas.

- During land-use classification habitation, vegetation and open land areas have been merged into a single category as in this scope of study we are trying to demarcate the land which can be acquired for industrial infrastructure.
- From the observation of study area, most of the area is covered by agricultural land. So, there is high prospect in producing crop. Then it is not healthy to create an industry in this particular area. There must have some social and political issues.
- Major criteria for industrial development is communication condition. In this area we can observe that Highway and Railway tracks are passing almost centre portion of this area.

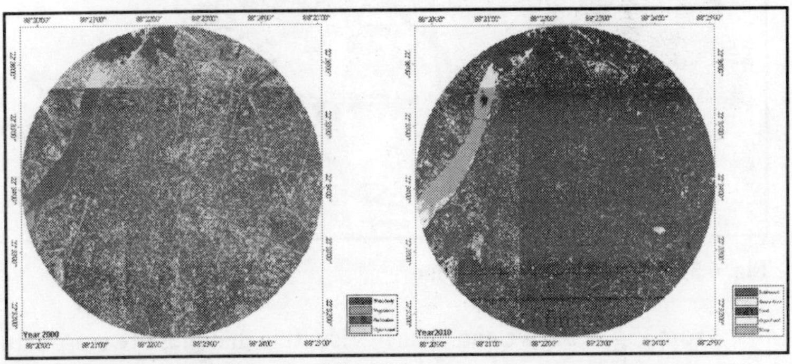

Fig. 6.30: FCC Classification of Sealdah

We can clearly see that the agricultural land has decreased to some extent (2000-2010) due to the significant increase in settlement areas and the decrease of waterbodies. Also, though there is potential industrial zones scattered throughout the aforementioned area, but scattered areas are not healthy for a potential industrial zone. At least 1 sq. km. continuous area is feasible for actual industrial zonation. So, here setting up large or small scale factories may not be viable.

Another issue arises up with settlement area. Here, we can observe that, in the year 2010, the percentage of population is very much higher than the year 2000. So, the scope of industrial expansion is not possible in this heavy population zone, so pollution issues are common. In the next map the potential industrial zones are depicted for the area of interest. (Fig. 6.31)

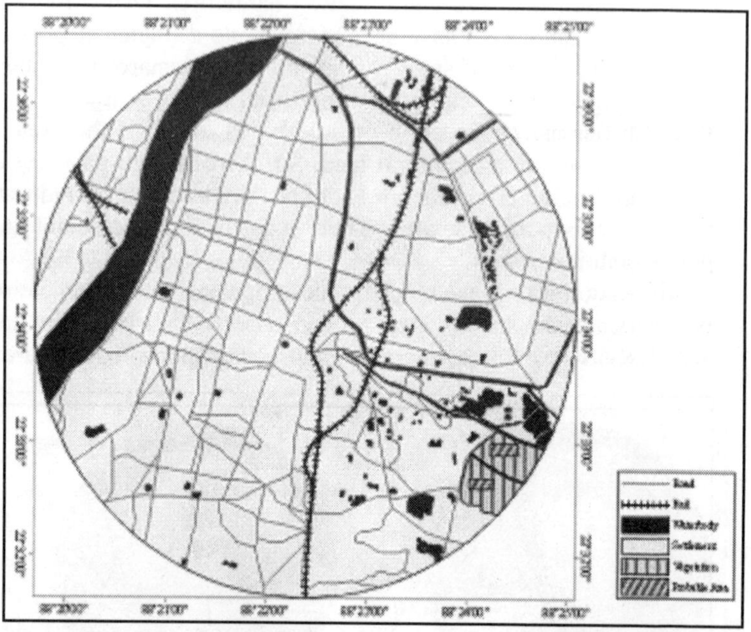

Fig. 6.31: Probable Industrial Zones

From Fig. 6.31. we can clearly visualize that these two probable zones are ideal for industrial area due to proper communication and availability of water. Areas of this prospective zones are 0.15 sq.km and 0.10 sq.km respectively. These two zones are under fallow land area, so, it cannot hamper the agricultural growth of this particular area. Due to good communication network and availability of water resource most of the areas are densely populated and prosperity of agricultural growth is very high. So, only these identified zones are feasible for industrial development within our region of interest.

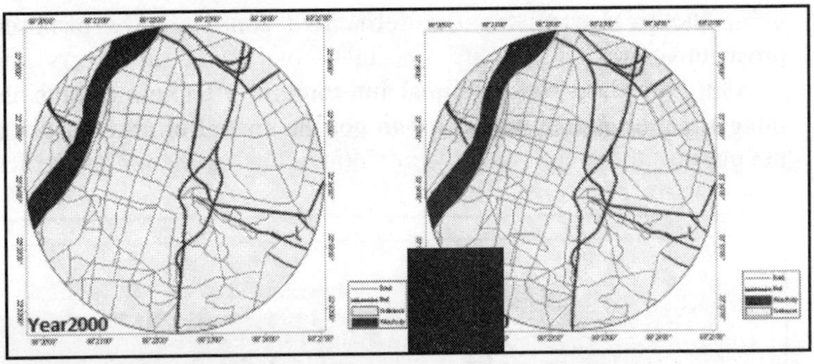

Fig. 6.32: Transport Network

From Fig. 6.32 we can interpret that the communication system has been drastically changed from 2000 to 2010 due to increase in population. So, probability of industrial zone is maximum in this zone.

In spite of other social issues, it can be concluded that this zone is superior for industrial growth. Considering all these factors, the actual suggested area for industrial area is shown in Fig. 6.33.

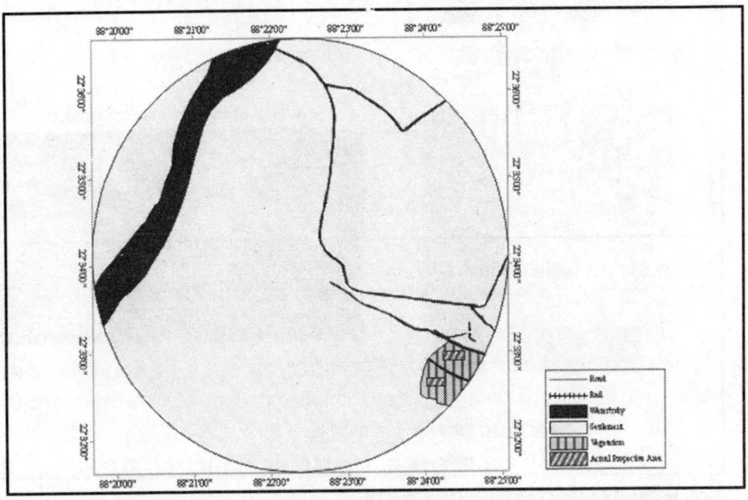

Fig. 6.33: Actual Prospective Industrial Area

Conclusion: In the present status of study all the parameters related to industrial suitability had not been considered. The zones, which had been delineated as prospective area, should be verified using the field data. So, the delineated zones are the probable prospective area.

So, using the same manual interpretation technique both the images were visually classified to get the spatial changes between the years.

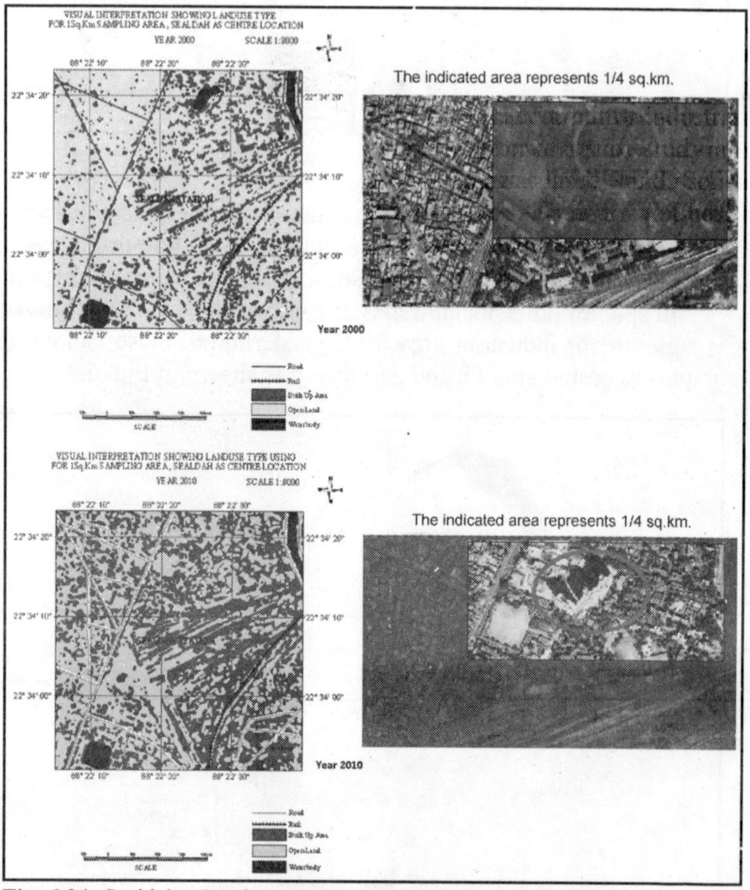

Fig. 6.34: Sealdah—Land-use Pattern

At the other hand, same images have been used for digital image classification. The study area has been passed through hybrid classification technique, where the unsupervised classification has been followed by supervised classification method and finally, the spurious classes were deliberately merged to get the intended result.

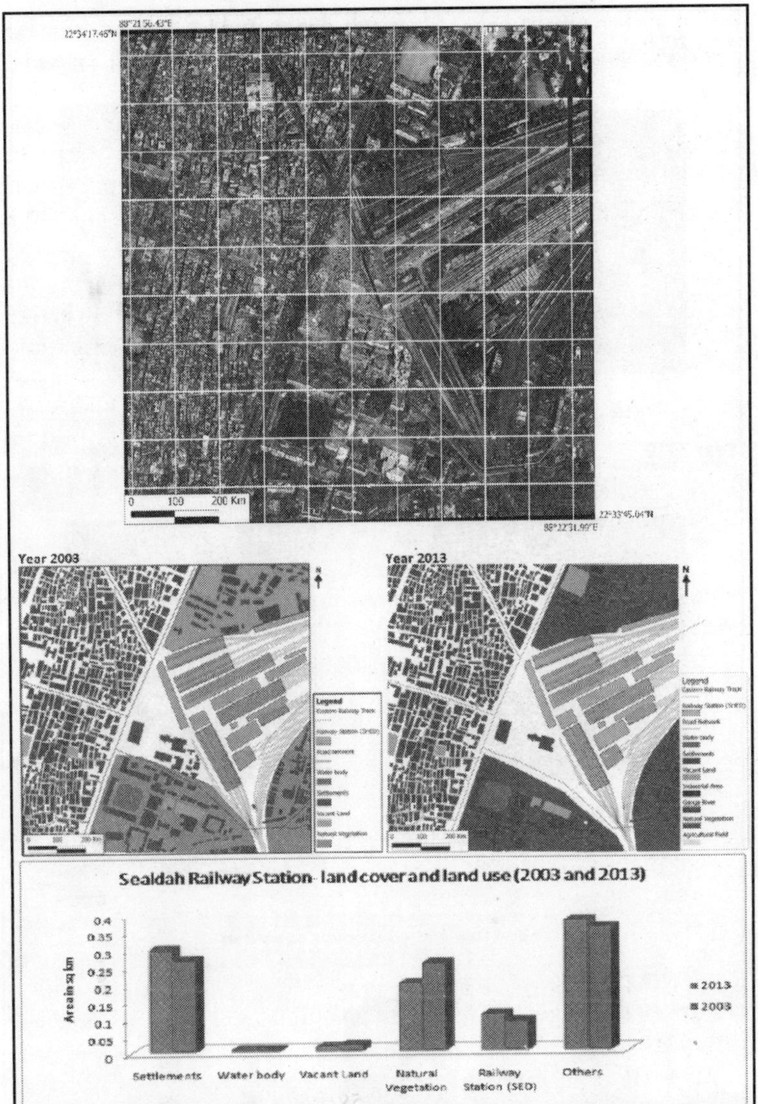

Fig. 6.35: Land-use and Land-cover Map—Sealdah Railway Station (Kolkata, West Bengal)

At Sealdah Railway Station, there is increase in station area and settlement and decrease is noticed in waterbody, vacant land, natural vegetation in the year 2013 compared to 2003. (Fig. 6.35)

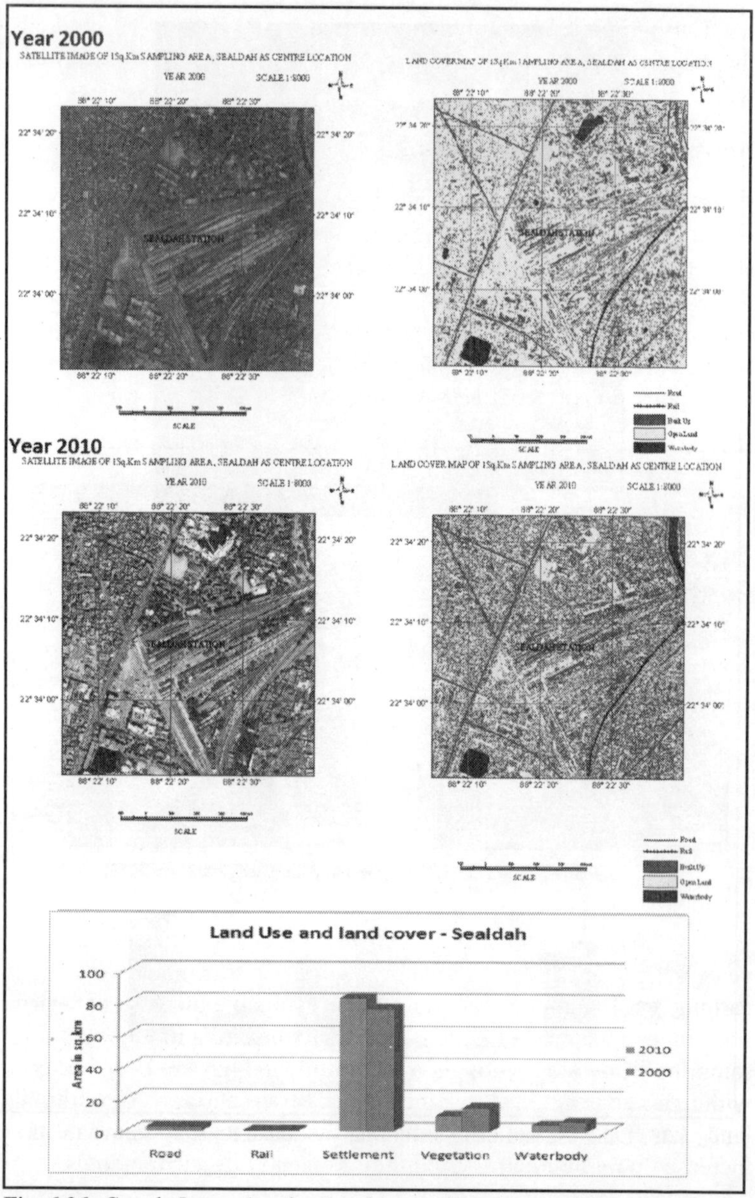

Fig. 6.36: Google Image 1 sq.km Land-use and Land-cover Map

Cartographical map preparation with suitable scale. Throughout the mapping we have tried to use A4 page where maps were fitted with 1:8000 scale.

Interpretation and Discussion

So, the procedural steps with the rigorous interpretation with both visual and digital technique for the study area between the years 2000 and 2010 this can be clearly interpreted that the '*Open Land*' has decreased to huge extent due to the significant increase in 'built-up' area and the decrease of water bodies is quite obvious. As this zone belongs to one of the impotent industrial city of West Bengal, naturally the population is dramatically increased during last 10 years.

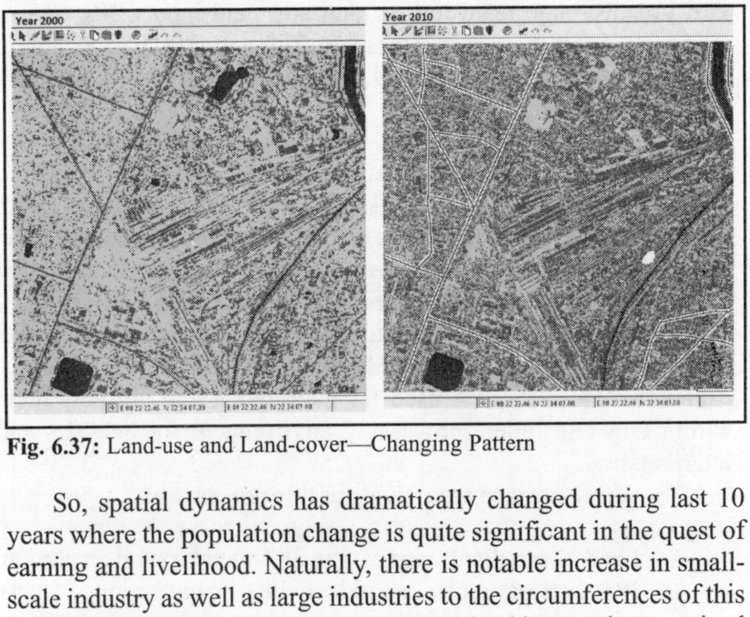

Fig. 6.37: Land-use and Land-cover—Changing Pattern

So, spatial dynamics has dramatically changed during last 10 years where the population change is quite significant in the quest of earning and livelihood. Naturally, there is notable increase in small-scale industry as well as large industries to the circumferences of this sampling study area. Though, agricultural land has not been noticed within this zone but in sequel the general observation is 'Agricultural land' has been occupied throughout the year to accommodate the increased population pressure in this zone and its surroundings.

Source: Chatterjee, K. 2015, UGC Major Research Project on "RS and GIS application in spatial dynamics of agriculture and industry along Sealdah-Maldah Transact, West Bengal."

Case Study V: Land-use Identification along Bardhaman Station, West Bengal by RS and GIS

Economic development and population growth have triggered rapid changes to Earth's land-cover over the last two centuries, and there is every indication that the pace of these changes will accelerate in the future. The present study shows the utility of remote sensing techniques integrated with GIS to study the spatial dynamics of Agriculture and Industry in the selected specified study area and its surroundings along Bardhaman Station, Bardhaman District. Various satellite image data were analyzed within a digital image processing system to provide up-to-date information of the whole area. The extracted information from remotely sensed data was then integrated with visually interpreted information and field inputs in a GIS to create a comprehensive spatial database. This permitted the integration of several layers of information with the remotely sensed data in both temporal and spatial dimensions.

Remote sensing technology has been recognized as a useful means of supplying up-to-date information and have the potential to respond to the growing and urgent demand for timely and accurate land-cover information over large areas. In the recent past, land-cover mapping from satellites has come of age. Through research on various issues regarding data pre-processing, classification and accuracy assessment, new and unique data/land-cover products are being generated which could not be produced by earlier techniques. Various data set of the area were used for interpreting and unifying them within GIS and Image processing environment for analysis and interpretation.

The following data were used for this project work:

- Landsat satellite Image having 28.5 metre spatial resolution.
- IRS Cartosat multi-spectral satellite image having 5 metre spatial resolution.
- Digital Globe high resolution image (0.5 m) from Open Source Google Earth repository for Visual interpretation and as a supplementary data for interpretation.

TNTmips Pro 2014, the integrated GIS and Image Processing platform were used in the present study.

Workflow

- Satellite Images were imported in a project file within TNTmips Pro platform.
- The Images were geometrically rectified with the GCP by using Geographic coordinate system and World Geodetic System 1984 (WGS 84) as Datum. Affine transformation model has been deliberately selected for this sampling area to maintain the geometric area and shape accuracy.
- The sampling location extends from North 23°14′ 55.398″ to North 23°14′ 25.670″ and East 87° 52′ 09.921″ to East 87°52′ 42.268″.
- As per the present scope of study to meet the temporal data requisite two different years data have been collected.
- Image pre-processing was implemented on both the images to improve the quality and interpretability.
- 2 Extraction model was implemented on the scenes to get the 1 sq.km sampling an area as decided to process within the buffer zone of 5 kilometre both of the railway track from Sealdah to Maldah at the location of Bardhaman station to get the surroundings bird's eyeview.

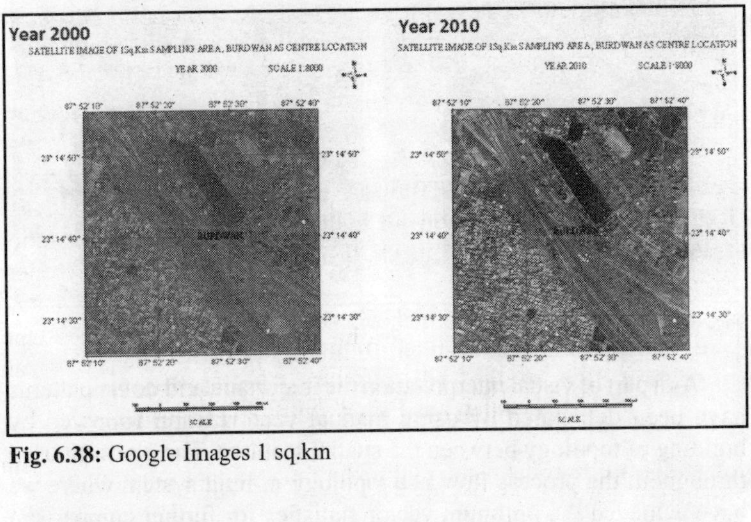

Fig. 6.38: Google Images 1 sq.km

The given area extends from North 23° 12′ 11″ to North 23°17′ 09″ and East 87°55′07″ to East 87° 49′44″. The area of interest is shown in Fig. 6.39.

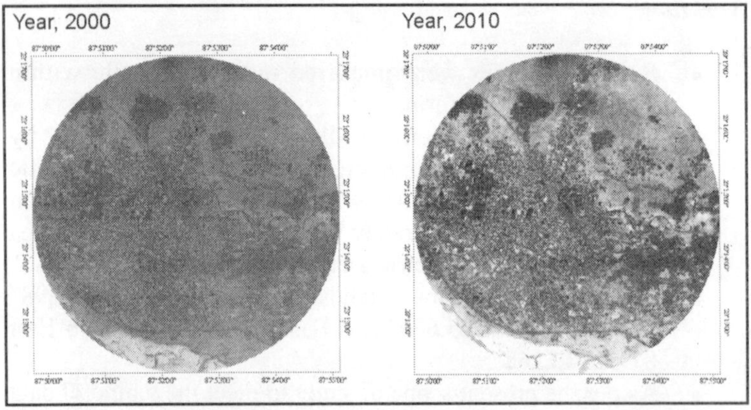

Fig. 6.39: Google Images 78 sq.km

Once we have the processed image for both the years the remarkable change between reflectance values were quite obvious study though this factor is highly dependent on the solar illumination of that particular time and date Here, is a comparative diagram of those values of particular location. (Fig. 6.40)

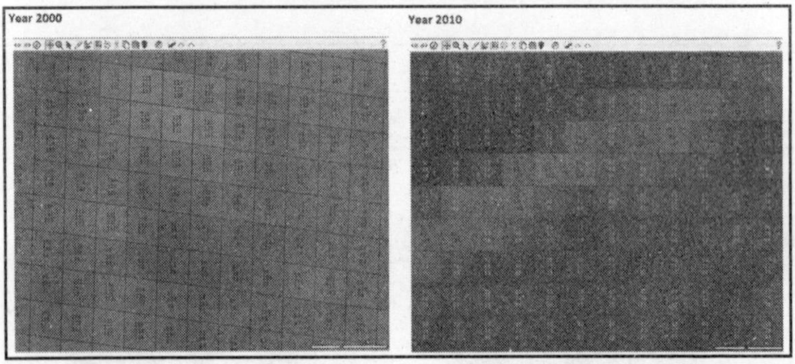

Fig. 6.40: RGB Values

As a part of visual interpretation the important land-cover patterns have been delineated by using manual vectorization followed by building of topology between the spatial features. The platform used throughout the process flow is a topology in-built system where we have achieved the optimum vector statistics for further comparison with digital interpreted result.

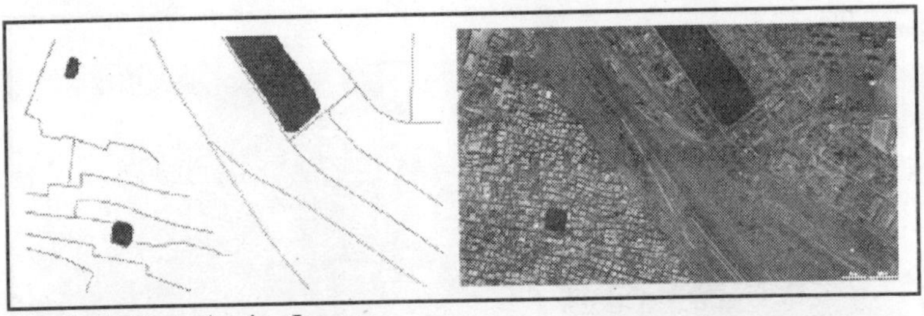

Fig. 6.41: Vectorization Layer

So, using the same manual interpretation technique both the images were visually classified to get the spatial changes between the year.

The implementation of the visual image interpretation technique, the areas having proper land-use differentiation had been delineated. Areas are shown in Fig. 6.42.

Factors Considered: Following factors were taken into consideration for delineating the zones of interest:

- In order to create a balanced and sustainable industrial growth in any zone and maximize use of uncultivable land in any area, it is felt that some parts of this zone can be identified as industrial growth poles, because of such factors such as availability of non-agricultural land, historical industrial presence and availability of good infrastructure. This will mean optimal use of the existing industrial infrastructure and upgradation of infrastructure where required and create new industrial infrastructure for project in backward areas.
- During land-use classification habitation, vegetation and open land areas have been merged into a single category as in this scope of study we are trying to demarcate the land which can be acquired for industrial infrastructure.
- From the observation of study area, most of the area covered by agricultural land. So, there is high prospect in producing crop. Then it is not healthy to create an industry in this particular area. There must have some social and political issues.
- Major criterion for industrial development is communication system. In this area we can observe that Highway and Railway tracks are passing almost centre portion of this area.

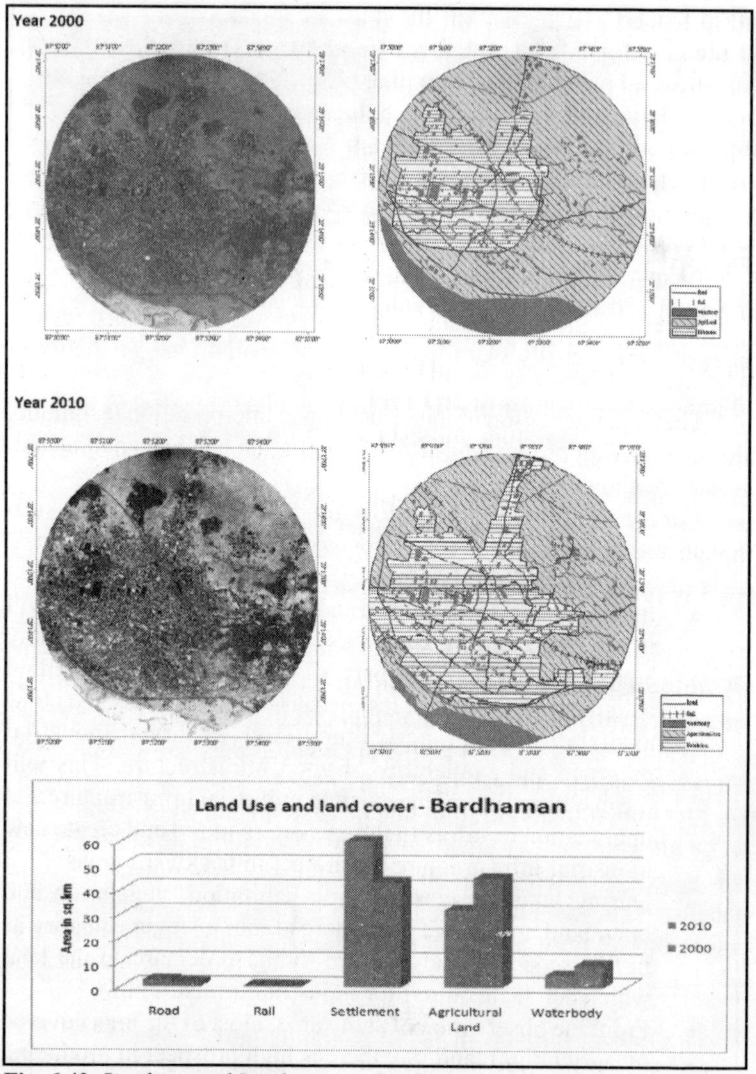

Fig. 6.42: Land-use and Land-cover— Bardhaman

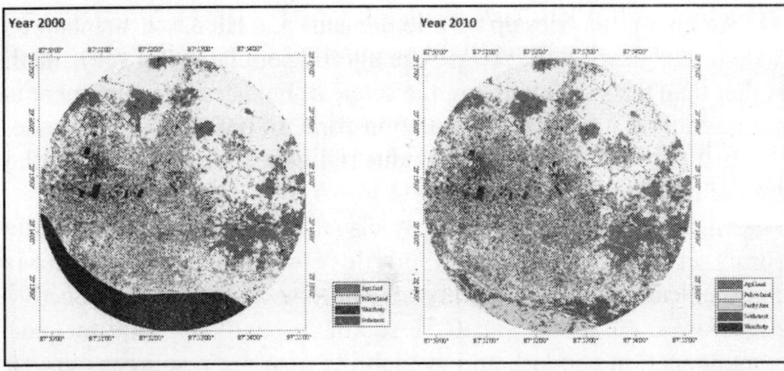

Fig. 6.43: FCC Classification

As we compare the FCC Classification image data of the desired area between the year 2000 and 2010 we can clearly see that the agricultural land has decreased to some extent due to the significant increase in settlement area and the decrease of water bodies. Also, though there is potential industrial zones scattered throughout the aforementioned area, but scattered area are not healthy for built up a proper industrial zone. At least 1 sq. km. continuous area is feasible for actual industrial zonation. So, here setting-up large or small-scale factories may not be viable.

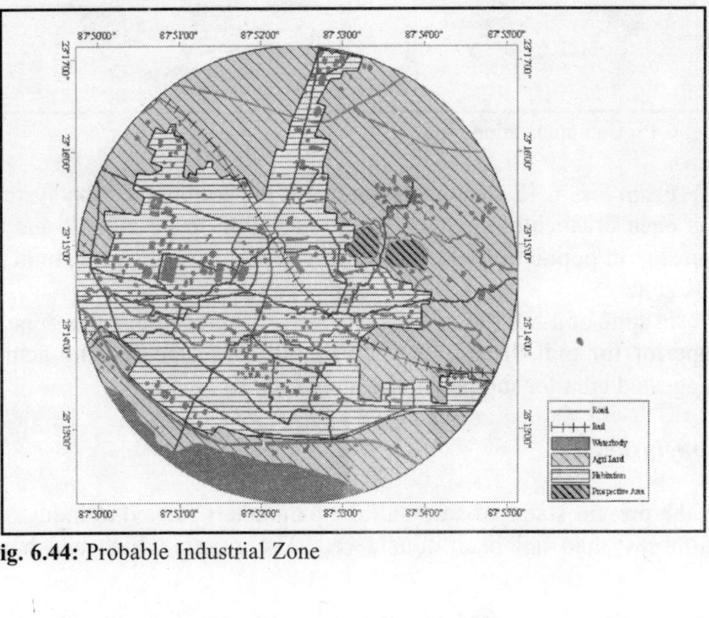

Fig. 6.44: Probable Industrial Zone

Another issue rises up with settlement area. Here, we can observe that, in the year 2010, the percentage of population is very much higher than the year 2000. So, the scope of industrial development is not possible in this heavy population zone, so pollution issues arise.

In Fig. 6.44, the potential industrial zones are depicted for the area of interest.

From Fig. 6.44 we can clearly visualize that these two probable zones are ideal for industrial development due to proper communication and availability of water. Areas of these prospective zones are 0.40 sq.km and 0.51 sq.km respectively. Due to good communication network and availability of water resources most of the areas are densely populated and prosperity of agricultural growth is very high. So, only these identified zones are feasible for industrial development within our region of interest.

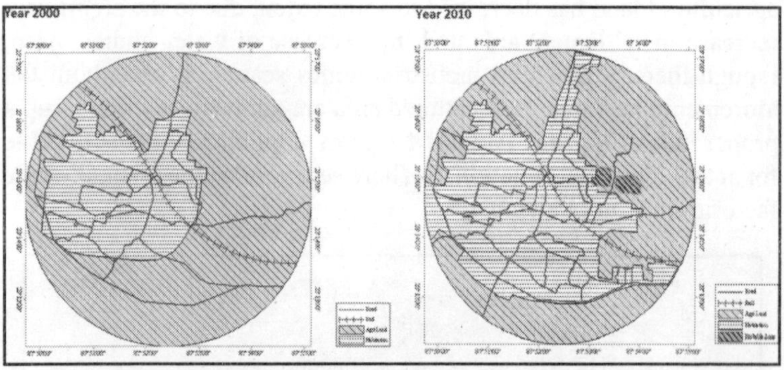

Fig. 6.45: Communication Map

From Fig. 6.45 we can interpret that the communication system has been drastically changed from year 2000 to year 2010 due to increase in population. So, probability of industries is maximum in this zone.

In spite of other social issues it can be concluded that this zone is superior for industriaes. Considering all these factors, the actual suggested area for industries has shown in Fig. 6.46.

Conclusion

In the present status of study all the parameters related to industrial suitability had not been considered. The zones, which had been

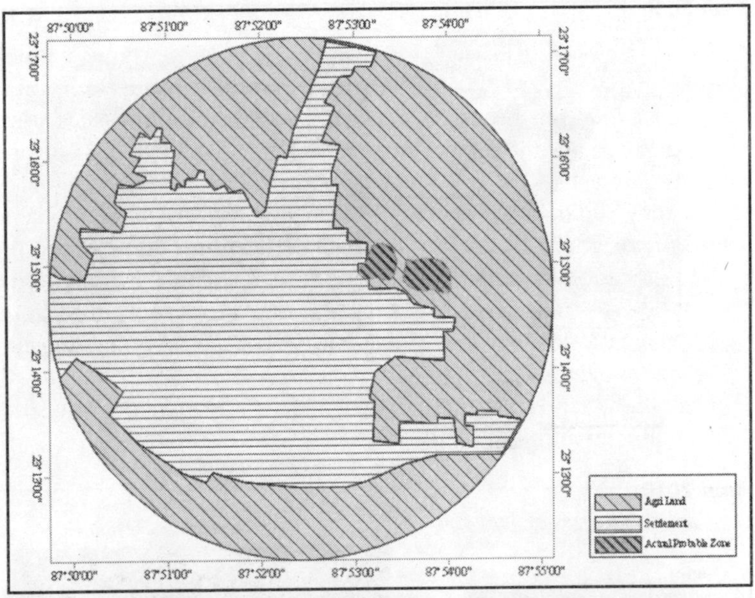

Fig. 6.46: Actual Prospective Industrial area

delineated as prospective area, should be verified using the field data. So, the delineated zones are the probable prospective area.

So, using the same manual interpretation technique, both the images were visually classified to get the spatial changes between the years (Fig. 6.47).

At the other hand same images have been used for digital image classification. The study area has been passed through hybrid classification technique, where the unsupervised classification has been followed by supervised classification method and finally, the spurious classes were deliberately merged to get the intended result.

Cartographical map preparation with suitable scale. Throughout the mapping we have tried to use A4 page where maps were fitted with 1:8000 scale.

Interpretation and Discussion

So, the procedural steps with the rigorous interpretation with both visual and digital technique for the study area between the years 2000 and 2010, this can be clearly interpreted that the '*Open Land*' has

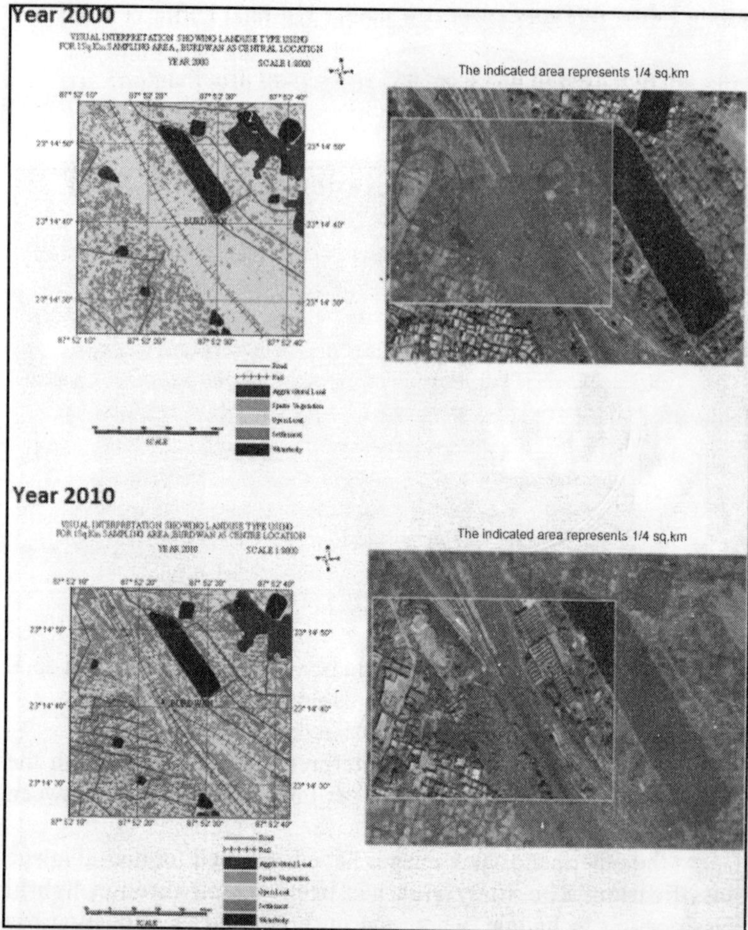

Fig. 6.47: Bardhaman—Land-use Pattern

decreased to huge extent due to the significant increase in 'built-up' area and the decrease of water bodies is quite obvious. As this zone belongs to one of the important industrial cities of West Bengal naturally the population has dramatically increased during last 10 years. (Fig. 6.49)

So, spatial dynamics has dramatically changed during last 10 years, where the population change is quite significant in the quest of earning and livelihood. Naturally, there is notable increase in small scale industry to the circumferences of this sampling study area. The

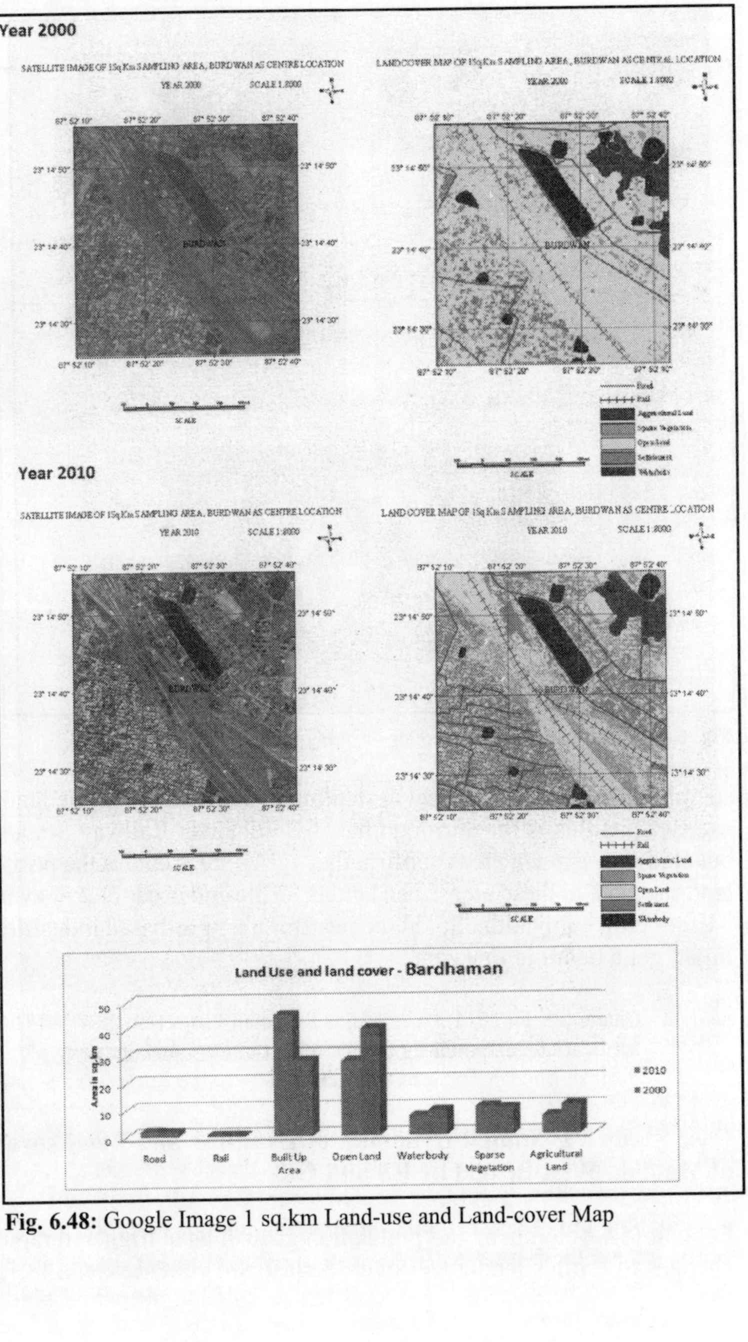

Fig. 6.48: Google Image 1 sq.km Land-use and Land-cover Map

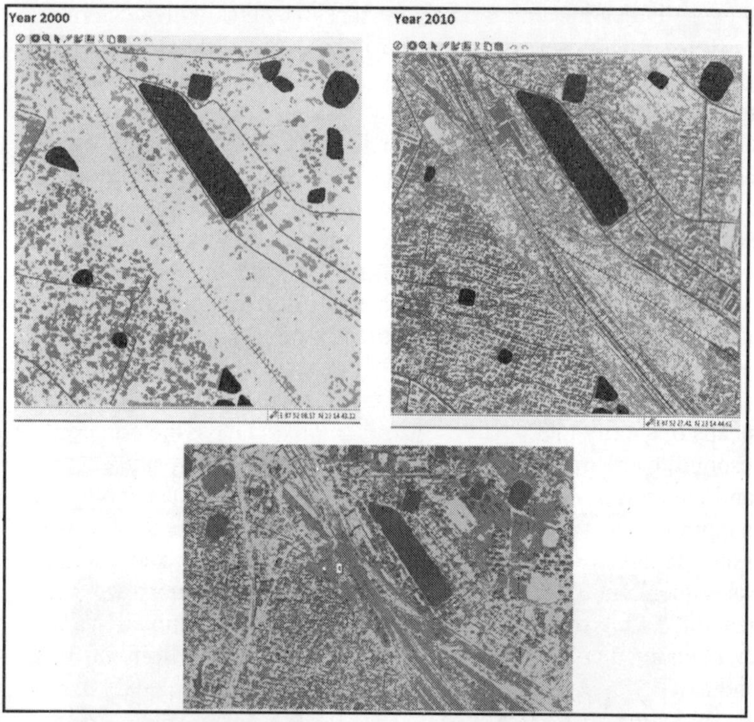

Fig. 6.49: Land-use and Land-cover—Changing Pattern

sampling area does not reveal agricultural as one of the prime land-use type, as this is the surrounding of Bardhaman Railway Station but study of adjacent areas confirm that agricultural land is the prime land-use type in these areas. The land is fertile and used for 2 or even 3 times crop cultivation. So, in the near future, agro-based industries might get a boom in this zone.

Source: Chatterjee, K. 2015, UGC Major Research Project on "RS and GIS application in spatial dynamics of agriculture and industry along Sealdah-Maldah Transact, West Bengal".

Case Study VI: Spatial Dynamics of Land-use and Land-cover at Maldah, West Bengal by RS and GIS

Economic development and population growth have triggered rapid changes to Earth's land-cover over the last two centuries, and there is every indication that the pace of these changes will accelerate in the future. The present study shows the utility of remote sensing techniques integrated with GIS to study the spatial dynamics of agriculture and industry in the selected specified study area and its surroundings in Maldah, Maldah District, West Bengal. Various satellite image data were analyzed within a digital image processing system to provide up-to-date information of the whole area. The extracted information from remotely sensed data was then integrated with visually interpreted information and field inputs in a GIS to create a comprehensive spatial database. This permitted the integration of several layers of information with the remotely sensed data in both temporal and spatial dimensions.

Remote sensing technology has been recognized as a useful means of supplying up-to-date information and have the potential to respond to the growing and urgent demand for timely and accurate land-cover information over large areas. In the recent past, land-cover mapping from satellites has come of age, through research on various issues regarding data pre-processing, classification and accuracy assessment, new and unique data/land-cover products are being generated which could not be produced by earlier techniques. Various data sets of the area were used for interpreting and unifying them within GIS and Image Processing environment for analysis and interpretation.

The following data were used for this project work:

- Landsat satellite image having 28.5 metre-spatial resolution.
- IRS Cartosat multi-spectral satellite image having 5 metre spatial resolution.
- Digital Globe high resolution image (0.5 m) from Open Source Google Earth repository for visual interpretation and as a supplementary data for interpretation.

TNTmips Pro 2014, the integrated GIS and Image Processing platform were used in the present study.

Workflow

- Satellite Images were imported in a project file within TNT mips Pro platform.

- The Images were geometrically rectified with the GCP by using Geographic coordinate system and World Geodetic System 1984 (WGS 84) as Datum. Affine transformation model has been deliberately selected for this sampling area to maintain the geometric area and shape accuracy.
- The sampling location extends from North 25°00′ 08.741″ to North 25° 01′ 12.776″ and East 88°07′ 33.068″ to East 88°08′ 08.741″. The area of interest is shown in Fig. 6.50.
- As per the present scope of study to meet the temporal data requisite two different years' data have been collected.
- Image preprocessing was implemented on both the images to improve the quality and interpretability.
- Extraction model was implemented on the scenes to get the 1 sq.km sampling area as decided to process within the buffer zone of 5 kilometre both of the railway track from Sealdah to Maldah at the location of Maldah Railway Station to get the surroundings bird's eyeview.

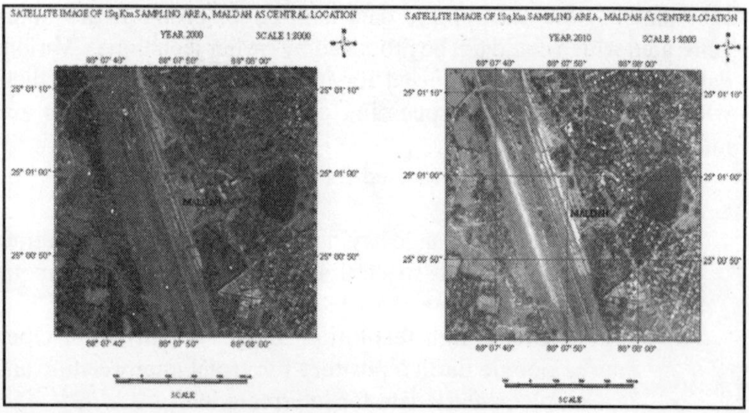

Fig. 6.50: Google Image 1 sq.km

The given area extends from North 24° 58′ 29″ to North 25° 03′ 22″ and East 88°05′08″ to East 88°10′ 32″. The area of interest is shown in Fig. 6.51.

Once we have the processed image for both the years, the remarkable change between reflectance values were quite obvious study though this factor is highly dependent on the solar illumination of that particular time and date. Here is a comparative diagram of those values of particular location (Fig. 6.52).

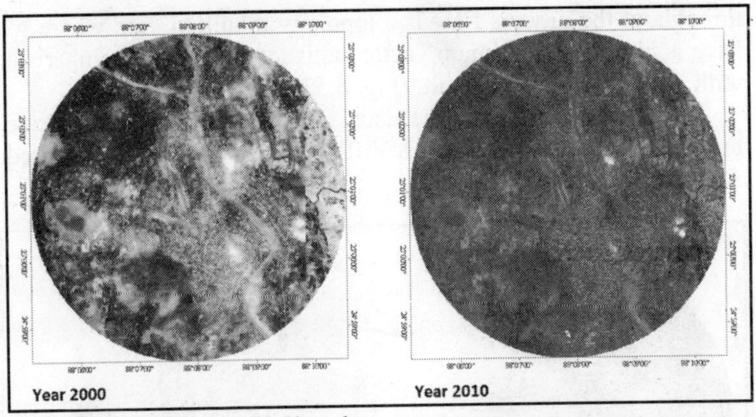

Fig. 6.51: Google Image 78.51 sq. km

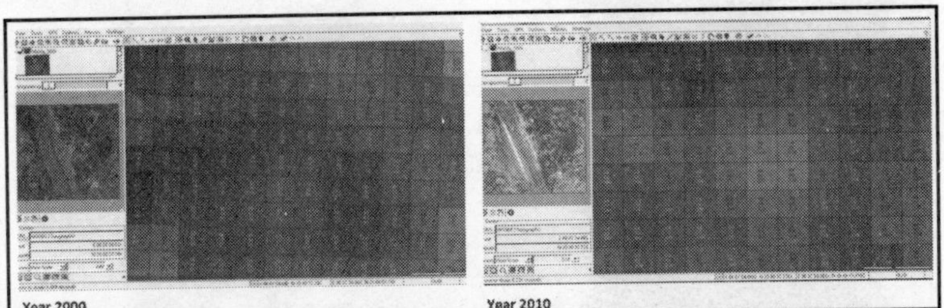

Fig. 6.52: RGB Values

As a part of visual interpretation the important land-cover patterns have been delineated by using manual vectorization followed by building of topology between the spatial features. The platform used

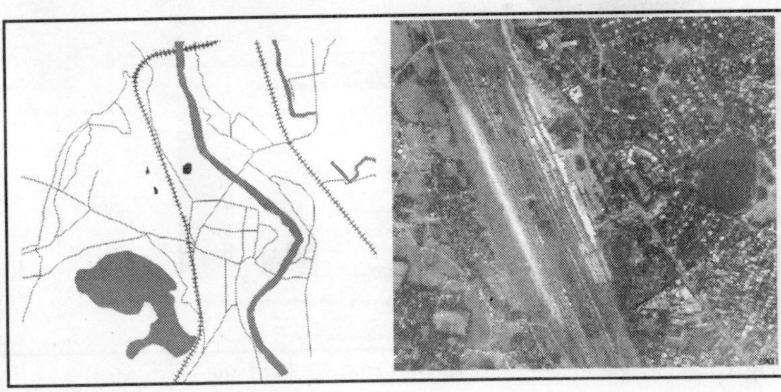

Fig. 6.53: Vectorization Layer

throughout the process flow is a topology inbuilt system where we have achieved the optimum vector statistics for further comparison with digital interpreted result. (Fig. 6.53)

The implementation of the visual image interpretation technique, the areas having proper land-use differentiation had been delineated. Areas are shown in Fig. 6.54

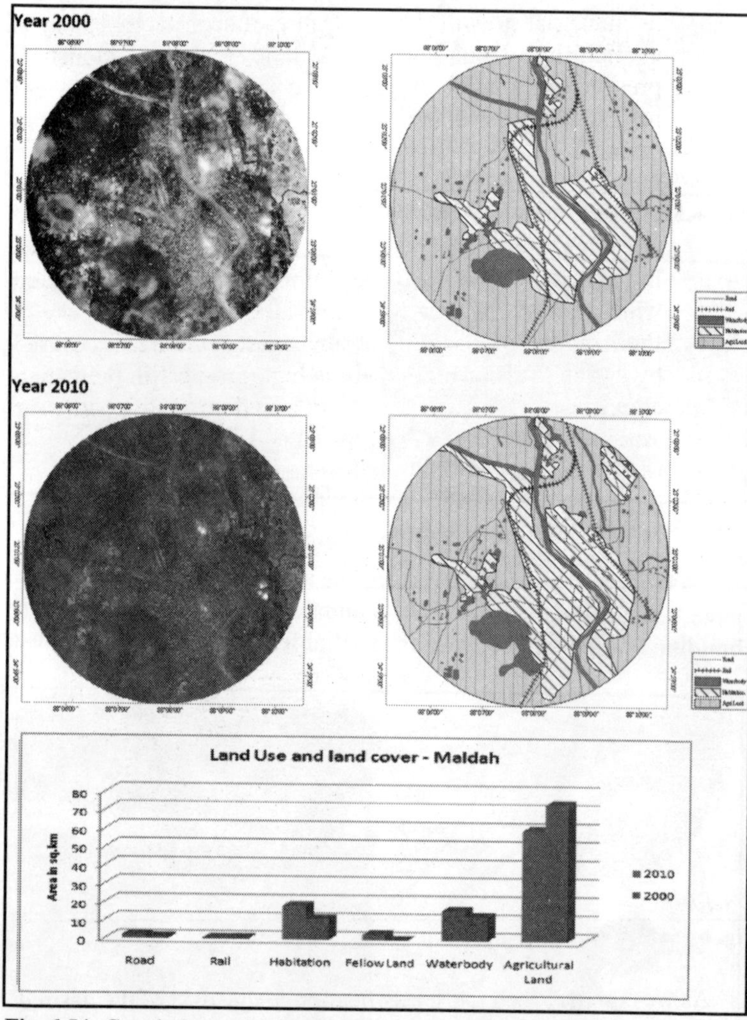

Fig. 6.54: Google Image 78.51 sq km Land-use and Land-cover Map

Factors Considered: Following factors were taken into consideration for delineating the zones of interest—

- In order to create a balanced and sustainable industrial growth in any zone and maximize use of uncultivable land in any area, it is felt that some parts of this zone can be identified as industrial growth poles, because of such factors such as availability of non-agricultural land, historical industrial presence and availability of good infrastructure. This will mean optimal use of the existing industrial infrastructure and upgradation of infrastructure where required and create new industrial infrastructure for project in backward areas.
- During land-use classification habitation, vegetation and open land areas have been merged into a single category as in this scope of study we are trying to demarcate the land which can be acquired for industrial development.
- From the observation of study area, most of the area is covered by agricultural land. So, there is high prospect in producing crop. Then it is not healthy to create an industry in this particular area. There must have some social and political issues.
- Major criteria for industrial development are communication condition. We can observe that Highway and Railway tracks are passing through almost centre portion of this area.

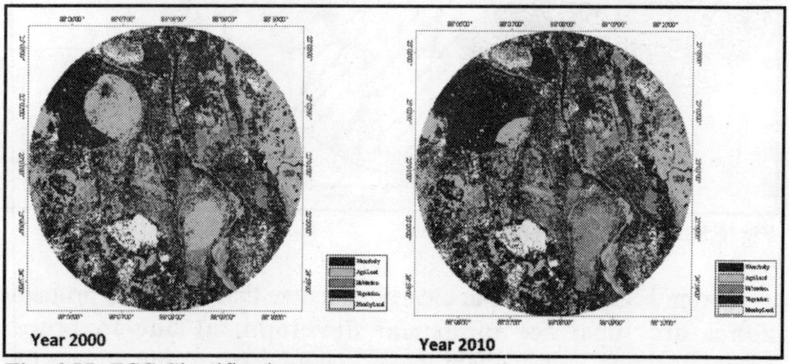

Fig. 6.55: FCC Classification

As we compare the FCC Classification image data of the desired area between the years 2000 and 2010 we can clearly see that the agricultural land has decreased to some extent due to the significant increase in settlement area and the decrease of waterbodies. Also, though there is potential industrial zones scattered throughout the aforementioned area, but scattered area are not healthy for built-up a proper industrial zone. At least 1 sq. km continuous area is feasible for actual industrial zonation. So, here setting-up of large or small-scale factories may not be viable. (Fig. 6.55)

Another issue rises up with settlement area. Here, we can observe that, in the year 2010, the percentage of population is very much higher than the year 2000. So, the scope of industrial development is not possible in this heavy population zone, so, pollution issues arise.

In the next map the potential industrial zones are depicted for the area of interest. (Fig. 6.56)

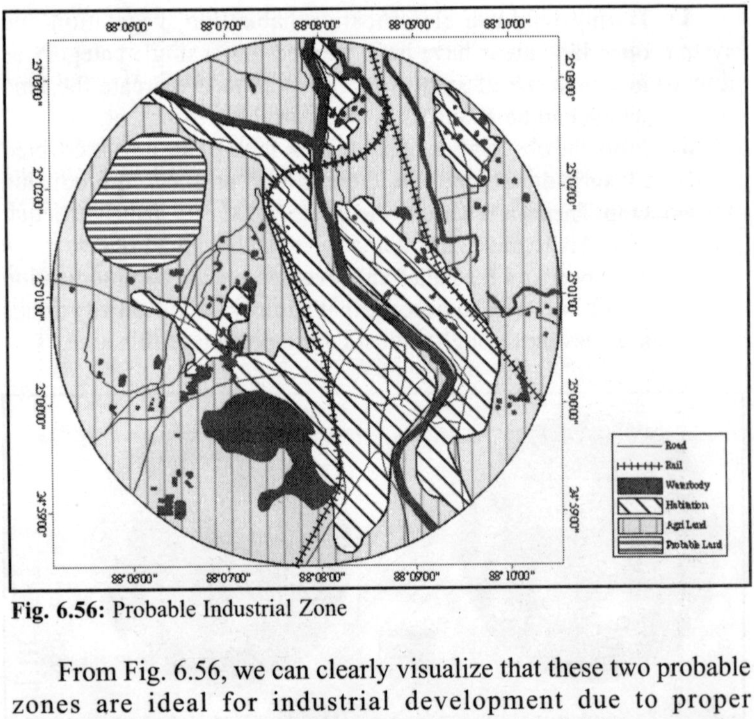

Fig. 6.56: Probable Industrial Zone

From Fig. 6.56, we can clearly visualize that these two probable zones are ideal for industrial development due to proper communication and availability of water. Area of this prospective zone is 4.70 km. This is more healthy for built-up an industrial zone. Due to good communication network and availability of water resource most of the areas are densely populated and prosperity of agricultural growth are very high. So, only this identified zone is feasible for industrial development within our region of interest.

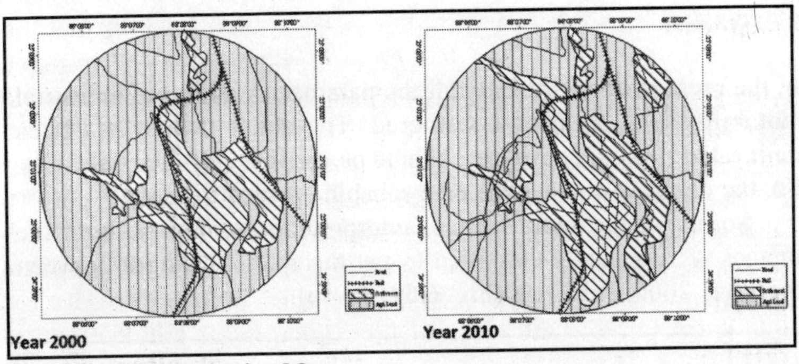

Fig. 6.57: Communication Map

From above two maps, we can interpret that the communication system has been drastically changed from year 2000 to year 2010 due to increase in population. So, probability of industrial development is maximum in this zone. (Fig. 6.57)

In spite of other social issues it can be concluded that this zone is superior for industrial development. Considering all these factors, the actual suggested area for industrial development has been shown in Fig. 6.58.

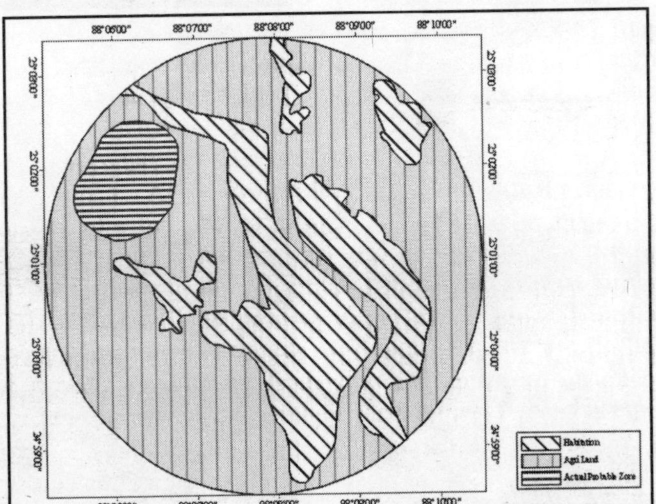

Fig. 6.58: Actual Prospective Industrial Area

Conclusion

In the present status of study all the parameters related to industrial suitability had not been considered. The zones, which had been delineated as prospective area, should be verified using the field data. So, the delineated zones are the probable prospective area.

So, using the same manual interpretation technique both the images were visually classified to get the spatial changes between the years 2000 and 2010. (Fig. 6.59)

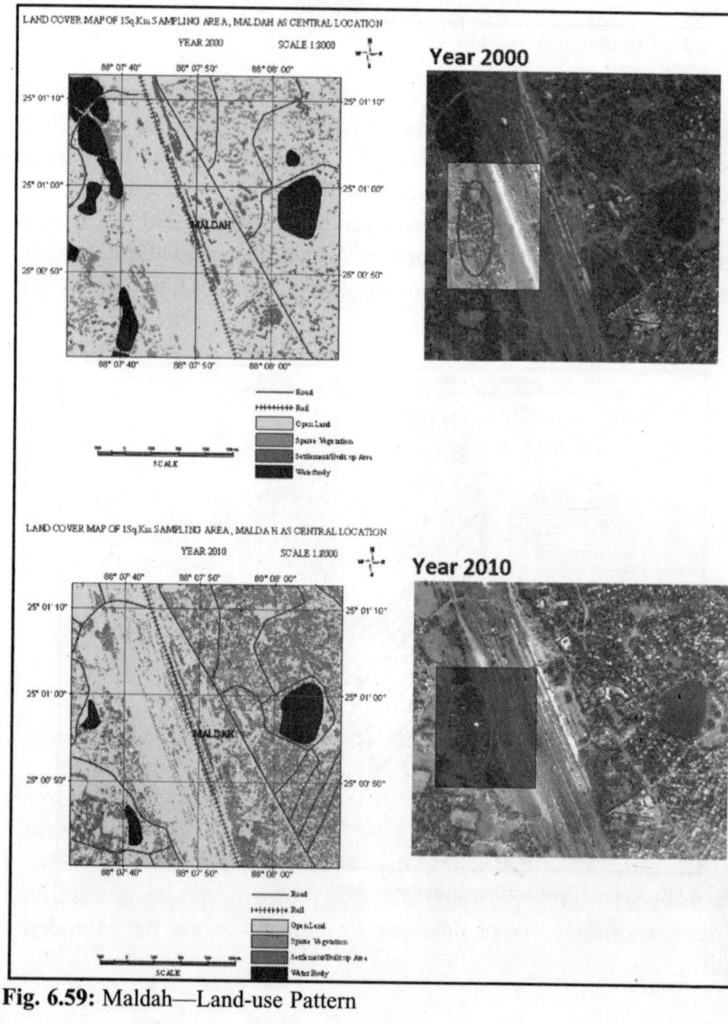

Fig. 6.59: Maldah—Land-use Pattern

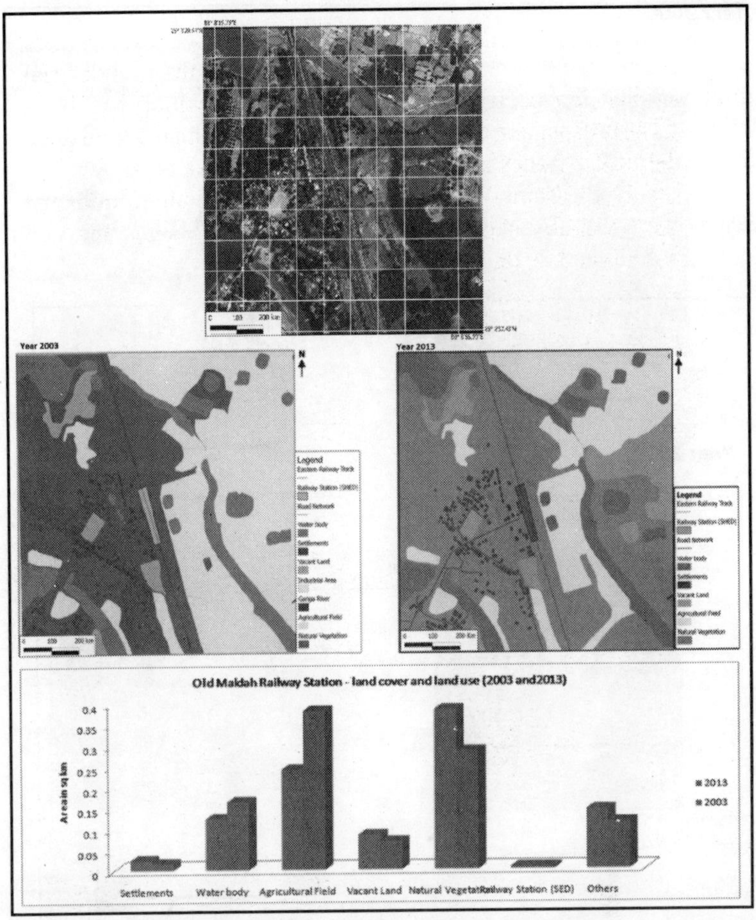

Fig. 6.60: Land-use and Land-cover Map

At Old Maldah Railway Station, there is increase in Settlement, vacant land, natural vegetation and decrease is noticed in waterbody and agricultural fields in the year 2013 compared to 2003.

At the other hand same images have been used for digital image classification. The study area has been passed through hybrid classification technique, where the unsupervised classification has been followed by supervised classification method and finally, the spurious classes were deliberately merged to get the intended result.

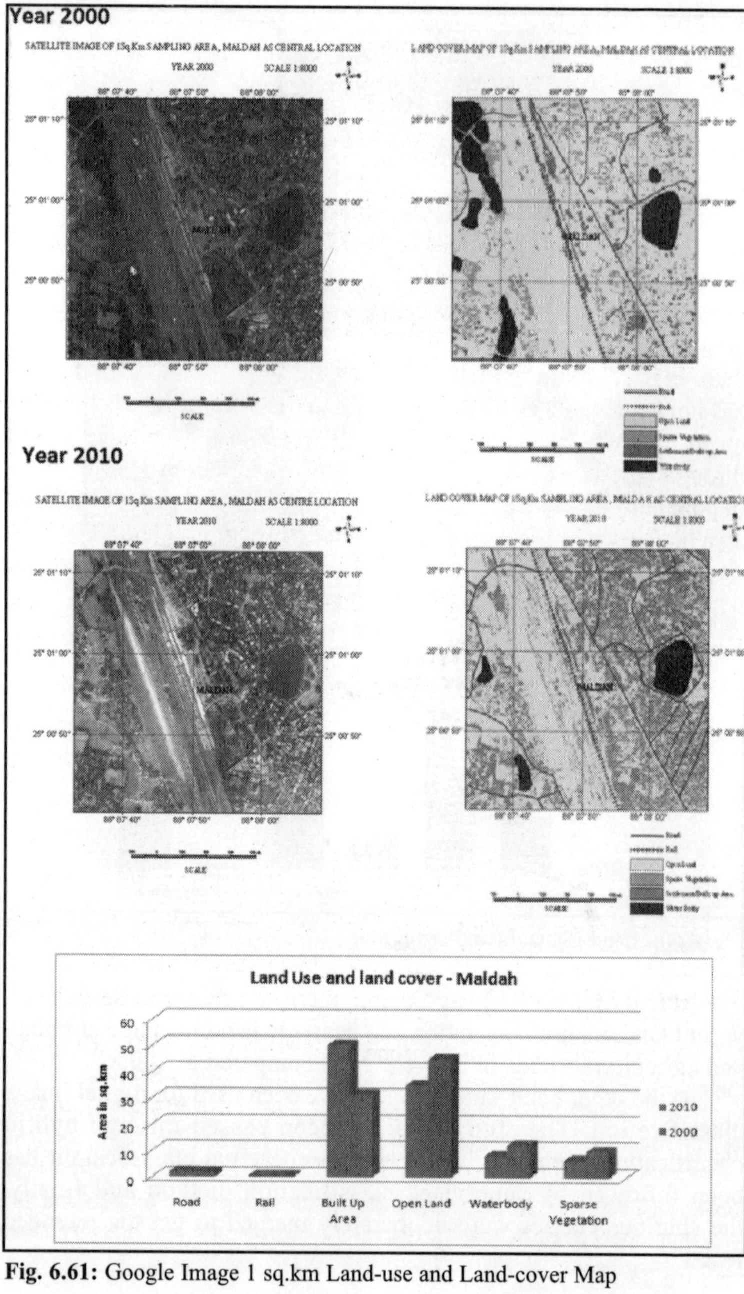

Fig. 6.61: Google Image 1 sq.km Land-use and Land-cover Map

Cartographical map preparation with suitable scale. Throughout the mapping we have tried to use A4 page where maps were fitted with 1:8000 scale.

Interpretation and Discussion

Though the study area is concentrated within the periphery of Maldah station in context to the spatial dynamics study this sampling zone is noticed to go through huge change for the land-cover type over the year of 2000 to 2010, where settlement and waterbody is the prime land-cover type noticed to be changed. But, within this buffer zone there is no existence of agricultural field so, agricultural dynamics has not been considered here as mapable land-cover which does not mean that no changes occur over the agricultural land-cover type throughout the years for this zone. In obvious reason with increase of population pressure the open land, waterbody and agricultural land area has gone through massive tress and 'Agricultural land' has been occupied throughout the year to accommodate the increased population pressure in this zone and its surroundings.

Fig. 6.62: Land-use and Land-cover - Changing Pattern

On the other hand still this zone has sufficient open land which can be considered for utilizing small scale industrial establishment because this zone is equipped with other necessary amenities of industrial development like communication, human resource, waterbody etc.

Source: Chatterjee, K. 2015, UGC Major Research Project on "RS and GIS application in spatial dynamics of agriculture and industry along Sealdah-Maldah Transact, West Bengal".

Chapter 7
Regional Planning—Development Strategies and Possibilities

Introduction

Among the backward areas, the need to accelerate development of areas inhabited by certain social groups like the tribal's, who had been bypassed during the development process, had become a priority issue. Simultaneously, the need was felt for directing effort towards building elements of special assistance to small and marginal farmers and agricultural labourers in the area development programmes. Planning is a future-oriented activity that links "scientific and technical knowledge to actions in the public domain" (Friedmann, 1987). It happens through a public discourse between all groups and individuals interested and affected by urban development and management activities pursued by the public or private sector. Urban and regional planning agencies are rich and dynamic arenas where many societal problems and solutions are explored and addressed in a direct and tangible way. Urban growth; unemployment and economic revitalization; transportation; environmental degradation and protection; neighbourhood decline and re-development; historic preservation; provision of open space, parks, and recreational facilities; and conservation of land and natural resources are examples of such problems and solutions. Planning-related decisions are made daily through a complex, often politically charged process involving plurality of interests. Moreover, the implementation of those decisions makes a long-term imprint on the urban structure, functionality, and quality of life in urban environments. While most of urban and regional planning happens at the local level, planning activities are often influenced by national and state policies and legislation. Policy research in the area of regional development has been undertaken from a variety of substantive standpoints such as land-use and physical planning, infrastructural development, urban institutional development and so on. Essentially, urban planning gives direction to the human habitation patterns. Its basic character is directional and it affects community living and hence an assessment of urban planning has to look into the changes that are brought about in the human settlement pattern through planned action. It is widely known that this Third World Metropolis suffers from acute scarcity of essential civic facilities, overcrowding and lack of housing space for a large number of people.

For most purposes, there is a need to convey detailed observations into groups, using some classification process. There is no one ideal classification of land-use and land-cover, and it is unlikely that one could ever be developed. There are different perspectives in the classification process, and the process itself tends to be subjective, even when an objective numerical approach is used. There is, in fact, no logical reason to expect that one detailed inventory should be adequate for more than a short time, since land-use and land-cover patterns change in keeping with demands for natural resources. Each classification is made to suit the needs of the user, and few users will be satisfied with an inventory that does not meet most of their needs. The fundamental question remains, however, how do we compare surveys if they use different terms and different categories to describe their data? If we cannot do this, then each survey becomes an island, separate in space and time from all other surveys. In practice, much land-use survey leads not to classification in a statistical sense but to a discriminated analysis—rather than grouping the geographical individuals on the basis of similarity to provide groups of individuals for which names are then sought, each individual is compared with a prior scheme; the individuals are then slotted into pigeon holes ('residential', 'manufacturing' etc.) one at a time. This distinction, however, says more about the differences in terminology between laymen and statisticians than anything of practical importance. Geographers should proceed on two fronts: firstly, by considering the functions, which a classification should meet, and secondly, by comparing some existing and widely used schemes. As the Twentieth Century drew on, many opportunities became articulate. Congestion inspired variety of proposals. Probably, the most popular theme was to acquire absolute accessibility.

It is quite natural that population growth increases the pressure on the land, and the non-urban land is converted into urban areas. Population growth and city expansion ultimately influence the land-use pattern. Knowledge of the patterns and intensity of land-use is very important in urban planning, but the preparation of a land-use inventory by conventional methods is expensive and time consuming. The advantage of satellite imagery interpretation in terms of accuracy, timeliness and cost is indisputable in comparison to the conventional methods. In this study, Land use/land-cover map for 1986, 1998 and 2002 is prepared covering the entire Dehradun city and its surroundings. Land-use classification was adopted with seven major categories, i.e. residential, commercial, institutional, industrial, traffic, agriculture and vacant etc.

Regional Development includes some key components like:

- Public participation;
- Decentralization and empowerment;
- Self-reliance;
- Self-management through collective voluntary action; and
- Polycentric industrial development.

Evaluation is a critical stage in urban and regional planning and development. The full impact of well-intentioned initiatives are rarely anticipated, and evaluation of alternative proposals is essential for informal debate and decision. Evaluation in planning has become even more important with the new paradigm attempting to integrate economic efficiency with equity, sustainability and social responsibility. The craft of pre-development evaluation has long been influenced by Nathaniel Lichfield. The conceptual foundations and subsequent development, its strengths and persisting dilemmas, its best practices and their potential are needed for improving future planning and development.

Conclusion

There is a growing awareness of the need for regional planning in many countries of the world. This awareness has provoked positive action. The need for regional planning is now widely accepted—even in government circles—it still only represents a start and there are many fundamental problems. There is a need to define regions which are satisfactory for planning at this intermediate level. The problem is to find areas suitable for interregional resource allocation and intra-regional planning providing a framework for more local plans. The next problem relates to the hazy nature of regional goals and objectives. There is a lack of general guidelines on the most desirable future inter- and intra-regional distribution of population and employment. Another problem concerns the relationship between the principles of regional analysis and the practice of regional planning. The principles provide a valuable insight into regional growth and change and spatial structure of region; yet there is a wide gap between theoretical possibilities and the *ad hoc* rule-of-thumb practice. Finally, there is problem of administration. This constitutes a major constraint on effective regional planning in many countries and certainly in India. However, despite the problems, significant progress has been made in regional planning in many countries and India in particular. But the problems should not be ignored. They can provide a guideline to future research priorities. Research is needed into technical areas—such as the role of growth centres, industrial location factors in practice and regional information systems and into institutional areas—such as the relationship between the regional planning and adjacent planning level and the most satisfactorily form of regional machineries. All of this require more regional planner and improved educational programmes.

Regional development and planning cannot perform a positive function in the economy and society unless it is properly related to economic and social development at the national level. Regional planning cannot be reduced to partial and sectoral solution and approaches. Modern regional planning should be of a comprehensive nature and should concentrate on inter-sectoral problems and on the interrelations of different patterns emerging in the process of development generated by economic, social and cultural activities of society.

The future regional planning strategies will be used to improve the coordination with national planning, the regional spatial development plans and the planning in neighbouring municipalities. The municipal planning strategy is an obvious place to describe the region's own vision and activity in relation to the regional and national spatial development strategies. The municipalities can make proposals for the inter-municipal planning, regional spatial development planning and national planning in their municipal planning strategies.

The regional planning strategies can be developed into an important tool for cooperation and dialogue with citizens, neighbouring municipalities, the regional council and the state about the development of the municipality.

It is stated that actual planning involves careful integration of backward areas with areas of growth potentialities so that the trickledown effect reaches to its maximum. Regional planning deals with the efficient placement of land-use activities, infrastructure, and settlement growth across a larger area of land than an individual city or town. The related field of urban planning deals with the specific issues of city planning. Both concepts are encapsulated in planning. This idea proposes statutory alternatives for the formation and organizational structure of regional planning agencies. The model legislation describes a full range of functions and duties for such agencies. It details the contents of regional comprehensive and functional plans (such as those for housing and transportation) and procedures for their adoption. A special feature of this chapter is model language for the designation of urban growth areas within a regional comprehensive plan. The chapter also proposes a variety of implementation tools, including the review of plans of state agencies, local governments, and special districts and of major capital projects of extra-jurisdictional or regional significance. Further, the chapter includes model legislation for agreements between the regional planning agency and other governmental units to implement regional plans. Finally, a model statute is provided for the designation of the regional planning agency as a sub-state district organization. Although the term "regional planning" is nearly universal in English-speaking countries the areas covered and specific administrative set-ups vary widely. In North America, regional planning may encompass more than one state, such as the Regional Plan Association, or a larger conurbation or network of settlements. North American regional planning is likely to cover a much larger area than the Regional Assemblies of the UK; both, however, are equally "regional" in nature. Regions require various land-uses; protection of farmland, cities, industrial space, transportation hubs and infrastructure, military bases, and wilderness. Regional Planning is the science of efficient placement of infrastructure and zoning for the sustainable growth of a region. Advocates for regional planning such as new urbanist Peter Calthorpe, promote the approach because it can address region-wide environmental, social, and economic issues which may necessarily require a regional focus. A 'region' in planning terms can be administrative or at least partially functional, and is likely to include a network of settlements and character areas. In most European countries, regional and national plans are 'spatial' directing certain levels of development to specific cities and towns in order to support and manage the region depending on specific needs, for example supporting or resisting polycentrism.

Regional Planning is considered to be draft proposals for the organization of the territory of a country's economic or administrative regions in conformity with a plan. Regional Planning is based on a wide range of social, economic, public health and sanitation, and urban development measures. Natural conditions are taken into account in implementing a regional plan. The principal task of regional planning is the comprehensive territorial and economic organization of a planned region and the shaping of its planned structure, in order to provide for the rational location of the productive forces and the best conditions for the labour, everyday life, and recreation of the population. To accomplish these objectives, regional planning envisages the creation of interrelated settlement systems, the rational location of new towns and rural settlements, the proportional development of existing towns and settlements, and the optimum development and location of industry, agricultural production and the other sectors of the national economy.

Bibliography

Alley, John. 1993. *Using 3-D CAD Perspective Images as Evidence in Planning Hearings*, Plan Canada, pp. 27-30.

Anselin, Luc. SpaceStat - *Spatial Statistics Software*. http://www.spacestat.com.

Arbeit, David. 1993. Resolving the Data Problem: A Spatial Information Infrastructure for Planning Support. Proceedings of Third International Conference on Computers in *Urban Planning and Urban Management*, Volume One, pp. 2-26.

Armstrong, Mark P. 1993. Perspectives on the development of group decision support systems for locational problem solving. *Geographical Systems* 1, no.1, pp. 69-81.

Asproth, Viveca, Anita Hakansson, and Peter Revay. 1995. Dynamic information in GIS systems. *Computers, Environment and Urban Systems* Vol. 19, no. 2, pp.107-116.

Azad, Bijan. 1998. *Management of Enterprise-wide GIS Implementation: Lessons from Exploration of Five Case Studies*, doctoral dissertation. Cambridge, MA: Massachusetts Institute of Technology.

Batty, Michael, and Yichun Xie. 1994. Modelling inside GIS. Part 1: Model structures, exploratory spatial data analysis and aggregation. *International Journal of Geographical Information Systems* Vol. 8, no. 3, pp. 291-307.

Bhattacharya, B. (2010) *Geography of Deprivation: An Unfair World*, Concept Publishing Company, (P) Ltd, ND-110059, pp.1-21, 32-34, 51-101, 197-198.

Bollens, Scott A., and Godschalk David R. 1987. Tracking Land Supply for Growth Management. *Journal of the American Planning Association* Vol. 53, no. 3, pp. 315-327.

Boudeville Jacques (1970), *Les Espaces économiques*, Paris, P.U.F. pp. 2-4, pp. 10-16.

Brail, Richard K. 1987. *Microcomputers in Urban Planning and Management*. New Brunswick, New Jersey: Center for Urban Policy Research.

Brown, Mary Maureen. 1997. An empirical assessment of the hurdles to geographic information system success in local governments. *State and Local Government Review* Vol. 28, no. 3, pp. 193-204.

Budic, Zorica D. 1993. GIS Use Among Southeastern Local Governments—1990/1991 Mail Survey Results. *URISA Journal,* Vol. 5, no. 1, pp. 4-17.

Budic, Zorica D. 1994. Effectiveness of Geographic Information Systems in Local Planning. *Journal of the American Planning Association*, Vol. 60, no. 2, pp. 244-263.

Budic, Zorica D., and David R. Godschalk. 1994. Implementation and Management Effectiveness in Adoption of GIS Technology in Local Governments. *Computers, Environment and Urban Systems,* Vol. 18, no. 5, pp. 285-304.

Campbell, Heather, and Ian Masser. 1995. *GIS and Organizations*. London: Taylor and Francis, pp. 1-35, 38-41.

Chand, M. and Puri, V.K. (2004), *Regional Planning in India*, Allied Publishers Pvt. Limited, Kolkata, pp. 1-38.

Chandra, S. 2004. *Introduction to Agricultural Extensions-Rural Development Programme*, Indian Agricultural Research Institute, New Delhi, p.3.

Chatterjee, K. 2011, U.G.C. Major Research Project on "Industrial area use of land monitoring through RS and GIS"

Chatterjee , K. 2015, U.G.C. Major Research Project on ?RS and GIS application in spatial dynamics of agriculture and industry along Sealdah-Maldah Transact, West Bengal.?

Chisolm M. *Rural Settlement and Land-use: An Essay in Location* 3rd Edition Publ. by Hutchinson & Co. (Publishers) Ltd, 1979, 18-25, 29-30, 61-67.

Chun, K. J., and H. K. Park. 1998. *Examining the conflicting results of GDSS research. Information & Management*, pp. 313-325.

Clark, M. J. 1998. GIS—Democracy or Delusion? *Environment and Planning A 32*, pp. 303-316.

Clercq, F. Le. 1990. *Information Supply to Strategic Planning. Environment and Planning B: Planning and Design* 17: pp.429-440.

Coleman, D. and Khanna, R. 1995. *Groupware: Technologies and Applications. Upper Saddle River*, NJ: Prentice Hall.

Coroza, Oliver, David Evans, and Ian Bishop. 1997. *Enhancing runoff modeling with GIS. Landscape and Urban Planning*, Vol. 38, no. 1, pp. 13-23.

Couclelis, Helen and Monmonier, Mark. 1995. Using SUSS to resolve NIMBY: how spatial understanding support systems can help with the "not in my backyard" syndrome. *Geographical Systems*, Vol. 2, no. 2, pp. 83-101.

Craig, William J. 1998. The Internet Aids Community Participation in the Planning Process. *Computers, Environment, and Urban Systems*, Vol. 22, no. 4, pp. 393-404.

Densham, P. J. 1991. Spatial decision support systems. In D. J. Maguire, M. F. Goodchild, D. W. Rhind (eds.), *Geographical Information Systems: Principles and Applications*, New York: John Wiley & Sons, pp. 403-412.

Densham, P. J., Armstrong, M. P., and K. Kemp. 1995. Report from the Specialist Meeting on Collaborative Spatial Decision Making. Initiative 17, National Center for Geographic Information and Analysis. U C Santa Barbara, September 17-21, 1995.

DeSanctis, G. and Gallupe, R. B. 1987. A foundation for the study of group decision support systems. *Management Science*, pp. 589-609.

Devogele, Thomas, Christine Parent, and Stefano Spaccapietra. 1998. On spatial database integration. *International Journal of Geographical Information Science* Vol. 12, no. 4, pp. 335-352.

Diamond, J. T., and J. R. Wright. 1988. Design of an Integrated Spatial Information System for Multiobjective Land-use Planning. *Environment and Planning B,* Vol. 15, no. 2, pp. 205-214.

Doyle, Simon, Martin Dodge, and Andy Smith. 1998. The Potential of Web-based Mapping and Virtual Reality Technologies for Modelling Urban Environments. *Computers, Environment, and Urban Systems*, Vol. 22, no. 2, pp. 137-155.

Dueker Kenneth J., and P. Barton DeLacy. 1990. GIS in the Land Development Planning Process. *Journal of the American Planning Association*, Vol. 56, no. 4, pp.483-491.

Edamura, T., and T. Tsuchida. 1999. Planning support system for an urban environment improvement project. *Environment and Planning B*, Vol. 26, pp. 381-391.

Esnard, Ann-Margaret. 1998. Cities, GIS, and Ethics. *Journal of Urban Technology*, Vol. 5, no. 3, pp. 33-45.

Esnard, Ann-Margaret, and E. Bruce MacDougall. 1997. Common Ground for Integrating Planning Theory and GIS Topics. *Journal of Planning Education and Research*, Vol. 17, no. 1, pp. 55-62.

Faber, B. G., J. Knutson, R. Watts, W. W. Wallace, J. E. Hautalouma, and L. Wallace. 1994. *A Groupware-enabled GIS, GIS '94 Symposium*, pp. 551-561.

Faber, B., Wallace, W., and Cuthbertson, J. 1995. Advances in collaborative GIS for land resource negotiation. Proceedings GIS'95, Ninth Annual Symposium on Geographic Information Systems, Vancouver, B. C., March 1995, *GIS World*, Inc., Vol. 1, pp. 183-189.

Faber, B.G., Wallace, W.W., and Miller, R.M.P. 1996. Collaborative modeling for environmental decision making. Proceedings GIS '96 Symposium, Vancouver, British Columbia, March. CD-ROM, no pages on proceedings published as compact disk.

French, Steven P., and Amy E. Skiles. 1996. *Organizational Structures for GIS Implementation*. URISA Proceedings, Mark J. Salling (Ed.). Washington, D.C.: Urban and Regional Information Systems Association.

French, Steven P., and Lyna L. Wiggins. 1990. California Planning Agency Experiences with Automated Mapping and Geographic Information Systems. *Environment and Planning B*, Vol. 17, no. 4, pp. 441-450.

Friedmann, John. 1987. *Planning in the Public Domain: From Knowledge to Action*. Princeton, NJ: Princeton University Press, pp.25-39, 85-89.

Friedmann, John, and Carol Kuester. 1994. Planning Education for the Late Twentieth Century: An Initial Inquiry. *Journal of Planning Education and Research*, Vol. 14, no. 1, pp. 55-54.

George, Varkki R. 1997. HyperSpace: Communicating Ideas About the Quality of Urban Spaces. *Journal of Planning Education and Research*, pp. 63-70.

Glasson, J. 1974, *An Introduction to Regional Planning, The Technical Journal*, Hutchinson of London, pp. 3-69, 319-322.

Godschalk, David R., Scott A Bollens, John S. Hekman, and Mike E. Miles. 1985. Land Supply Monitoring – A Guide for Improving Public and Private Urban Development Decisions. Boston: Oelgeschlager, Gunn & Hain in association with Lincoln Institute of Land Policy.

Godschalk, D. R., G. McMahon, A. Kaplan, and W. Qin. 1992. Using GIS for Computer-Assisted Dispute Resolution. *Photogrammetric Engineering & Remote Sensing 58*, no. 8, pp. 1209-1212.

Godschalk, David R., and Gerard McMahon. 1992. Staffing the Revolution: GIS Education for Planners. *Journal of Planning Education and Research* Vol. 11, no. 3, pp. 216-226.

Godschalk, David R. et al. 1994. Pulling Together: A Planning and Development Consensus-Building Manual. Washington, D.C.: Urban Land Institute.

Golay, F.. and Nyerges, T. 1995. Understanding Collaborative Use of GIS Through Social Cognition. In T. Nyerges, D. M. Mark, R. Laurini, and M. Egenhofer (eds.), Cognitive Aspects of Human-Computer Interaction for Geographic Information Systems, Proceedings of the NATO ARW, Mallorca, Spain, March 21-25, 1994. Dordrecht, Netherlands: Kluwer Academic Publishers, pp. 287-294.

Guhathakurta, Subhrajit. 1999. Urban Modeling and Contemporary Planning Theory: Is There a Common Ground? *Journal of Planning Education and Research* 18(4), pp. 281-292.

Hall, A. C. 1993. The use of computer visualisation in planning control. *Town Planning Review* 64, no. 2: pp. 193-211.

Harris, Britton. 1989. Beyond Geographic Information Systems: Computers and the Planning Professional. *Journal of the American Planning Association* 55, no. 1.

Holden, Robert, and Tom Turner. 1997. Western Europe, current city expansion and the use of GIS. *Landscape and Urban Planning*, pp. 315-326.

Harris, Britton, and Michael Batty. 1993. Locational Models, Geographic Information and Planning Support Systems. *Journal of Planning Education and Research*, Vol. 12, no. 3, pp. 184-198.

Harvey, Francis, and Nicholas Chrisman. 1998. Boundary objects and the social construction of GIS technology. *Environment and Planning*, pp. 1683-1694.

Heikkila, Eric. 1998. GIS is Dead; Long Live GIS! *Journal of the American Planning Association*, Vol. 64, no. 3, pp. 350-360.

Heywood, D. I., Oliver, J., and Tomlinson, S. 1995. Building an Exploratory Multicriteria Modeling Environment for Spatial Decision Support. In P. Fisher (ed.) *Innovations in GIS*, Vol. 2, 127-36, Taylor & Francis, London.

Holmberg, S. C. 1994. Geoinformatics for urban and regional planning. *Environment and Planning B*, Vol. 21, no. 1, pp. 5-19.

Hopkins, Lewis D. 1999. Structure of a planning support system for urban development. *Environment and Planning*, pp. 333-343.

Huxhold, William E. 1991. *Introduction to Urban Geographic Information Systems*. New York: Oxford University Press.

Huxhold, William E., and Allan G. Levinsohn. 1995. *Managing Geographic Information System Projects*. New York: Oxford University Press.

Hwang, C-L., M-J. Lin. 1987. *Group Decision Making Under Multiple Criteria*. Berlin: Springer Verlag.

Innes, Judith E. 1998. Information in Communicative Planning. *Journal of the American Planning Association*, Vol. 64, no. 1, pp. 52-63.

Innes, Judith E. 1996. Planning Through Consensus Building: A New View of the Comprehensive Planning Ideal. *Journal of American Planning Association*, Vol. 62, no. 4.

Innes, Judith E., and David M. Simpson. 1993. Implementing GIS for Planning: Lessons from the History of Technological Innovation. *Journal of American Planning Association*, Vol. 59, no. 2, pp. 230-236.

Isard W. (1956), *Location and Space Economy*, Cambridge, MIT Press, pp 3-52, 131-132.

Jankowski, P., T. L. Nyerges, A. Smith, T. J. Moore, and E. Horvath. 1997. Spatial Group Choice: a SDSS tool for collaborative spatial decision-making. *International Journal of Geographic Information Systems*, Vol. 11, no. 6, pp. 577-602.

Jankowski, P., M. Stasik. 1997. Design consideration for space and time distributed collaborative spatial decision-making. *Journal of Geographic Information and Decision Analysis*, Vol. 1, no. 1, pp. 1-8.

Jessup, L. and Valacich, J. (eds.). 1993. *Group Support Systems. New Perspectives*. New York: MacMillan Publishing Company.

Jones, R. M. 1998. An Analysis of Computer-supported Co-operative Work Systems to Support Decision-making in Regional Planning. Computers, *Environment, and Urban Systems*, Vol. 22, no. 4, pp. 335-350.

Juhl, Ginger M. 1993. Government Agencies Let Their Hair Down about GIS. *Geo Info Systems*, Vol. 3, no. 7, pp.20-26.

Kammeier, H. D. 1999. New tools for spatial analysis and planning as components of an incremental planning-support system. *Environment and Planning*, pp. 365-380.

Kaufman, Sanda, and Robert Simons. 1995. Quantitative and Research Methods in Planning: Are Schools Teaching What Practitioners Practice? *Journal of Planning Education and Research*, Vol. 15, no. 1, pp. 17-33.

Kent, Martin, Allan Jones, and Ruth Weaver, Editors. 1993. Geographical information systems and remote sensing in land-use planning. *Applied Geography "theme" volume*.

Kliskey, Andrew. 1995. The Role and Functionality of GIS as a Planning Tool in Natural-resource Management. *Computers, Environment, and Urban Systems*, Vol. 19, no. 1, pp. 15-22.

Klosterman, Richard E. 1990. Microcomputers in Urban and Regional Planning: Lessons from the Past, Directions for the Future. *Computers, Environment and Urban Systems*, Vol. 14, no. 3, pp. 177-185.

Klosterman, Richard E. 1997. Planning Support Systems: A New Perspective on Computer-Aided Planning. *Journal of Planning Education and Research*, Vol. 17, no. 1, pp. 45-54.

Klosterman, Richard E. 1999. The What if? Collaborative planning support system. *Environment and Planning*, pp. 393-408.

Knaap, Gerrit J., Lewis D. Hopkins, and Kieran P. Donaghy. 1998. Do Plans Matter? A Game-Theoretic Model for Examining the Logic and Effects of Land-use Planning. *Journal of Planning Education and Research*, Vol. 18, no. 1, pp. 25-34.

Landis, John D. 1994. The California Urban Futures Model: a New Generation of Metropolitan Simulation Models. *Environment and Planning*, pp. 399-420.

Landis, John D. 1995. Imagining Land-use Futures—Applying the California Urban Futures Model. *Journal of the American Planning Association*, Vol. 61, no. 4, pp. 438-357.

Landis, John D., Juan Pablo Monzon, Michael Reilly, and Chris Cogan. 1998. Development and Pilot Application of the California Urban and Biodiversity Analysis (CURBA) Model. Monograph 98-1.Berkeley, CA: Institute of Urban and Regional Development.

Langendorf, R. 1992. The 1990s: *Information Systems and Computer Visualization for Urban Design, Planning, and Management. Environment and Planning B*, Vol. 19, no. 6, pp. 723-738.

Laurini, Robert. 1998. Groupware for Urban Planning: An Introduction. *Computers, Environment, and Urban Systems*, Vol. 22, no. 4, pp. 317-733.

Lee, Y. C. 1990. Geographic Information Systems for Urban Applications: Problems and Solutions. *Environment and Planning B*, Vol. 17, pp. 463-473.

Levine, Jonathan, and John D. Landis. 1989. Geographic Information Systems for Local Planning. *Journal of the American Planning Association*, Vol. 55, no. 2, pp. 209-220.

Lo, C. P., and Robert L. Shipman. 1990. A GIS Approach to Land-Use Change Dynamics Detection. *Photogrammetric Engineering and Remote Sensing*, Vol. 56, no. 11, pp. 1483-1491.

Logsdon, Miles G., Earl J. Bell, and Frank V. Westerlund. 1996. Probability Mapping of Land-use Change: A GIS Interface for Visualizing Transition Probabilities. *Computers, Environment, and Urban Systems*, Vol. 20, no. 6, pp. 389-398.

Mandelbaum, Seymour J. 1996. Making and Breaking Planning Tools. *Computers, Environment and Urban Systems*, Vol. 20, no. 2, pp. 71-84.

Mannheim, Karl. 1940. *Man and Society in an Age of Reconstruction*. New York: Harcourt, Brace & World.

Matheny, rom, Laura Jackson, Tom Gunther, Fred Ducca, Robert Johnston, and Ricahrd Klosterman. 1999. Land-Use Change Model Inventory and

Evaluation. U.S. Environmental Protection Agency / Urban and Regional Information Systems Association Annual Conference Proceedings.

Mesev, Victor. 1997. Remote Sensing of Urban Systems: Hierarchical Integration with GIS. *Computers, Environment, and Urban Systems,* Vol. 21, no. 3, pp. 175-187.

Mishra, R.P. (ed.) (2002), *Regional Planning Concepts, Techniques, Policies and Case Studies*, Concept Publishing Company, New Delhi. pp.58-59.

Misra, R. P., Sundaram, K. V. and Prakasa Rao V. L. S. (1974), *Regional Development Planning in India: A New Strategy*, Vikas Publishing House Pvt. Ltd., Delhi, pp. 190-201.

Montagu, A. Simon. 1998. GIS and Natural Resource Planning in Papua New Guinea: A Contextual Analysis. Unpublished manuscript.

Nedovic-Budic, Zorica. 1998. *The Impact of GIS Technology. Environment and Planning B: Planning and Design*, Vol. 25, no. 5, pp. 681-692.

Nedovic-Budic, Zorica. 1999. Evaluating the Effects of GIS Technology: Review of Methods. *Journal of Planning Literature*, Vol. 13, no. 3, pp. 284-295.

Nedovic-Budic, Zorica, and David R. Godschalk. 1996. Human Factors in Adoption of Geographic Information Systems: A Local Government Case Study. *Public Administration Review*, Vol. 56, no. 6, pp. 554-567.

Nedovic-Budic, Zorica, and Jeffrey K. Pinto. Forthcoming. Understanding Interorganizational GIS: A Conceptual Framework. *URISA Journal*.

Nyerges, T, and Jankowski, P. 1997. Enhanced Adaptive Structuration Theory: A Theory of GIS-supported Collaborative Decision-Making. *Geographical Systems*, Vol. 4, no. 3, pp. 225-259.

Nyerges, T,. Moore, T J, Montejano, R., Compton, M. 1998a. Interaction Coding Systems for Studying the Use of Groupware, *Journal of Human-Computer Interaction*, Vol. 13, no. 2, pp. 127-165.

Nyerges, T., Montejano. R., Oshiro, C. and Dadswell, M. 1998b. Group-based Geographic Information Systems for Transportation Site Selection. *Transportation Research C: Emerging Technologies*, Vol. 5, no. 6, pp. 349-369.

Pickles, John. 1995. *Ground Truth: The Social Implications of Geographic Information Systems*. New York, N.Y.: Guilford Press.

Prospects for Expanding Regional Planning Efforts, Elisabeth R. Gerber, Ford School of Public Policy, Institute for Social Research, University of Michigan ,Carolyn G. Loh, Department of Urban and Regional Planning,Wayne State University,March 15, 2010.

Ranzinger, Monika, and Gunther Gleixner. 1997. GIS datasets for 3D urban planning. *Computers, Environment, and Urban Systems*, Vol. 21, no. 2, p.159

Reitsma, R. 1996. Structure and support of water-resources management and decision-making. *Journal of Hydrology*, pp. 253-268.

Reitsma, R., Zigurs, I., Lewis, C., Wilson, V., and Sloane, A. 1996. Experiment with Simulation Models in Water-Resources Negotiation. *Journal of Water Resources Planning and Management*, Vol. 122, no. 1, pp. 64-70.

Report on Twelfth Five Year Plan (2012-2017), 2013. *Economic Sectors*, Volume-II, Sage Publication India Pvt. Ltd., New Delhi, India, p. 317.

Sager, Tore. 1990. *Communicate or Calculate*. Stockholm: NORDPLAN.

Sarjakoski, T. 1998. Networked GIS for Public Participation – Emphasis on Utilizing *Image Data. Computers, Environment, and Urban Systems*, Vol. 22, no. 4, pp.381-392.

Sawicki, David S., and William J. Craig. 1996. The Democratization of Data – Bridging the Gap for Community Groups. *Journal of the American Planning Association*, Vol. 62, no. 4, pp. 512-523.

Sawicki, David S., and Patrice Flynn. 1996. Neighbourhood Indicators: a review of the literature and an assessment of conceptual and methodological issues. *Journal of the American Planning Association*, Vol. 62(2).

Scholten, Henk J., and Stillwell, John C.H. (Eds.) 1990. *Geographical Information Systems for Urban and Regional Planning*. Netherlands: Kluwer Academic Publishers. pp.10-13, pp. 15-17.

Schon, Donald A., Sanyal, Bish, and Mitchell, William J. (Eds.). 1999. *High Technology and Low-Income Communities: Prospects for the Positive Use of Advanced Information Technology*. Cambridge, MA: The MIT Press.

Schuur, J. 1994. Analysis and Design in Computer-aided Physical Planning. *Environment and Planning B*, Vol. 21, no. 1, pp. 97-108.

Schweik, Charles M., and Glen M. Green. 1999. The Use of Spectral Mixture Analysis to Study Human Incentives, Actions, and Environmental Outcomes. *Social Science Computer Review*, Vol. 17(1), pp. 40-63.

Shi, X., and A. G. O. Yeh. 1999. The integration of case-based systems and GIS in development control. *Environment and Planning B*, Vol. 26, pp. 345-364.

Singh, R. R. 1999. Sketching the city: a GIS-based approach. *Environment and Planning B*, Vol. no. 26, pp. 455-468.

Sui, Daniel Z. 1992. A Fuzzy GIS Modeling Approach for Urban Land Evaluation. *Computers, Environment, and Urban Systems*, pp. 101-115.

Sutton, Paul. 1997. Modeling Population Density with Night-time Satellite Imagery and GIS. *Computers, Environment, and Urban Systems,* Vol. 21, no. 3, pp. 227-244.

Talen, Emily. 1996. After the Plans: Methods to Evaluate the Implementation Success for Plans. *Journal of Planning Education and Research*, pp. 79-91.

Talen, Emily. 1998. Visualizing Fairness – Equity Maps for Planners. *Journal of the American Planning Association,* Vol. 64, no. 1, p. 22.

Talen, Emily. 1999. Constructing neighbourhoods from the bottom up: the case for resident-generated GIS. *Environment and Planning B,* Vol. 26(4), pp. 533-554.

Tellez, Bruno, and Sylvie Servigne. 1997. Updating Urban Database with Aerial Photographs: A Common Structuring Methodology. *Computers, Environment, and Urban Systems,* Vol. 21, no. 2, pp. 133-145.

Tulloch, David L., Bernard J. Jr. Niemann, and Earl F. Epstein. 1996. A Model of Multipurpose Land Information System Development in Communities: Forces, Factors, Stages, Indicators, and Benefits. GIS/LIS Proceedings, 325-48Bethesda, MA; Washington D.C.; Aurora, CO: ASPRS/ACSM, AAG, URISA, AM/FM International.

Urban Institute, Center for Public Finance and Housing. 1996. Democratizing Information: first year report of the national neighbourhood indicators project. Washington, DC: The Urban Institute.

Ventura, Stephen J., Lucy A. Buchan, Bernard J. Jr. Niemann, and Peter G. Thum. 1993. Evaluating Alternative Agricultural Land Management Policies for a Water Quality Perspective. *URISA Journal,* Vol. 5, no. 2, pp. 44-54.

Vernez-Moudon, Anne, and Michael Hubner (Eds.). Forthcoming. Parcel-based GIS for Land Supply and Capacity Monitoring. New York: John Wiley & Sons.

Warnecke, Lisa, Jeff Beattie, Kollin Cheryl, Winifred Lyday, and Steven French. 1998. *Geographic Information Technology in Cities and Counties: A Nationwide Assessment.* Washington, D.C.: American Forests.

Webster, Christopher J. 1994. GIS and the Scientific Inputs to Planning. Part 2: Prediction and Prescription. *Environment and Planning B*, Vol. 21, no. 2, pp. 145-157.

Webster, Christopher J. 1993. GIS and the Scientific Inputs to Urban Planning. Part 1: Description. *Environment and Planning B*, Vol. 20, no. 6, pp. 709-728.

Wellar, Barry, Cameron Nairne, and Sawada Michael. 1994. Progress in building linkages between GIS and methods and techniques of scientific inquiry. *Computers, Environment, and Urban Systems,* Vol. 18, no. 2, pp. 67-80.

Wong, David. 1996. Enhancing Segregation Studies Using GIS. *Computers, Environment, and Urban Systems*, Vol. 20, no. 2, pp. 99-109.

Worrall, Les. 1990. Information Systems for Urban and Regional Planning in the United Kingdom: a Review. *Environment and Planning B*, Vol. 17, pp. 451-462.

Yeh, Anthony Gar-On. 1998. Urban Planning and GIS. *Geographical Information Systems—Management Issues and Applications*. Second ed., Editors Paul A. Longley, Michael F. Goodchild, David J. Maguire, and David W. Rhind, 877-88. Vol. 2. New York: John Wiley & Sons, Inc.

Yiftachel, Oren. 1999. Planning Theory at a Crossroad: The Third Oxford Conference. *Journal of Planning Education and Research*, pp. 267-270.

Zhang, Zhiqiang, and Daniel A. Griffith. 1997. Developing User-friendly Spatial Statistical Analysis Modules for GIS: An Example Using ArcView. *Computers, Environment, and Urban Systems*, Vol. 21, no. 1, pp. 5-29.

Index